Longing, Belonging

Bishwanath Ghosh, born in Kanpur on 26 December 1970, is the author of the hugely popular *Chai, Chai: Travels in Places Where You Stop but Never Get Off*. He's also a Hindi poet, who has two well-received compilations—*Jiyo Banaras* and *Tedhi-Medhi Lakeeren*—to his credit. His other books include *Tamarind City: Where Modern India Began*; *Gazing at Neighbours: Travels Along the Line that Partitioned India* and *Aimless in Banaras: Wanderings in India's Holiest City*. He is an Associate Editor with *The Hindu* newspaper and lives in Calcutta.

Bishwanath Ghosh

Longing, Belonging

An Outsider
at Home in Calcutta

WESTLAND
NON·FICTION

First published by Tranquebar, an imprint of westland ltd, in 2014

Published by Westland Non-Fiction, an imprint of Westland Books, a division of Nasadiya Technologies Private Limited, in 2025

No. 269/2B, First Floor, 'Irai Arul', Vimalraj Street, Nethaji Nagar, Alapakkam Main Road, Maduravoyal, Chennai 600095

Westland, the Westland logo, Westland Non-Fiction and the Westland Non-Fiction logo are the trademarks of Nasadiya Technologies Private Limited, or its affiliates.

Copyright © Bishwanath Ghosh, 2014

Bishwanath Ghosh asserts the moral right to be identified as the author of this work.

ISBN: 9789371974592

10 9 8 7 6 5 4 3 2 1

The views and opinions expressed in this work are the author's own and the facts are as reported by him, and the publisher is in no way liable for the same.

All rights reserved

Typeset by SÜRYA

Printed at Manipal Technologies Limited, Manipal

No part of this book may be reproduced, or stored in a retrieval system, or transmitted in any form or by any means, electronic, mechanical, photocopying, recording, or otherwise, without express written permission of the publisher.

For my wife Shuvashree,
who introduced me to Calcutta

CONTENTS

Preface to the 2025 Edition ix

Author's Note xviii

Prelude 1

Spring 9

Summer 115

Autumn 185

Winter 219

Spring Again 311

PREFACE TO THE 2025 EDITION

WHEN I BEGAN work on *Longing, Belonging*, in March 2011, I was living in Chennai and would periodically visit Calcutta whenever I could afford leave. Chennai was a city I was faithful to, but Calcutta fascinated me. The iconic tram was still going strong. The yellow taxi dominated the roads. Good-quality whisky, something I couldn't do without back then and something almost impossible to find in Chennai, was easily available. Smoking, something I was addicted to, was not looked down upon and actually encouraged. The past and the present could be found having addas at every street corner. The communist government was trying to move on from the protest mode to the progressive. Religion and language didn't quite matter to people. There was general permissiveness in the air, no matter what the season. Above all, what fun it was to be in the city during Durga Puja and Christmas — you never saw celebrations of that scale anywhere else in the world.

When the book was released, in September 2014, I got irritated with Calcutta for the first time. I held the launch — at Park Hotel, with a cocktail party — on the auspicious day of Mahalaya, that is about six days before the formal beginning of Durga Puja, in the hope that Bengalis strolling into bookshops during the holidays would notice my book. Perhaps a few hundred — if not a few thousand — copies would sell and I would become a celebrity of sorts in Calcutta. But the very next morning the city got into the festival mode. The book got stranded outside bookshops because the process of transferring fresh arrivals onto the shelves was put on hold. Even the local newspaper I admired the most got busy covering premature pandal inaugurations and reported the book launch only about a month after it happened.

Much later I also found out that *Longing, Belonging* was selling the least in Calcutta. I wasn't surprised. A Calcuttan would rather tell me a thing or three about the city rather than read what I, an outsider, had to say about it. I moved on to write about other places. And then, in August 2018, I moved to Calcutta. For good. That's when I began to discover the city. Until then I had just been looking.

*

In Calcutta I got the ground floor of my in-laws' house in Salt Lake City to set up my study. They initially occupied this part when the house was constructed, in 1987, but soon moved to the second floor to get more breeze and a better view. They kept the ground floor locked with the intention that someday when they were too old to climb stairs, they would return there, with the place looking exactly how they had left it. That never happened. My father-in-law died in 2005, a year before I got married, and my mother-in-law, in order to keep breathing his memory, remained on the second floor. For me, a floor locked up for nearly thirty years was like a blank canvas to set up a study. But some of the fittings, such as the commode, needed immediate replacement.

PREFACE TO THE 2025 EDITION

One evening I set out commode-hunting and landed at a reputed shop run by a Bengali family. The Bengali manager showed me a catalogue and when I placed my finger on what I liked, he said, 'Yes, of course, we have that in stock. You will get it tomorrow morning.' Thereafter, he pulled me into a forty-five-minute conversation that began with what makes a good commode and ended with things nowhere connected to sanitaryware.

The following morning, I returned to the shop. The manager was not to be seen. Two elderly employees present there, when I showed them the catalogue, said the particular commode was not in stock. I found another sanitaryware shop, this one run by a Goenka, and was back home in thirty minutes, not only with a commode but also a plumber provided by the shopkeeper.

Once I settled down in the city, it didn't take me too long to realise that there are actually two Calcuttas. One is the public image, a place peopled by the bhadralok, where the presiding deities are Tagore and Satyajit Ray, where tastes are refined, be it for food or literature. The other you see on Bengali news channels like ABP Ananda: crude, cruel, corrupt. The cultured coexists with the crass, just as the present cohabits with the past.

*

Eleven years have passed since the launch of *Longing, Belonging*. Eleven years isn't long at all in the life of a city, particularly Calcutta or Kolkata, which has existed from the time when the Mughals were still around. But during these eleven years, from the time the book was released until today, Calcutta looks and feels quite different to me.

To begin with, the tram, around for more than a century and a half, is almost dead. A couple of routes that are still alive—only because of the noise made by activists and some concern shown by the court—may also get wiped off the map soon because the present government considers the tram to be a public nuisance rather than public transport. A charming, environment-friendly mode of commute will trundle into history at a time when it has made a comeback in several parts of the developed world.

The yellow Ambassador, for many years the instantly-recognisable doorman who let you into Calcutta, is also counting its days in the city. Most of these Bengal-manufactured cars have either reached or are about to reach retirement age, which is fifteen years.

But one icon of Calcutta has already disappeared into darkness, without any noise being made about his exit from the ecosystem: the bhadralok. To me he is — or, he was — the dhoti-clad dignified Bengali man, usually a communist by belief but not necessarily so, someone who spoke his mind but always watched his tongue, a walking encyclopaedia who could tell you the history of China and Chile with equal ease, who could be turned to for advice when difficult decisions had to be taken.

When I began work on this book, one could still find the bhadralok in some corner or the other of Calcutta, at least participating in neighbourhood communist meetings. Today he is nowhere to be seen. Not all bhadraloks were communists, but the exit of the Left from Bengal seems to have led to the extinction of the bhadralok. Looking back, the leftists who were at the helm in Bengal for close to thirty years were all ambassadors of ethnic fashion. You don't find such men today. Their departure from society has led to a cultural erosion.

Literature is another area where I notice a shift. The most popular genre these days—at least going by what's served in Durga Puja specials of most publications—happens to be *tantra-mantra*, or occult. For a city that once idolised the architects of revolution and makers of magic realism, one can coin a new category of literary production: magic spiritualism.

Connected to Bengali literature was the adda, which ignited movements and kindled creative fire. Today the adda stands replaced by WhatsApp exchanges, which is nothing but forwarding of fake or provocative information circulating throughout the country. Back then, the adda seemed a waste of time to me; today it appears as healthy as morning walk.

Also back then, perhaps at the end of 2012 or in the beginning of 2013, I remember running into a candlelight march somewhere near the Victoria Memorial one pleasant evening. It was a protest against the Nirbhaya rape that had taken place in Delhi but had shaken the entire nation. I walked past a man who was telling his female companion, 'One should cut off the dicks of rapists!' My admiration for Calcutta went up a few notches as I smelt the burning candles. Cut to August 2024. Protestors are once again out on the streets, this time in massive numbers, probably more women than men, because an on-duty young doctor has been raped and murdered in the RG Kar Medical College and Hospital, a well-known government institution. Nearly a year later, a student is raped in the South Calcutta Law College; protests begin but soon fade away. Considering that both the crimes took place not in deserted locations but in premier institutions, it was clear that the culprits possessed the courage that usually comes from either being in power or being close to it.

Not surprisingly, the two rape cases are now forgotten. As I write these lines, Durga Puja has just begun. Durga Puja now begins even before Durga Puja actually begins. Of the nine nights and ten days in autumn that are dedicated to the goddess in the Hindu calendar, it is on the sixth day — *sashti* — that the consecration of the clay idols takes place in the pandals, with the worship going on until the morning of the tenth day. But of late, particularly after the festival earned UNESCO's 'intangible cultural heritage' tag in 2021, the pandals are inaugurated—and pandal hopping begins—long before sashti, and the inaugurations are done mostly by West Bengal chief minister Mamata Banerjee. This year, she set off the inauguration process even before the nine-day holy period could begin, when Hindus were still honouring their ancestors during the inauspicious fortnight called *pitru paksha*.

Durga Puja will be followed by Kali Puja and finally it will be Christmas. Once 2026 sets in, political parties will begin sharpening their weapons for the Assembly elections. Will Mamata Banerjee be the chief minister again? That will be the question.

*

If Calcutta has changed in these eleven years, so have I. I no longer smoke and drink. Back then, I found the *bonedi baris*—palatial homes of the rich who once mattered in the city—most charming. Today, even though I value heritage more than before, I see these pillared buildings as monuments of discrimination.

Time has melted away much of their pride. Many of these houses, in order to remain relevant, now open the same gates that once kept out the common people to welcome those very people to their private Durga Puja. Some of these buildings, refurbished, now serve as luxury lodges where visitors spend a small fortune to step into the shoes, for a night or two, of a nineteenth-century aristocrat. If nothing else, such restorations help preserve Calcutta's architecture and also its olden days. Nostalgia, after all, is one tonic the city cannot do without: it is as important to its survival as mustard oil and Boroline. And that is why, of all my books, I have the softest corner for *Longing, Belonging*. It preserves in its pages the Calcutta that once fascinated me.

This is not to say that Calcutta no longer fascinates me. There are places that I still can't get over. Such as Park Street, College Street, Dalhousie Square. In these stretches you cross different eras during a short, single walk. To go further back in time, walk through Chitpore Road, also called Rabindra Sarani. Here, the pharmacy that supplied medicines to Rabindranath Tagore during his final days still survives. For that matter, a tuft of Tagore's hair, which he had himself gifted to one of his muses, remains preserved at the Academy of Fine Arts, evidence that the bearded bard was not entirely beyond narcissistic tendencies.

I like how, despite their problems, people are always looking forward to the next festival. As if to keep their spirits perennially up, some festival or the other is always round the corner. And a festival need not always be religious. Even the book fair is considered a mega festival. Then the handicraft fairs that light up winter evenings; they are more of a social occasion where the urban comes face to face with the rural.

Then there is something about its biggest festival. If Durga Puja was merely about Durga worship, Bengalis here would have built permanent Durga temples too. But Calcutta, in spite of Durga being its biggest cultural icon, is perhaps the only city in India that does not have a single Durga temple. Kali temples, yes. But not Durga. I have my own reasoning why this is so. The artisans work for months to create beautiful idols of the goddess and her four children, but after five days of worship the awe-inspiring artworks are all consigned to the river, so the message is clear: whatever comes, must go; whatever is created, must get destroyed; look forward to the next Puja and live on; looking forward is how you live on. I derive strength from this thought. This year, the look-forward, show-must-go-on spirit was particularly jaw-dropping. The nine-day holy period had hardly set in when almost all of Calcutta, lashed by a few hours of heavy rains, got flooded and remained waterlogged for an entire day. One thought Durga Puja had been washed away. But in a matter of hours massive crowds of pandal hoppers were back on the streets—as if nothing had happened.

The other day I read somewhere that the government, chuffed by UNESCO's recognition for the autumn festival, is considering building a Durga temple so that tourists get the feel of Durga Puja round the year. To that I would say that Durga Puja is far too big to need—or even acknowledge—validation from UNESCO. Also, if at all such a temple ever comes up, I would call it a Durga Puja temple—and not a Durga temple.

*

For all its flaws, Calcutta is the only city in India I would choose to live in. Mumbai is a struggle. Delhi is all about knowing how powerful—financially, officially, or politically—one's family is. And these days when you say Delhi, it is more likely to be Noida or Gurgaon, two places where I wouldn't mind visiting friends but would never, ever want to be a resident. Bangalore is now like the hosepipe that was watering your garden a few moments ago but is now blocked. Hyderabad I could never connect with. In Chennai I've lived long enough, about eighteen years, even though that would still be my first choice if Calcutta didn't exist. But right now—and it is too late in life anyway for the possibility of later—it is Calcutta. I may no longer long for it, but I certainly belong to it. Maybe because I belong, that I no longer long.

Bishwanath Ghosh
September 2025

AUTHOR'S NOTE

THE CALCUTTA PRESENTED in this book is what I experienced and encountered during my numerous visits to the city between the spring of 2011 and the spring of 2013.

Many of the experiences and encounters—and for them to add up to an ambitious book—would not have been possible without help from others. I would, therefore, like to thank:

Kausik Ghosh, Sharmistha Duttaroy, Satarupa Basu, Drimi Chaudhuri, Jayatri Nag, Sapratibha Mondal, Dripta Piplai, Arunima Bhowmick, Sudipta Dey—for finding time to take me around Calcutta and introduce me to its people;

Anubhuti Krishna, Debasish Mukherjee, Sudeep Chowdhuri, Sandip Chakroborty, Deboleena Chakraborty—all dear friends, who were my critics while the book was being written;

Gautam Padmanabhan, the CEO of Westland—without whose support, this book, or any of my earlier books, would not have seen the light. I only wish Gautam's father, KS Padmanabhan, who founded Westland, were alive today: he shared an emotional bond with Calcutta and I would have liked him to read this book. Unfortunately, he died a year ago, just when I was getting to know him better.

I am also grateful to my editors at Westland: Prita Maitra, for accepting the idea in the first place and setting me on track; and Sanghamitra Biswas, for meticulously combing through the final manuscript.

Several changes have overtaken Calcutta since I finished collecting material for the book. The state government machinery, for example, no longer functions out of Writers' Building, but out of a brand new high-rise called Nabanna across the Hooghly (this is supposed to be a temporary arrangement pending renovation of Writers', but one can't be sure). A new mall has come up in Park Circus, boasting of luxury international brands: Gucci, Armani and L'Occitane, to name a few. What has affected me personally is the closure of the Music World outlet on Park Street: I have spent countless evenings scanning its racks for Bengali music.

Such changes, for better or for worse, are laughably negligible when seen against the vicissitudes that Calcutta has been subjected to in its more than 300 years of existence. Calcutta, forever driven by a spirit of celebration, goes on.

BG
August 2014

PRELUDE

I HAD NEVER thought Calcutta would figure on the map of my adult life until, at the age of thirty-five, I married a woman from the city.

Like most non-resident Bengalis—*probashi Bangali*—I had grown up in the absence of Calcutta, and was certain that I could do without the city, just as it could without me.

I had no special affinity for the place, no compelling connections beckoning me. Calcutta, at best, had been a piece of old furniture stored away in the attic.

As a child I would pay a visit nearly every year with my parents to see my grandmother, always taking the steam-pulled Toofan Express from Kanpur, where I was growing up. But I absorbed almost nothing of Calcutta from those trips. The memories that I have relate mostly to our stay in the homes of various paternal uncles and aunts, who were scattered across the city and took turns in looking after my grandmother.

Each uncle and aunt had a set of studious children who were on the verge of becoming doctors, engineers and civil servants; comparisons between me and my cousins were inevitable.

One of these cousins had already joined the Indian Administrative Service, or IAS, for as long as I could remember. He would rarely be home during our visits (I've seen him only twice in my entire life. After four or five years in service, he had proceeded on study leave to the US, never to return to India), but a black-and-white picture, taken during his IAS Academy days in Mussourie, marked his presence in my aunt's Lake Gardens home.

The photograph, which showed him posing with his arm around a fellow Bengali probationer (a young man who belonged to a very poor family), was the ultimate depiction of the fabled Bengali studiousness. My parents, particularly my mother, would regard the picture with great reverence. It would stay in their minds long after our return to Kanpur, and I would often be chided for not studying hard enough to follow in my cousin's footsteps.

By the time the IAS-officer cousin left for the US, his younger brother, a graduate of the Indian Statistical Institute, was already there for higher studies (he, too, never returned to India). Soon, colour pictures of the two brothers, striking poses in the sanitised environs of America, began adding to my aunt's family album—and to my Calcutta woes.

My aunt's husband—a lean and learned man I called *pishomoshai*—would dutifully write a caption, in neat cursive hand, behind each photograph ('Taken in Minneapolis, Minnesota; March 1980'). He would also carefully preserve his sons' textbooks and notebooks. Wrapped in brown paper, they would remain meticulously arranged on shelves; and he looked displeased if I happened to show any curiosity about them.

Over time, our visits became less frequent. As a family

we made one last trip from Kanpur to Calcutta in 1987, when I was seventeen. The occasion was the *annaprashan* (the first feeding of solid food to an infant) of the child of yet another bright cousin. Nearly all relatives were in attendance and they were inquisitive about my future. At seventeen, I was next in line: it was my turn now to prove that my brain was nourished by the same blood. Fortunately, I was not to return to Calcutta for years to come.

The next visit took place only a decade later, in 1997, when I flew in from Delhi with a fellow journalist to follow LK Advani's chariot in Bengal.

Advani was then heading the Bharatiya Janata Party, which had finally come within striking distance of a majority in Parliament. To garner votes for his party, he was travelling the length and breadth of the country in the name of commemorating fifty years of Independence. The party's spin doctors had wanted Delhi journalists to see, first hand, the rousing reception his procession was evoking in Marxist Bengal.

Upon landing in the city, we were picked up by a white Ambassador which deposited us at a cheap hotel in north Calcutta—the room was fitted with the front-panel of an air-conditioner, without the actual machine—where we sat up all night drinking before setting out the next morning in search of Advani's chariot.

We traced it to a village near Burdwan and followed it back to Calcutta, even getting a chance along the way to climb onto the deck of the motorised chariot. It remains one of the most exhilarating moments of my life, to stand behind Advani as his chariot ploughed through the lanes of Bengal and had all kinds of gifts—from clothes to coins—flung at it by people waiting all day long for him to show up. It was the closest I've ever come to experiencing public adulation—although vicariously.

But I had remained blind to Calcutta during that trip, possibly because at the time I was a citizen of New Delhi, who looks through all cities other than his own.

That there is an India beyond Delhi, I realised when I moved to Chennai in 2001. I began exploring the south: Kerala, Bangalore, Hyderabad. Calcutta was now more distant than ever.

Then, in the summer of 2006, I got married. Calcutta became my hometown-in-law. I was no longer the poor cousin from Kanpur.

Annual visits began all over again; sometimes more than once a year. I began to like the city. It smelt of my childhood. The dishes were all too familiar, so were the habits and mannerisms of people. The local language was no longer just background sound—which happens to be the case for me in Chennai—but my mother-tongue. At the same time, it bore comforting similarities with Chennai: simplicity, absence of ostentation, pride in culture, spiritual bent of mind, worship of knowledge. I felt rooted.

Calcutta was no longer an old piece of furniture in the attic. It was an antique whose value I had realised.

THEN ONE EVENING, in the autumn of 2010, I found myself in the dimly-lit confines of Trincas, the restaurant on Park Street.

I was sharing a table—laden with bottles of beer and varieties of kebabs—with two men who were distantly related to my wife but were now my friends. The live band was in attendance, and all eyes were on the singer—a small woman, mildly plump, wearing a black cocktail dress that was short and tight.

'How old do you think she would be?' one of my companions asked.

'Twenty-five, or twenty-six?' guessed the other.

'Are you out of your mind? I first came here some fifteen years ago and she was here even then. She couldn't have been singing here at the age of ten.'

'Then how old do you think she is?'

We all looked at the woman. Under the soft lights, it was impossible to even guess. We returned to the beer and the kebabs.

Later that evening, as we stepped out of Trincas, I asked the liveried doorman who had just saluted us, 'That woman singing inside, how old do you think she is?'

'I don't know, sir.'

'Since when has she been singing here?'

'Since a long time ago.'

'How long?'

'Very long.'

'And since when have you been working here?'

'Since a long time ago.'

'How long?'

'Very long.'

'You must have some idea?'

'I don't remember the year, sir. All I remember is that Usha Uthup was still singing here. That was a long time ago.'

A long time ago. This was an expression I was coming across often in Calcutta. And the 'long time' would invariably be traced back not to a particular year but to the lifestyle indicators of the time.

A waiter I had spoken to in Olypub, a lively but somewhat rundown pub also situated on Park Street, had come from Orissa at a time when a peg of whisky cost Rs 1.75 and a cotton vest was sold in the market for Rs 1.25.

An elderly vendor on Camac Street, who runs a popular *vada* stall called Victoria Vada, once told me that he had started off by hawking wares outside the Victoria Memorial a long time ago—when the rail fare from Jaunpur, the town in Uttar Pradesh he migrated from, was seventeen rupees and a hearty meal cost ten annas.

And now the doorman at Trincas was telling me that he had come from Bihar when Usha Uthup, who later became famous by singing in Hindi films, was still the crowd-puller at the restaurant.

Men like these expected me to do back-calculation on the basis of nuggets their memory could serve. But how was I to know which year a cotton vest cost Rs 1.25?

As I prodded them for more clues about how long was a long time ago, I realised that these people have been living in Calcutta, doing the same thing they are still doing, from the time I was born—or sometimes even before. They are still around, so are the places. This meant I could still, in some small ways, make up for not having grown up in Calcutta.

At the same time I could not think of relocating to Calcutta, mainly for the fear that its charm may begin to wear off once I become a resident. Surely there must be other ways of knowing a city where I could not be born but would like to die—someday—to eventually be one with the soil that had given me my surname?

So that night, even as the age of the singer remained

undetermined, I became determined to write this book. That way I could return to Calcutta soon—and return more often.

By the time I hailed a taxi from outside Trincas, my mind had already begun working on a synopsis, even though I had barely finished researching a book about Chennai I had signed a contract for and was a long away from delivering the manuscript. Looking at one city as a subject had given me the courage to look at another.

SPRING

SPRING

1

THE SULTRY WOMAN looms in front of Howrah Station, selling men's deodorant to a city long associated with the smell of decay.

The billboard has been strategically placed, right at the mouth of the iconic bridge that is gleaming like a giant silver artefact under the March sun. You cannot enter the bridge, and therefore Calcutta, without noticing the advertisement.

The model, clad in a short red strapless dress, is seductively holding up a shiny cricket ball, as if asking the stream of humanity gushing out of the station: What would you prefer, the ball or my charm?

Her presence on the skyline is so overwhelming that you barely notice the product she is peddling, a fluorescent blue can of deodorant spray. But the tag line is impossible to miss: 'When the match ends, your game begins.'

The 2011 cricket World Cup, being hosted jointly by India, Sri Lanka and Bangladesh, has just begun. Forty-nine matches across forty-three days. Since the important matches start at 2.30 pm and finish typically around 11 in the night, the deodorant company (promoting a new brand called Googly to cash in on the cricket mood) has decided to play on the timings. Its message to the Calcutta man, who can readily sacrifice sex for sport during such tournaments, is explicit: Don't miss out on the match, but once it has ended, go ahead and seduce your woman (with the help of our deodorant, of course).

Looking at the billboard from the taxi, I suddenly recall a remark a friend had made some time ago. Returning to Calcutta after spending three years in conservative Chennai, she had written to me, 'How I missed Calcutta! There's a lot of love, sex and eroticism in the air.'

I have never looked at Calcutta that way. I have hardly known Calcutta for that matter. My visits to the city, first as a boy and much later as a son-in-law, have been too brief and protected to look beyond the visible.

But I can now see what my friend had possibly meant. Maybe these things were always in the air, just that I hadn't noticed them because I wasn't required to. And I can see them now because I have come with a notebook and a pen.

When you are carrying a notebook, it becomes your job to look around and listen. In Calcutta, you don't have to try very hard.

A minute out of the station and you realise this is not a city that requires peeping into. It lays bare its entrails for you. Poverty, riches, anger, joy, despair, failures, successes, beliefs—they are all exhibited on its pavements, walls and billboards. The visitor registers the unpleasant and quickly forgets the pleasant.

Calcutta is the most sneered-at, most maligned metropolis of India—and also the one most battered by the swing of the pendulum. Just until a century ago, it was the capital of Imperial India, the city of palaces, the city of cities, the Indian London.

The stage for its decline was set in 1912 when the British, faced with rising nationalist sentiments in Bengal, moved the seat of governance away to the more centrally-located Delhi. Over the next two decades, a brand new administrative capital—which they called New Delhi—was constructed and Calcutta ceased to be the most important address in India. By the 1940s, the film industry too began moving its base to Bombay. Then a crippling famine struck in 1943.

In 1947, when India became independent at the cost of a partitioned Bengal, Calcutta was flooded by a river of refugees fleeing the newly-carved East Bengal, which had now become a part of Pakistan. Even before this river could reduce to a trickle, yet another wave of refugees swept into the city in 1971, when East Bengal fought for freedom from Pakistan to become Bangladesh.

With the two successive influxes, Calcutta's population exploded. Its civic infrastructure nearly collapsed. Shortages grew, opportunities shrank. The city had far too many poor and unemployed than it could ever handle. There was hopelessness all around.

With the British now gone, the collective Bengali anger came to be trained against the new rulers and Calcutta, having long baked in the flames of revolution, easily transformed into a hub for communists. It became a city of protests and strikes, witnessing frequent upheavals and violence on its streets over political ideology. Business houses moved out as red hammer-and-sickle flags took over factories.

Its most famous resident, during these turbulent times, happened to be Mother Teresa, the 'saint of the gutters.' Her much-acclaimed work for the poor, for which she was given the Nobel Peace Prize in 1979, ended up drawing the world's attention to the unflattering side of

Calcutta. It came to be seen as a city of the destitute and the dying.

But a lot of water has flown under the Howrah Bridge since the days of Mother Teresa.

Today the man on the street appears sufficiently nourished and content. Political violence has moved to the hinterlands. Calls for *bandhs*, or closures, are far less frequent than before and succeed only in arousing public anger rather than sympathy. Students are a lot calmer. Unemployment is no longer a burning issue. Calcutta, if anything, looks enticing and charming—a delightful salad of the colonial and the Bengali with a dash of the global.

The information technology industry has established its presence in the city, creating a small but visible population of the young and the upwardly mobile. Shopping malls, considered a sign of prosperity, are filled with celebratory air round the year. Restaurants are forever packed and so are the nightclubs, whose floors pulsate to trance music and bhangra beats.

Tagore's compositions, meanwhile, have been set free from the custody of Viswa-Bharati because their copyright has expired. They are being reinvented by the younger generation of musicians, much to the horror of purists who believe Tagore is too sacred to be tampered with.

The Ambassador car is no longer the undisputed king of the road. Load-shedding is now a common feature in other cities, not anymore in Calcutta. Traffic is a breeze when you compare it with Bangalore's. Tram doors no longer bulge with office-goers; on the contrary, the trams run almost empty—but they still run.

The empty trams, in a way, define Calcutta. That they mostly run empty means the city has long moved on; but that they continue to run despite poor patronage shows that the city, even as changing times push it into the future, finds great comfort in its past.

Calcutta's eagerness to hold on to the days bygone—perhaps born out of the Bengali's inherent love for nostalgia—is what sets it apart. It's a once-upon-a-time-city.

One of its FM channels, Radio One, proudly calls itself a '100 per cent retro station' and shuns new songs. And if Trincas keeps the tradition of the live band alive, Flurys retains its colonial-era menu: both are located diagonally across from each other on Park Street, which boasts of many other eateries as well as shops that have been around as long as any Calcuttan can remember.

What's more, the city continues to be called Calcutta by its most popular English daily, *The Telegraph*, even though it was officially renamed Kolkata in 2001. Hardly anyone seems to have a problem with the paper's deliberate defiance of the rechristening, certainly not the nostalgia-loving Bengalis who have long been comfortable using both the names: Kolkata in their mother-tongue, and Calcutta in English.

And so Calcutta—the name and the city—lives on.

2

YOUR FIRST IMPRESSIONS of Calcutta may differ diametrically, depending on how you come to Calcutta—by train or plane.

If you come in a train, you will arrive invariably at the red-brick Howrah Station, which stands separated from the city by the width of the Hooghly River. Though there is another old station called Sealdah, it is the red-brick station, built during the time of Lord Curzon over a century ago, where nearly every train coming from outside Bengal terminates.

From the station, you will take the Howrah Bridge across the river and emerge straight into a Calcutta that you have read about or seen in the pictures—a city long fallen into disrepair and as if about to collapse.

The sense of an impending collapse will grip you even when you are still on the iconic bridge, where the load-bearers briskly trotting alongside your taxi will appear to tumble any moment under the weight of the merchandise they are transporting. The bridge, known to carry half a million pedestrians daily, is a stream of such load-bearers. The load, placed on their heads or balanced on bamboo poles across their shoulders, is often so heavy that it propels their feet into a jog.

Once you cross the bridge and enter the city, you will find the same load-bearers now turning into two-legged trucks that are required to follow traffic rules. In spite of the momentum induced by the loads on their heads, they squeeze their calf muscles to bring themselves to a halt each time the light turns red.

Then you will find other things that are about to collapse. Such as the decaying colonial-era buildings that now have trees growing out of their walls, or the multi-storeyed residential blocks where tenants continue to pay the same rent they paid sixty or seventy years ago. On the pavements you will find families of migrant labourers who sleep, bathe and cook by the road: their worlds too will seem to be teetering on the edge of collapse.

On the road you will find the most unusual assortment

of vehicles—from eighteenth-century modes of transport, such as trams and hand-pulled rickshaws, to the twenty-first century luxury cars and SUVs, not to mention the countless Ambassadors and buses of indeterminable age. So chaotic is the traffic that you will expect constant collisions: buses ramming into track-bound trams and impatient taxis running over rickshaw-pullers.

But nothing ever collapses. No collisions ever take place. No one ever dies in the madness that you meet outside the Howrah Bridge.

Instead, this Calcutta wakes up every dawn with renewed vigour, washing away the previous day's uncertainties and hardships in the river or in the water gushing from taps installed on the streets. The climbing sun lends a fresh glint to the old decay, the pavements soon begin to smell of food, the crowds erupt once again—and the city adds one more day to its more than three centuries of existence.

You may hate this Calcutta at the first sight—and may even hate it for the rest of your life. Conversely, you may fall in love with its chaotic charm and want to come back again.

But if you fly into Calcutta and from the airport take the Rajarhat Road into the city, you could be rubbing your eyes in wonder—is this Calcutta or Gurgaon?

You will tear through a global landscape, mile after mile, represented by upscale apartment complexes, state-of-the-art offices of information technology giants, plush malls and retail outlets. This Calcutta is called New Town—a technopolis, as some of the signboards.

Your wide-eyed ride will continue even after you have reached Salt Lake City, a planned township resplendent with prosperity and greenery. You won't find the mention of Salt Lake City in any of the acclaimed books that describe (mostly the horrors of) Calcutta. That's because it did not exist when Calcutta still interested writers from the West.

Salt Lake—the 'City' is rarely suffixed—was founded in 1962, reclaimed from saltwater lakes on the eastern fringes of the city, but it wasn't until the eighties that it came to be fully populated. Today this mini-Chandigarh, covering almost twelve square kilometres and divided into sectors and blocks, is also home to several government departments and Bengal's information technology industry.

The official name of Salt Lake is Bidhan Nagar—after its creator, Dr Bidhan Chandra Roy, the legendary chief minister—but is almost never used except in government signboards.

Only once you've crossed Salt Lake will you slowly begin to recognise the Calcutta you've read about in the books or seen in Satyajit Ray's films. Salt Lake, thirty times the size of Vatican City and six times that of Monaco, effectively sits between new and old Calcutta.

But even as you drive through New Town, often to the sight of an aeroplane or construction cranes looming on the horizon, you will find yourself in the lap of a vast emptiness.

Many of the high-rise apartment buildings are already occupied, the offices of the information technology giants are fully functional, while the malls and retail outlets display the newest arrivals in the world of fashion and gadgets—yet you will feel as if you are driving through a ghost city. You will find the soul of Calcutta missing from this modern landscape.

You can carve New Town out of a barren stretch of

land, but you cannot lend it the character of Calcutta by merely incorporating it in the geographical boundaries of the city. New Town, like Gurgaon, denotes the future; whereas Calcutta, once upon a time the greatest of Indian cities, finds comfort in its past. To be cut off from the past—and therefore cut off from the sense of belonging and familiarity provided by the past—is not being Calcutta enough.

Imagine living on a street that is identified by a set of digits and not named after a famous Bengali (or a Calcutta-loving Westerner); where you see more uniformed security guards than vendors, where access for visitors is so controlled that friends cannot drop in unannounced; where you don't spot a single dilapidated red-brick colonial-era mansion with green or grey slated windows; where you don't see political graffiti on the walls; where residents follow the time zone of their employers in America and work through holidays and can't even protest by shouting the all-too-familiar slogan, *Cholbe na! Cholbe na!*—This can't go on! This can't go on!

How can such a place be Calcutta?

Over time, New Town may get culturally assimilated into Calcutta. But as of now, die-hard Calcutta loyalists don't consider New Town, for that matter even Salt Lake, to be part of their dear city. They rather look down upon the residents of these recent townships for living on soil that has not been blessed by the footprints of either the colonial masters or any of the great Bengali nationalists.

Salt Lake, unfortunately or fortunately, happens to be my home in Calcutta. My mother-in-law lives there.

3

STARTLED, I LOOK out of the window yet again—is it raining?—only to find the curtains afloat in the air and the branches of the mango tree outside swaying wildly in the breeze, the rustle of its leaves mimicking the sound of a sudden downpour.

No way can it rain on a morning as pleasantly sunny as this. But the rustling leaves keep tricking me out of concentration as I recline on the bed with a cup of tea and the *Telegraph*, having arrived in Calcutta just an hour ago.

My fault: I've lived far too long in tropical Chennai to remember that back in the north, a fragrant breeze picks up at this time of the year to blow away not only drying leaves but also harsh memories of the winter.

And so what if it rains? I have no clothes drying on the balcony, no specific plans of going out, no appointments to honour and, above all, no job to keep. Back in Chennai, I've just quit my job with one newspaper and will return to join another only after a month.

To make the most of this unusually long break, I had spent a few days with my father in Kanpur before taking the Rajdhani Express to Calcutta.

Rajdhani Express isn't what it used to be once upon a time, when even its tickets would resemble the boarding card of an airline. Only the well-to-do would travel by it. Today it is just another respectable train. Maybe it is still a special train; just that other trains have caught up with it over the years, not to mention the budget airlines that have dealt a severe blow to the exclusivity of superfast trains such as the Rajdhani.

The excitement for me, however, lay in the destination:

I was taking a train from Kanpur to Calcutta after twenty-five years. The journey was a rerun of a tiny clip of childhood.

My immediate neighbours in the train happened to be two young bespectacled Bengali men who seemed to be studying in Kanpur and were now headed home on holiday. I was curious to know where exactly they were studying—IIT or the medical college—and had hoped to get a clue by eavesdropping on their conversation. I could have asked them directly, but I feared being held hostage to a long-drawn conversation.

But the two young men had spent their waking hours on the train talking mostly about food—how uninspiring the breakfast was at the hostel ('How can you have *poha* the first thing in the morning!'); how they missed the food they were used to having in Calcutta; the most memorable meals they'd had in recent times.

There was little doubt that they were going to pamper their taste-buds as soon as they reached Calcutta. The two were still fast asleep when, in the morning, I had woken up to something that pampered mine: the railways breakfast of buttered bread, cutlet and omelette.

Later, sipping the railways tea, I had watched the countryside of Bengal glide past: the fields, the green ponds, the hyacinths, the Communist slogans painted on brick walls, humans and animals moving about with an air of melancholy. Soon the landscape tapered into a bed of rail tracks, signalling the arrival of Howrah station—the gateway to Calcutta.

And now, after another round of breakfast at home, I am in bed with the paper, drinking tea and looking out of the window every now and then to see if it is raining.

Just then the indicator on my phone blinks. I have received a message on Facebook. The message is from a stranger—a woman—who says she has just finished reading my first book, *Chai, Chai*, and that she enjoyed it and would like to be friends with me. The eerie coincidence: she is a Bengali and lives in Calcutta.

Clicking open her profile page on my phone, I find myself looking at the picture of an attractive woman, who has listed herself as married—to another woman. I click open the profile of her spouse as well: a young bespectacled woman with bobbed hair.

I can't believe my luck. What better way to begin the Calcutta book than by interviewing two young lesbians who have shown the courage to get married to each other.

I instantly message her back, asking for her number, and soon we are chatting on the phone. She turns out to be a journalist too, with a Bengali TV channel. We decide to meet in the evening at Oxford Bookstore on Park Street.

At Oxford it turns out to be an unending wait for me. On a normal day I would have been only too happy to kill time in a bookshop but right now I am eager to get on with the evening. I try calling her but her phone is switched off.

Am I the victim of some kind of a prank? All this was too good to be true after all: that I should receive a message from an unknown woman living in Calcutta on the very day I arrive in the city—that too from a woman who is pretty and who has liked my book and who wants to be friends with me.

After an hour of browsing through books and looking at fountain pens, I step out onto the pavement. I give myself ten more minutes: if she doesn't call or show up by then,

I am going home. I decide to take a short walk on Park Street in the meantime.

Just a few paces from Oxford I am flagged down by a man seated on a piece of concrete by the pavement. He is fat and clad in a white vest and checked lungi. He is sitting down there with an air of lazy authority, as if he owns the whole of Park Street and is surveying his property from that lowly perch. 'Yes sir, what do you want?' he asks me.

'Me? I don't want anything.'

He motions me to come closer to him. 'But we have everything that you might want,' he tells me, 'College girl, call girl, housewife—whoever you choose.'

'Housewife?' I ask him surprised. I have heard of housewives moonlighting as prostitutes and always nursed a desire to meet one someday so that I can tell her story: what makes a coy homemaker—someone you'd run into in the supermarket or at the puja pandal—enlist herself in the sex market? Such stories not only arouse the sympathy (or indignation) of the audience but also titillate a large number of them, though few would ever admit to that.

'Yes, you get housewives too,' replies the fat man.

'And how much will I have to pay?'

'Rs 1,500 for a regular call girl, Rs 2,500 for a housewife, and Rs 3,500 for a college girl. You will get one full hour. We have rooms inside,' he says, pointing in the direction of a large grille gate which seems to be leading into a housing complex. (I later learn the complex is called Karnani Mansion.)

I have the money, but not the courage. What is the guarantee that the housewife will tell me her story? In all probability, she will have me thrown out if I were to take out my notebook. Then, other fears: what if the police decide to raid the place when I am with the woman; or what if she doesn't turn out to be a housewife after all, but a con woman who takes away my wallet, watch and phone?

But I like the idea that such a conversation is taking place in the open on Park Street at eight in the evening, when respectable (and fashionable) Bengalis are walking past us in desperate search for a table in one of the restaurants. Calcutta, clearly, believes in living and letting live.

'So you want housewife? College girl?' the fat man asks me.

'Not now, I don't have the money.'

'How can people like you not have the money?' he says sarcastically and waves me away with disdain.

Just when I begin to walk away from the laziest pimp on earth, I feel a tap on my shoulder. My Facebook friend has arrived.

The first thing that I notice are her eyes: alive, alert and resolute. She has worn a white top and a long printed skirt and has a sling bag across her shoulder.

'I am so sorry!' she is panting, 'You must have waited for long.'

'But why was your phone switched off?'

'I was in the editing studio. I had loads of work today. Tagore's 150th birth anniversary is coming up, you see. Now tell me, where would you like to go?

'You tell me. This is your city.'

'Peter Cat? Mocambo? Olypub?'

'Isn't there any restaurant by the river?'

She thinks for a while and says, 'There is one place. It's

actually a boat that has been turned into a restaurant. Would you like to go there?'

'Why not?'

'Taxi!' she yells at the top of her voice. An Ambassador screeches to a halt and we get in.

The boat turns out to be a floating luxury hotel, called The Floatel, anchored by the Strand. The deck serves as an open-air restaurant and offers, from a height of eighty feet, calming views of the river.

Behind me is the fortress-like State Bank of India building; to my right the familiar silhouette of Howrah Bridge; to my left the silhouette of Vidyasagar Bridge; in my front the woman with beautiful eyes. Her nose-pin sparkles in the candlelight.

'Would you mind if I smoke?' I ask her.

'Please go ahead,' she says and digs out a packet of Classic Milds from her bag. I light her cigarette as well.

'I wish you had brought your wife along,' I tell her.

'I did ask her,' she laughs, 'but she is tied up this evening.'

'Never mind, but I would like to meet her sometime.'

'But how did you decide that she is the wife? She could be the husband and I could be the wife.'

'I am so sorry, it never struck me. What I meant was spouse.'

'It's okay, not everybody understands people like us.'

I feel my ears turning red. I take a sip of whisky and say, 'But I must admire your courage. It mustn't have been easy to come out in the open, that too on Facebook.'

'So you really fell for that?' she laughs out loud.

'Excuse me?'

'She is not my wife or spouse or whatever. She is just a good friend.'

'What do you mean?'

'No, we are not lesbians. We just decided to have some fun on Facebook, just to shock people.'

A cool breeze sweeps up the river and across the deck.

Two hours and two drinks each later, we get into a taxi once again. She is going to drop me back to Park Street on her way home to Tollygunge.

As the taxi turns left from the Strand and speeds through the wide empty road along the Maidan, she puts a cigarette between her lips. When I lean towards her to light it up, her hair blows over my face.

'I am sorry about that,' she says.

'About what?'

'For making you believe that you had a juicy story. You came all the way for that, didn't you?'

'That's okay. I had a good time.'

'No really, I am sorry,' she says, 'I am going to make up for it. What time is it?'

'Ten-thirty.'

'Come with me to my place for another drink?'

4

CALCUTTA IS LIKE no other city in India. Give a third-world look to London, spray it with the permissive air of Paris, lend it the temperament of Latin America, people it with Bengalis—Calcutta would be that city.

This uniqueness is lost on most Bengali men who seem far too concerned with what's happening around the world than in their own backyard. And the world being what it is, Bengali men, since they read the newspaper cover to cover, always find some cause or the other to be angry about and debate. If there's anything that their anger does not make them blind to, it's food.

The night India lose to South Africa in one of the early World Cup matches, a distant relative at whose house I manage to catch the tail-end of the game is furious with the Indian captain, Mahendra Singh Dhoni.

He fumes, 'India *te ektai captain chhilo, shey holo* Sourav Ganguly!'—India has had only one able cricket captain, Sourav Ganguly (a Bengali).

He carries his anger along like an unfinished glass of drink as he leads his guests—three fashionable couples apart from me—to the dining table. The anger turns out to be infectious. Over a delightful meal of rice and mutton curry, the men make a mince-meat of Dhoni for having trusted Ashish Nehra, not the most accurate of bowlers, with the final (and decisive) over:

'Why did Dhoni have to give the ball to that ass?

'Sourav would have never done that.'

'What a shame.'

'Didn't I just tell you,' the host repeats, 'India has produced just one good captain, and that was Sourav Ganguly.'

The women at the table remain unaffected by the mourning. They carry on a parallel conversation among themselves: about the difficulties in readying their children for school early in the morning, about the maids not being efficient enough, about the new restaurants in Calcutta, about the adulterous activities of various men and women they know.

Bengali women love to talk, but unlike the men, stay clear of subjects that do not have a direct bearing on their lives. They are always articulate and assertive—besides being attractive. Some are soft-spoken yet firm, some others outspoken and bold, but they always have their say and, very often, their way.

5

'BODON SINGH! O BODON SINGH!'

My mother-in-law's heavy voice wakes me up every morning. I open my eyes to find her standing at the window by my bed. With her forehead pressed against the grille, she calls out, 'Bodon Singh! O Bodon Singh!'

Badan Singh, the one-eyed watchman, lives in a small room in the backyard, which this window overlooks. She calls out to him every morning to let him know that the tea is ready and that he should come up and get it.

Badan Singh was one of the many Bihari labourers involved in the construction of this house back in 1987, when Salt Lake was still a developing neighbourhood. For some inexplicable reason, my in-laws took a liking for him and had retained him as the watchman once the house was built. His perks included a glass of tea every morning and evening, and breakfast on Sundays.

Ever since my father-in-law passed away in 2005—this was a year before I got married—Badan Singh's presence in the house became even more assuring for my mother-in-law. If there is anyone she trusts the house keys with, it is Badan Singh. He calls her *ma ji*, or mother. She refers to him as *buro*—the old man. They must be the same age, about seventy.

'You know something,' my mother-in-law tells me over tea every morning, 'I've set aside a certain sum for *buro*. It is my duty to give him some money once he retires.'

'How much have you set aside for him, *ma*?' I ask, pretending this is the first time I am hearing about the retirement benefits that await Badan Singh.

'One lakh rupees. He has served us long enough. I can't send him away empty-handed, can I?'

'Of course you can't.'

'My daughters laugh at me. They say I am tight-fisted. But had I been a spendthrift, would they be living in such a palatial house today? True that I don't spend on myself, but have I deprived them of anything?'

'No, you haven't.'

'Tell me, do you save money?'

'No. Never.'

'Very bad. You are just like your father-in-law. He was a spendthrift too. But he was a nice man, very large-hearted. I wish you could've met him. You know, some 300 people came for the feast the day we moved into this house. He had invited just about everybody. Would you like to have some more tea?'

I indulge her because I quite like her: she is one of those forthright, upright people from the bygone era who have come up in life the hard way without seeking obligations or taking shortcuts, and who like to measure others with the principles they themselves had adhered to all their lives.

She is blunt enough to call a spade a spade, no matter how polite the occasion. During the lunch she had hosted at home the day before my wedding, she publicly warned one of the guests, even as he was delightfully tucking into the various varieties of fish, that he should watch his weight.

'You must control your diet,' my mother-in-law, who

holds a doctorate in physical education, had sternly told him. It had not mattered to her that the guest belonged to the groom's side. The man gorging on fish happened to be one of my own elderly cousins: a food-loving doctor who had come all the way from New Alipore to Salt Lake only because he couldn't resist the menu.

Quite ironically, the cousin died some months after, within hours of undergoing a bypass surgery.

It is impossible to imagine my mother-in-law having a soft, social conversation with anyone on this earth. The moment a conversation begins, she assumes the role of a teacher, an instructor—which is what she had been all her working life.

But there is a soft side which remains shadowed by her matronly self. As a teenager she wrote poems, in Bengali as well as in English, which remain preserved in her diaries. Since I am a good listener, she reads them out to me from time to time. What do poets want other than a patient pair of ears?

At times I feel sad that such body of work should remain unweighed and unexamined for literary merit, dug out of the almirah only when someone is willing to lend an ear.

But at the dining table she is more of a matron than a poet.

The conversation over morning tea, even though it largely revolves around Badan Singh and my late father-in-law, occasionally meanders to other subjects, such as the weather or the headlines of the day. But what is spoken over lunch repeats itself with unbelievable sameness every afternoon that we eat together—as if dictated by a written script.

'Come sit,' she will command me in an indulgent manner, as if I were her favourite student and not son-in-law. 'You don't eat prawns, do you?'

'No, *ma*.'

'Not even *ilish*?'

'No. Only mutton and *rui* fish, that too preferably after I've had a few drinks.'

'Had your mother been alive, I would have told her that she hadn't taught her son anything about the art of eating.'

'You cannot teach such things, *ma*. It is all about temperament. I have never been particularly fond of meat or fish.'

'No, you need to be taught from childhood, only then you learn.'

As we start eating, she will begin telling her story, right from her childhood.

Mahamaya, my mother-in-law, was born in 1940 in a town in Assam, where her father, a doctor who had graduated from the Calcutta Medical College, ran a practice. When she was seven or eight, she was put under the care of a rich uncle living in Mirzapur in East Bengal.

The uncle, an Army officer-turned-industrialist-turned-philanthropist called Ranada Prasad Saha, had just built a hospital and a residential school for girls (they still run, Kumudini Hospital and Bharateswari Homes, both well-known names in Bangladesh).

He was particularly fond of Mahamaya, who grew up in awe of him. For her, the uncle—or *jethamoshai*, as she called him—was a model man: dynamic, disciplined, larger-than-life. He wanted her to take up a job in one of his institutions once she had finished studying, but

Mahamaya, even though she idolised him, did not want to live off his benevolence forever.

In 1964, she left Bangladesh and landed in Gwalior, where she found herself a job in a big college as a physical education teacher. *Jethamoshai*, his ego hurt, stopped talking to her. But they patched up some years later in Calcutta, where he had taken ill during a visit and was looked after by Mahamaya, who also happened to be in Calcutta at the time. That was the last time she saw *jethamoshai*.

In 1971, when East Bengal fought for independence from Pakistan—in a war that led to the formation of Bangladesh—*jethamoshai* and his newly-married son were taken away from their home by uniformed men. They never returned. They were presumed to have met the same fate as tens of thousands of other Bengalis who were murdered by Pakistani soldiers during the nine-month-long war.

By then, Mahamaya was teaching in a Delhi college. She was pregnant with her first daughter—the one I was to marry—when she read about her *jethamoshai*'s abduction in a newspaper in the college library.

I know the story by heart. Yet it is narrated with undiluted earnestness, give or take a few anecdotes, each afternoon we sit for lunch.

And on evenings she spots me pouring a drink:

'How many pegs do you have in a day?'

'It depends, *ma*. But mostly two,' I lie.

'I have nothing against drinking. But you must never exceed two pegs. *Jethamoshai* used to drink every evening, and he used to drink in style. But he never went beyond two pegs.'

Fortunately she retires for the night when I am still on my first drink. Writing through the night, I invariably exceed the number of pegs prescribed by her and go to sleep around four in the morning, only to be woken up shortly after by the call: 'Bodon Singh! O Bodon Singh!'

6

SOON MY DAYS arrange themselves into a pattern.

As soon as I wake up, I sit with the *Telegraph*, which I think is the best sub-edited English paper in the country. I read the paper over two cups of tea, simultaneously listening to my mother-in-law's plans for Badan Singh's retirement and stories about my father-in-law's spendthrift ways.

Then I go for a long walk at Central Park, which is a stone's throw from home. In the afternoons, after lunch, I set out with no particular destination in mind; occasionally, though, I have an appointment. Evenings, if I am not home, are invariably spent on Park Street.

It is the walk at Central Park and the stroll on Park Street that I look forward to the most. The park, maintained by the forest department, is almost like a miniature wildlife sanctuary, complete with a large lake, but without the wild animals. The greenery stretches as far as eyes can see, and far in the horizon loom buildings that house various departments of the government of West Bengal.

From five till nine in the morning, when entry is free, the park is overrun by walkers. From ten o' clock onwards, when the entry becomes ticketed—twenty rupees a person—it turns into a lovers' paradise. Couples start arriving even before the clock can strike ten, getting out of weathered taxis that would have brought them from various corners of Calcutta.

Right outside the gate of the park are two shops—each competing with the other—selling chips, biscuits and soft drinks. They also rent plastic mats to couples for a deposit of twenty rupees, of which ten are returned once the mat is handed back.

Since I am rarely able to leave home before ten, I invariably pay to enter the park. The ticket is issued by a clerk who seems disinterested in his job and who always has a packet of cigarettes and a matchbox placed next to the ticketing machine. The ticket is then examined—and torn slightly, in order to prevent reuse—by a beedi-smoking gatekeeper.

The plus side of making a late entry is that you have the entire park to yourself—not a soul in sight except lovers trying to hide in cosy corners.

Each time I walk past an amorous pair, I avert my gaze just in time so that they don't catch the voyeur in me red-handed. Only once did my ears pick up a part of a conversation between two lovers, that too because the woman happened to be too loud. She was telling the man: 'You know what my son said this morning? He said, "Mother, I have an exam today. Where are you off to?"'

I had wanted to pause and have a good look at the woman and also at the man—whether he deserved the sacrifice made by the woman—but I walked on.

One morning I run into a man—rotund, bald and sunburned—who makes no bones about being a voyeur. Holding a large black umbrella to shield his tanned pate from the sun, he is going from one tree to another just to ogle at couples who are cosying up in the shade.

Imagine lying on your lover's lap under a tree and suddenly noticing a pair of large lustful eyes—embedded on the face of a bald, sunburned man—slowly emerging from behind the trunk, along with the black umbrella.

Couples react differently to his intrusion: some stand up with alacrity, as if they have spotted a snake; while others merely break away from the embrace and sit straight. The voyeur then moves on to the next tree to unsettle another unsuspecting pair of lovers. I am not sure what gives him the kick: watching the intimate moments between lovers from close, or watching them react to his presence.

Such brazen voyeurism would have earned him a slap or two, if not a sound thrashing, in any other location; but in a park, where lovers themselves are little better than thieves hiding from the world outside, he can afford to be bold. No sane couple would want a confrontation with him for the fear of being discovered—and the voyeur knows that very well.

'That man with a black umbrella, does he come here often?' I ask the gatekeeper on my way out of the park.

'Almost every day, around the same time,' the gatekeeper replies.

'Why don't you stop him? He disturbs people.'

'How can we? He buys a ticket.'

The gatekeeper tells me that once upon a time, Central Park used to be frequented by families. But once it transformed into a lovers' haunt, the families began to keep away. The state government decided to act. It built, on an adjacent piece of land, a smaller park, complete with play equipment, for families. Couples were barred from entering the new park.

The voyeur soon becomes part of my morning-walk

routine. On days I don't spot his umbrella, I look for him. Once I almost smiled at him as he walked past me.

Park Street, meanwhile, has become my second home in Calcutta. When I don't go there I feel I am missing out on an event that I should be part of.

Park Street *is* an event: an elegant dance of the colonial times in the courtyard of contemporary.

The show begins at seven-thirty in the morning when Flurys opens. It serves, among other things, English breakfast and therefore remains a living link to the British days.

By the time the first set of patrons wash down their breakfast with first-class Assam tea, the rest of Park Street stirs awake. Magazine-sellers take their positions on the pavement, cigarette shops open, parking attendants show up and so do the women beggars. Soon after, other eateries and shops begin to raise their shutters.

By noon, Park Street is dancing to its practiced rhythm— and is ready for lunch.

The festive air that descends during lunchtime continues to hang thick until well after midnight, when all other shutters are down but the gates of Park Hotel still spit out smartly-dressed young women who are flagging down taxis to get home. Their perfumes linger long after they are gone, and by noon the smell of food once again takes over Park Street.

Park Street's energy comes from food. Every eatery here is legendary, and finding a table in the most popular ones is always a challenge. A manager in suit and tie, standing at the door, will take down your name and phone number and ask you to wait.

The wait can last even up to an hour, especially during

dinner time, but you endure it because each time the door opens to let in or let out a group of diners, the aroma of food that wafts out makes you hungrier and even more determined to stay put. Moreover, there is no guarantee that you will have it easier at another restaurant—the wait could be even longer there.

People who make the mistake of wandering away during the waiting period often return to find their name already called out by the suited manager, who now gives preference to those who had chosen to hang in there. When he finally invites you in after the long wait, you are so overcome by gratitude that you already like the food.

Bengalis are discerning eaters. The dishes come under scrutiny as soon as they are laid on the table and a serious discussion ensues: Isn't the mutton excellent? Don't you think they should have added some more mustard to the fish? Isn't the chicken curry a little bland unlike what we ate the last time?

Every Bengali dining out is a food critic. Their opinion may not make it to the papers, but it certainly reaches the ears of people next table.

One evening at Mocambo, I find myself flanked by two divergent sets of diners. The table to my left has a bunch of boisterous journalists who celebrate the arrival of their sizzlers by taking pictures of the food. The table to my right is occupied by a family consisting of an elderly gent and three women of varying ages—the oldest must be around sixty and the youngest about twenty.

The old man is unhappy from the start—he is irritated by the noise in the restaurant. The noise is nothing but the collective drone generated by excited conversations taking place at the various tables.

'Once I went to a restaurant in London,' the old man tells the women, 'people there were eating in silence, as if they were mute.' He puts a finger to his lips to demonstrate the silence of the London diner.

The women pay scant attention to him and are scanning the menu. All three settle for continental fare, while the old man orders *tandoori rotis* and *paneer butter masala*.

The *rotis*, when they come, harden in no time and the old man has a tough time tearing them—and also chewing them. Already the noise is killing him. The women, meanwhile, gleefully attack their food with forks and knives.

At another table nearby, a young woman is protesting as her companion transfers some sliced onions and capsicum onto her plate along with *seekh kebabs*. She squeals, '*Ei, amake ghaas-phoos dibi na*'—Don't give me *ghaas-phoos*.

Ghaas-phoos, or weeds, is an insulting term non-vegetarians accord to vegetables. This woman wants to concentrate on the meat alone. Looking at her devotion to the *kebabs*, I summon the waiter and order some for myself.

But it is not very often that I get into these restaurants when I come to Park Street. I usually begin with the Oxford bookstore, where I spend about an hour. Then I walk down the length of the street and cross over to the opposite side and get into Music World. There I am invariably looking for a Bengali song I would have heard on one of the FM channels and taken a fancy to.

Occasionally, if I am hungry, I step into Flurys and order masala omelette along with toast and Assam tea, and through its glass panels watch Indian sahibs and memsahibs walk past at a leisurely pace, often with a determined beggar in tow.

The beggars are always either emaciated women jingling coins in a steel tumbler or small girls telling you that they haven't eaten all day. They can chase you for long distances, unlike the fat lungi-clad pimp who is forever seated on his throne near Oxford Bookstore, waiting for custom to fall on his lap.

He no longer calls out to me when I walk past him. His trained eyes can perhaps tell that I am no longer new in Calcutta.

7

CALCUTTA, AS OF 2011, is 321 years old. That is if you go by the popular story that the city was founded by East India Company merchant Job Charnock on 24 August 1690 when he landed at Sutanuti, a village by the Hooghly, with the intention of building a fortified trading base for the British.

But it would not be entirely right to call Charnock the founder of Calcutta, just as it would be entirely wrong to think of Calcutta as India's first British city.

Madras—or Chennai—is India's first British city, founded by the Company in 1640 with the construction of Fort St George. Practically every modern institution in the country—army, judiciary, education, engineering—traces its origins to the fort at Madras.

By the 1650s the Company had expanded its trade from the east coast to Bengal; but it was not until the 1680s that it began to feel the need for a Madras-like fortified settlement in Bengal as well in order to protect its interests in the region.

Among the locations that were considered to build a

fortified base was Chittagong. But Job Charnock, who had spent nearly his entire career in Bengal, rooted for Sutanuti. He was familiar with the riverside village, which not only offered deep anchorage but also had a thriving textile trade.

Charnock finally had his way, but not before he had half-heartedly participated in an expedition to forcibly take Chittagong from the Mughals. The expedition got botched and the Company had to shut shop in Bengal and retreat to Madras.

It was from Madras that Charnock, once the Mughals agreed to restore the Company's trading rights, had led his men back to Bengal, landing at Sutanuti, amid heavy rains, on the morning of 24 August 1690.

Charnock, almost sixty at the time, lived only two and a half years more, and during this period not a brick was laid to build a fort or even a factory because the Mughal governor had still not given formal consent. He died on 10 January 1693.

Eight months later when Sir John Goldsborough, the president of Madras presidency who was now also responsible for Bengal, arrived in Sutanuti on inspection, he found the settlement in utter disorder.

He was incensed that neither Charnock nor his successor Francis Ellis had thought of marking out a site for the proposed fort, which was the least they could have done pending permission from the Mughals. This lapse on their part, Goldsborough believed, had allowed the British settlers to build themselves dwellings where and how they pleased, even on plots that would have been most suitable for the fort.

He sacked Ellis and replaced him with Charles Eyre,

Charnock's son-in-law, as the chief agent for Bengal. He also ordered a piece of land in the neighbouring village of Kalikata (which was not as populated as Sutanuti) to be enclosed with a mud wall so that the fort could be built on it once permission was granted.

Before he could achieve more, Goldsborough died of a fever in November 1693—barely three months after arriving in Sutanuti—and joined Charnock in the graveyard, which was a stone's throw from the piece of land he had just ordered to be enclosed.

It was Charles Eyre who, in 1696, began the construction of Fort William on the site marked by Goldsborough. It was also Eyre who, in 1698, formally leased Sutanuti, Kalikata and the adjoining village, Gobindapur, from the Sabarna Roychoudhury family, which had been given the zamindari rights for these villages by the Mughals.

These three riverside villages, which sat close to each other on the east bank of the Hooghly—Sutanuti to the north, Gobindapur to the south, and Kalikata between them—got merged into a single entity over a period of time. The new township—since Fort William, the administrative centre, was located in Kalikata—came to be called Calcutta.

It wasn't until 1710 that letters sent by the Company from Bengal to its headquarters in London began carrying the address, 'Fort William in Calcutta.' Charnock, by then, had been in the grave for seventeen years.

The foundations of the city were, therefore, effectively laid by Goldsborough and Charles Eyre. Charnock had only shown the way to Sutanuti.

In Calcutta, at least officially, Charnock is no longer considered its founder and August 24 no longer considered its founding day. An order to this effect was passed by the Calcutta high court in 2003 following a case filed by the descendants of the Sabarna Roychoudhury family, who contended that the three villages were already flourishing under the patronage of their ancestors even before Charnock's arrival.

Charnock's Calcutta no longer exists anyway. The Calcutta we see today bears the unmistakable stamp of another East India Company employee who was born nearly a century after Charnock and who, with his courage and cunning, single-handedly elevated the status of the British from that of traders to rulers: Robert Clive.

In mid-1756, the Nawab of Bengal, the young Siraj-ud-Daula, realising that the British traders had become too big for their boots, invaded Calcutta and captured Fort William. While most of the inhabitants fled the fort before the Nawab's army took it on 20 June 1756, those who could not were locked up overnight in a tiny cell so that they could be interrogated the next morning. Of the 146 said to be held, only twenty-three survived the detention; the remaining died of suffocation and the cell at Fort William came to be known as the Black Hole.

Though the death toll was disputed by latter-day historians, who argued that it would have been physically impossible to pack 146 Europeans into a cell fourteen by eighteen feet, the Black Hole lent a moral justification to Robert Clive's campaign as he set out from Madras in late 1756 to free Calcutta from the Nawab of Bengal.

Clive, by then, had already built himself an impressive CV during a decade-long stint in Madras, rising from a lowly clerk to being hailed as 'a heaven-born general' during the siege of Arcot.

He not only recaptured Calcutta but also went on to engage the Nawab in a battle at Plassey, not far from Bengal's capital Murshidabad, on 23 June 1757. The Nawab, betrayed by his own men, not only lost the battle but also his life.

Clive, thus securing Bengal for the British, set out to build a new Calcutta. He demolished the village of Gobindapur to construct a new, stronger Fort William, and cleared the jungle around it to leave a vast empty space so that in case of future attacks the approaching enemy would have no cover. The empty space became the Maidan. Charles Eyre's Fort William became the custom house before it was pulled down in 1818.

Today, Clive's Fort William serves as the headquarters of the Indian Army's Eastern Command. The village of Kalikata, where the old Fort William stood, grew into Dalhousie Square, now BBD Bagh, with the infamous Black Hole said to be buried under the General Post Office.

The village of Sutanuti, where it all began, has become notional. On the present-day map, it would occupy chunks of Shobhabazar and Shyambazar in north Calcutta. The only mention you will find of it is in the signage at the Shobhabazar metro station, which is officially called 'Shobhabazar Sutanuti.' Otherwise, there is no place today in Calcutta called Sutanuti.

Yet, the story of Calcutta continues to begin with Charnock's landing at Sutanuti on the morning of 24 August 1690. That's how it has begun for over three centuries now. That's a nice way to begin a story, though, for it was a rainy morning—and a Sunday morning at that.

8

CHARNOCK'S ACCOUNT OF his arrival at Sutanuti is showcased in a gallery at the Victoria Memorial:

> 'This day at Sankraul [Sankral, a village on the west bank of the Hooghly] ordered Capt. Brooke to come up with his Vessell to Chutanutte [Sutanuti] where We arrived about noon, but found ye place in a deplorable condition, nothing being left for our present accommodation & ye Rains falling day & night.'

The Victoria Memorial, built to match the grandeur of the Taj Mahal, is easily the most imposing statement of British power to stand in Calcutta, even though it was inaugurated a little too late in the day, in 1921, when India was almost at the doorstep of freedom.

I have been inside Victoria Memorial only once before, on a scorching afternoon in 1981 when my Lake Gardens aunt, who is now dead, had brought me here on my insistence. I was eleven years old then, and the building only sixty. All I remember is lingering at the weapons gallery.

In the recent years, ever since I got married and started visiting Calcutta all over again, I have been watching the Victoria Memorial only from outside its gates—either while taking a buggy ride around the Maidan or having *phuchkaas* from one of the vendors stationed across the road.

Set against the vast emptiness of the Maidan, the white-marble structure—complete with the Figure of Victory atop its dome—is one of the most majestic sights of

Calcutta and somehow makes me proud of the city even though I am neither British nor a Calcuttan.

But now that I am inside, after thirty years, I soon find myself running out of patience as I stare at the exhibits on the walls. The weapons do not interest me anymore, the paintings are barricaded a bit too far to be lingered upon, the precious books I would like to leaf through are—quite understandably—locked up in glass cases.

I spend some time at the Calcutta gallery, which traces the birth and the growth of the city, starting with Charnock's account of his arrival. I learn, among other things, that *babus*—cultured Bengalis who made enormous wealth from their association with the British—were "inveterate ladies' men with lax morals", and that Gobindram Mitter, Calcutta's first *babu*, draped goddess Durga in gold and silver.

What particularly interests me is the facsimile of an advertisement for Kali Cigarettes, marketed as '*bishuddha swadeshi*' (purely Indian-made) at a time when anti-British sentiment was picking up in the city. I have also read somewhere about Kali brand of alcohol being sold in local watering holes around that time.

Kali, the dark goddess with her tongue sticking out, has always loomed over Calcutta: her temple at Kalighat predates the arrival of the British by several decades, and it is quite likely that she gave her name to the village of Kalikata, which eventually gave its name to the city. She evokes fear most of the time, but is sometimes invoked, as one can see, as a nationalist brand name.

But Victoria Memorial, which was Lord Curzon's idea of paying tribute to Queen Victoria when she died in 1901, was built with Indian money. The cost of its construction—one crore and five lakh rupees—was borne entirely by rich Indians, the numerous princes included, who were eager to please the British.

Preserved in bronze, Victoria sits on her throne in the garden, facing the gates of the memorial and the Maidan beyond. The idea is that anyone visiting the Victoria Memorial should not fail to notice her or escape her gaze.

As I climb down the steps of the museum and walk across the garden to the exit gate, I turn back to look at Victoria one more time. She looks grandmotherly and rather glum—just like one of those elderly Indian women who, once they consider themselves too old to do anything else, sit on the verandah or balcony all day to watch the world go by, showing no emotion even when visitors arrive or leave.

I walk out of the memorial into the Maidan and seat myself on a grassy patch. To describe the Maidan in physical measurements would make no sense for it is simply too huge. From where I am sitting right now, amid the smell of horse dung, Calcutta appears to have been put on the mute mode. I can see vehicles moving along the perimeter of the Maidan but cannot hear their engines because of the distance separating us.

All I can hear now is the sound of cricket. Dozens of matches are in progress, the players being young boys from nearby neighbourhoods. A new pitch comes up right in front of where I am sitting and a boy goes about placing bricks on the grass to mark the boundary. He is about to place one brick very close to me when another boy who is hammering the stumps into the ground shouts at him: '*Okhane dibi na, okhane foreigner ta boshe achhe*'—Don't place the brick near the foreigner.

There is no way I can be mistaken for a foreigner—read Westerner—but I guess he takes me to be one because I am sitting all by myself in the Maidan, wearing sunglasses and scribbling in my notebook.

The boy who is marking the boundary ignores him and places the brick near my feet. He then runs in the direction of the pitch, shouting back to the other boy, 'O foreigner na, o Bangali'—He is not a foreigner, he is a Bengali.

So what if I didn't grow up in Calcutta. I easily belong here. I have the looks.

9

AS THE DAYS pass, the sun begins to get hotter. Not hot enough yet to prevent you from loitering in Calcutta, but enough to make you crave for another glass of *aam panna*—that tangy raw-mango drink—being sold on College Street.

College Street is not a street, but an institution by itself: nearly every Bengali that India reveres rose from this street. It is not a street even by municipal standards, but a wide road where trams still jostle with buses and yellow Ambassadors.

On one side are the temples of learning: Calcutta Medical College, which is India's oldest; University of Calcutta; Presidency College. On the other side, where the entire pavement is occupied by booksellers, stands the Coffee House—directly opposite Presidency College.

The Coffee House too is an institution by itself; not just because it belongs to College Street, but also because it has institutionalised the Bengali's favourite pastime: *adda*.

Adda, loosely defined, means chit-chat. More precisely, it is the exchange that takes place when a group of people with similar interests and aspirations—they could be writers or students or housewives—gathers at a particular place in the evening with the sole purpose of chit-chatting.

The exchange, depending on the composition of the group, can be intellectual in nature or just plain gossip. The idea is to meet up and talk. The venue can be the neighbourhood park, the local tea-shop, someone's home, or the Coffee House.

Your credentials as a Bengali intellectual aren't impressive enough if you haven't done *adda* at Coffee House at some point in your life. You should have spent numerous evenings there with your buddies, sitting around cups of tea or coffee, engulfed in cigarette smoke: each time one took a drag and exhaled the smoke, he also discharged in the air his ambitions and anxieties for the others to inhale. Many a famous Bengali had once upon a time spent his evenings in Coffee House and had lit his cigarettes with the fire burning in his belly.

There is even a song, in the voice of Manna Dey, which pays a poignant tribute to the culture of *adda* at Coffee House and which, needless to say, enjoys cult status in Calcutta:

> *Coffee House-er shei adda ta aaj aar nei, aaj aar nei*
> *kothaye hariye gelo shonali bikel gulo shei aaj aar nei . . .*

> That *adda* at Coffee House no longer happens,
> Those golden evenings are lost, they no longer happen.

The song is about seven friends who would meet for *adda* at Coffee House during their younger days but who now lay scattered and are no longer in touch—the artist is in Paris, the journalist in Dhaka, the guitarist has gone to the grave, the poet is battling cancer, and so on—and the seven chairs they once sat on are now occupied by fresh faces.

It mourns the fading of a generation and therefore gives voice to the Bengali's perennial aching for the bygone.

Coffee House is situated on the first floor of a historic building called Albert Hall. If not for the signboard of Coffee House, the building would go unnoticed, eclipsed by the shops selling textbooks. Heritage structures are a dime a dozen in Calcutta: no one cares for them unless they are attached to a tradition.

Stepping into Albert Hall, I nearly trip because of a cavity in the floor. Seeing me stumble, two girls who are on their way out stifle their laughter. I climb up the stairs. On the landing, the aged walls have political posters pasted on them. They have been put up by students' unions belonging to various ideologies.

Nearly all the posters are in Bengali, a language I can read only haltingly even though it is my mother tongue. As I stand there deciphering their contents—most of them are seething with anger against the Congress-led government at the Centre—I can hear the buzz emanating from Coffee House. Multiple *adda* sessions must be in progress.

I am a little nervous entering the hall because I have no idea what to expect in a place so romanticised as this. I imagine myself being surrounded by groups of bearded men and gorgeous women, cigarettes between their fingers, and being sneered at for knowing nothing of Nietzsche or

Foucault. For that matter, I've read very little of Tagore—and now I see a larger than life portrait of a young Tagore, wearing a black beard, looming over the tables in the high-ceilinged hall.

Coffee House, however, turns out to be more of a lovers' hangout.

Young men and women, just into college, like to linger here because they pay next to nothing for killing time in the hallowed premises—the most expensive dish on the menu, baked fish, comes for fifty-five rupees. A cup of coffee costs eight.

Older people drop by too every now and then, not just for the cheap food but also the experience. Coffee House, after all, is also a museum of memories. The curators are the waiters who still wear Raj-era white uniforms, which include a cummerbund and turban.

One such waiter comes over with a glass of water. I try to initiate a conversation with him but he is not interested. All I get to know is that he is from Bihar and has been working here since—quite predictably—a long time ago. He is impatient to take my order. I ask for Mughlai Paratha.

Seated at the table next to mine is a young couple. They are sitting in total silence, and that's because the woman is gazing lovingly into the man's eyes. Books are placed on their table: not Nietzsche or Foucault, but college textbooks.

At another adjacent table is another couple. If their body language is anything to go by, the man is trying to persuade the woman into something. Eavesdropping is not a possibility here because of the noise; Coffee House is noisier than a college canteen.

I look around. I want to witness, first-hand, an *adda* of the intellectual kind in progress. But even at tables that have large groups, I only detect banter and not heated debates. People are talking, laughing, smoking and eating.

Maybe this is how *adda* sessions look from a distance, who knows. I have not seen Sunil Gangopadhyay or Mrinal Sen warming the chairs in Coffee House to be able to tell the difference.

I am still looking around when a tall grey-haired man, carrying a *jhola*—or sling bag—enters. He dispenses with the courtesy of asking whether he could share my table, drags a chair and seats himself. He looks angry—not the kind of angry when you have a spat with someone, but when you are angry with the system, with the whole world. His mind is somewhere far away; and with his eyes still set on an unspecified object at a distance, he pulls out a packet of cigarettes from his pocket and lights one.

Emboldened, I light up too. Not everywhere in the country can you smoke in a public place, that too in an eatery, ever since a ban came into effect in 2008. Calcutta is the only city that makes concessions for smokers by looking the other way if you happen to be breaking the rule.

Communism and the habit of smoking go back a long way, when one could bond with a rank stranger by offering him a cigarette or even bumming one from him, and convert him into a comrade over a smoke.

The idea may not work today because the risks of smoking stand far more successfully propagated than any political ideology, but communism did romanticise the habit and create several generations of hardened smokers.

Coffee House, by giving its patrons the freedom to

smoke, is only insisting on preserving its old self. If a regular from the 1960s were to return to Coffee House today, he would find the place smelling just the same—the combined smell of cigarette smoke, fried food and coffee.

I have to put out the cigarette prematurely because the Mughlai Paratha has arrived. It doesn't look as inviting as it had in the pictures that a friend—a non-resident Bengali living in America—had posted on Facebook after a visit to Coffee House. Even the plate and spoon can do with another round of washing.

But never mind—this is Coffee House. You can't fall ill by eating in a place where legends have eaten before. Its reputation is a powerful germ-killer.

I wonder for a moment if I should start eating in front of the grey-haired man while he is still waiting for his order. Then I quickly remind myself that I do it all the time in Chennai, where perfect strangers share tables in eateries and one has no choice but to ignore the other's presence.

The food is good, but then, I am not the best judge of food. But I can now boast that I've eaten at Coffee House.

As the waiter collects the bill—a measly twenty-four rupees—I ask him if I could visit the back office. I want to know more about Coffee House. So far all I know, from information already available, is that it was started in 1942 and that it earned its reputation as the meeting point of Calcutta's intelligentsia during the tumultuous 1960s and 70s, when the vacuum created by the departure of the British was filled by home-grown anger and creativity.

The waiter points to a door in one corner of the hall. Walking through that door, I enter a passage that seems to serve as a resting area for off-duty waiters. White uniform shirts hang from hooks on the wall, and there are so many shirts on each hook that they have assumed the girth of a rice sack. And they stink. On the floor, a turban-less waiter is half-asleep. He is somewhat taken aback at my appearance.

He asks me, '*Kothaye jaaben?*'—Where do you want to go?

'The office, where is it?'

He motions me towards a glass panel door at the end of the passage.

Inside the small office, tables are joined sideways to save space and act as a barricade between staff and visitors. They are laden with files, registers and calculators. But the chairs are all empty at this hour: it is lunchtime. The lone clerk I come across is also about to leave; I beg him to spare me a few minutes.

'This place we are sitting in,' he suddenly transforms into a story-teller who has all the time in the world, 'is called Albert Hall. Very historical building, founded in 1876. Tagore came here for meetings four to five times; Chittaranjan Das came here; Subhas Bose came here.

'In 1942, when Coffee Board was set up by the government, Coffee House was started here to promote coffee. Until then, coffee was not very popular among Indians; it was considered the drink of the sahibs.

'On the ground floor they had the godown, and the hall on the first floor, where Tagore and Subhas Bose had addressed meetings once upon a time, served as the cafeteria.

'But in 1958, Coffee Board shut down the place. They must have had their reasons—maybe they were running into losses. But the workers of Coffee House were rendered jobless. Some of the prominent patrons of Coffee House, who understood the historical value of the place, got together and petitioned the chief minister for its reopening.

'The chief minister at the time was Dr Bidhan Chandra Roy, and one of the patrons, Professor Nirmal Chandra Bhattacharya of Scottish Church College, happened to be his friend. Dr Roy suggested that Coffee House be run as a cooperative society, and so it reopened the very year it had shut down—1958.

'Ever since then it has run as a cooperative society, which means the workers are also the owners. Be it a waiter or an administrative staff, we all draw the same salary, between six to seven thousand rupees a month.

'But paying salaries is a challenge these days because we are running into losses. We lose seven to eight lakh rupees every year but we are somehow managing. We are not here to make profits; we are here to keep Coffee House alive.'

The clerk looks at his watch and is about to get up.

'One last question,' I plead, 'has your clientele changed over the years?'

'Of course,' he settles down once again, 'Now we get only the student crowd. But once upon a time, we had only intellectuals coming over, very few students. Barristers, professors, writers, journalists, poets, singers—they would all gather here every evening for *adda*.

'Oh, the kind of people who used to come: Rudraprasad Sengupta, Soumitra Chatterjee, Sunil Gangopadhyay, Shakti Chattopadhyay, Mrinal Sen, Aparna Sen and so many more.

'There is so much one stands to gain from *adda*.

People come together, exchange ideas, discuss their problems, debate on important issues. *Adda* keeps our culture alive.

'But times are changing. In those days people had the time, you see. Coffee House now sees less of *adda* and more of *prem alaap*.'

Prem alaap—mushy exchange between lovers—is what I too got to see this afternoon.

I step out of the office, back into the noise of the hall, and walk down the stairs into the noise of College Street.

I enter one of the bigger bookshops, wondering if it would have anything for me. But they are all textbooks. Suddenly I remember a textbook from my younger days, Wren & Martin, something that might still come in handy, and ask for it.

The Wren & Martin that I am shown, alas, is not the one I had known in school—compact, serious-looking with an old-fashioned red cover—but a magazine-sized textbook with coloured illustrations.

'The one you are talking about is a very old edition,' the shopkeeper tells me, 'they stopped it a long time ago. This is how Wren & Martin looks these days.'

Suddenly, there is a commotion out on the street. People are running and shouting. I drop the book and rush out. Are they chasing a pickpocket, or is it something more serious? I walk behind the crowd cautiously, bracing myself for a spectacle.

Soon I feel foolish for getting alarmed. They are only shouting: '*Ei, ke* bat *dhorechhe?! Ke* bat *dhorechhe?!*'

Ke bat *dhorechhe*. Literally translated, it means: 'Who is holding the bat?' But in the context of the ongoing World Cup tournament, its means: 'Who is batting first?' Talk of Bengali wordsmithery.

Needless to say, the crowd is not chasing a pickpocket but is rushing to the nearest TV set. Today India are taking on the invincible Australia in a do-or-die contest. The team that wins will move into the semi-finals. And from what I gather from the excited crowd, Australia have decided to hold the bat.

I had forgotten all about the match until now. I cross the street to take a taxi home. I hardly watch cricket on TV ever since advertisements took over the game—it makes me wonder whether I am watching commercials in between cricket, or cricket in between commercials—but I don't mind catching up on this match. There are already far less people on College Street than there were when I had arrived a couple of hours ago, and I don't want to be left behind.

The thing with taxis in Calcutta is that you never find one when you need it badly: you see a taxi approaching and desperately wave at it thinking it is empty, but as it comes closer, you notice a head or two propped up on the backseat. But on days you don't need one, you notice several yellow Ambassadors parked by the road or drone past you, passenger-less.

I am still waiting for a taxi when the slogan-shouting begins. I look behind: a crowd of students has suddenly formed, out of the blue, inside the gate of the University of Calcutta building.

The students—nervous-looking boys and girls with rucksacks hanging from their shoulders—stand facing a young leader who has parts of his hair coloured magenta and who is now making a speech. I try to listen in but the action is taking place inside the gate, which I am not supposed to enter. Not that anyone is likely to stop me if

I do: which speaker minds an extra pair of ears, that too the ears of a journalist. But who wants to listen to yet another angry speech in Calcutta?

The speech lasts for about ten minutes, after which the students obediently disperse and their leader comes out onto the pavement for a smoke. Only a moment ago, he had looked like a lion as he commanded the attention—and perhaps admiration—of hundred-odd students. But now, as he stood all alone and took long puffs from the cigarette, he looked as nervous and vulnerable as the students he had just addressed.

I am about to walk up to him when a young bespectacled man comes over and puts his arm around him and says, '*Khoob bhalo bolli kintu*'—No matter what, you spoke really well.

Then the two go into a huddle and I step back to look for a taxi.

10

'THERE IS ONE thing about Calcutta,' the writer Sunil Gangopadhyay tells me, 'If you come here for two or three days, you may not like the city; you might even hate it. But live here for a month and you will fall in love with it.'

Sunil Gangopadhyay, at seventy-six, is Bengal's most famous living writer—and still relevant. Only months before, a film based on his novel *Moner Manush* won the award for the best film at the International Film Festival of India.

You will find him even on hoardings, endorsing Emami brand of mustard oil. In the advertisement, the pudgy-faced writer is shown all teary, his eyes supposedly smarting from the vapours of the oil. Pungency, after all, is the true test of mustard oil: if it makes your eyes water, it is pure.

Nowhere else in the world will you see a writer, not even a Nobel laureate, endorsing a product. The fact that Sunil Gangopadhyay is doing so, that too at the age of seventy-six, not only testifies to his own popularity as a writer in Calcutta but also the trust that Calcutta places on its writers.

Gangopadhyay has published over 200 literary works in a career spanning six decades. I haven't read any of them because I can barely read Bengali, but English translations of two voluminous historical novels—*First Light* and *Those Days*—find respectable slots on the bookshelf back home. I admire him most for the two novels that were made into films by Satyajit Ray: *Aranyer Din Ratri* and *Pratidwandi*.

Aranyer Din Ratri—Days and Nights in the Forest—remains my favourite Ray film. It released in 1970, but sells an idea that is far more relevant today—the idea of taking a break, of escaping the grind of city life. Most importantly, the escape is *not* plotted. Four friends from Calcutta, eager to cut themselves away temporarily from civilisation, just hop into a car one fine morning and set off for the tribal country of Palamau, in neighbouring Bihar: no tickets are booked, no rooms reserved in advance.

To *not* plan, but simply surrender to the urge to travel, the moment it seizes you—it's a luxury most of us can only dream of, what with targets and deadlines (and appraisals) constantly staring us in the face. Only the courageous and the carefree, who do not like to worry about where the next meal is going to come from, can afford to hop into the next available bus or train.

I've called on Sunil Gangopadhyay on a Sunday

morning, when his ninth-floor flat in south Calcutta is receiving a steady stream of visitors. People are coming from far and near for a few minutes of his time. They are armed with invitations, job applications, petitions, self-published books. I take a seat, right under the painting of a bare-breasted woman playing the sitar and await my turn.

Gangopadhyay, clad in a loose-fitting blue kurta and white pyjamas, is busy writing on the official letterhead of the Sahitya Akademi, of which he is currently the president. He then tears off the sheet and hands it over to a waiting man, who bows in gratitude and makes an exit.

Another man steps forward, along with his wife. She has written a book and wants to present a copy to the writer. Gangopadhyay accepts the copy and makes polite enquiries, after which the wife touches his feet and the couple withdraws.

A young woman now presents herself. She wants a job in Sahitya Akademi as a junior clerk.

'No, no, no, I can't help you,' the writer refuses to accept her CV, 'Please go through the proper channel.'

'Please, sir. If you don't help me, who will? I have also attached my OBC certificate. Here, please take a look.'

'Please try to understand,' he refuses to touch the pieces of paper, 'I cannot help you. You must go through the proper channel.'

'Please, sir.'

'Don't put me in a spot. I really can't help you.'

'If you can't, who else can, sir? I badly need the job.'

'Oh well,' he finally gives in to her perseverance and accepts her application—along with the OBC certificate, 'let me see what I can do.'

'Thank you, sir.' She swiftly touches his feet and leaves.

When I introduce myself, he realises I've come to walk with him down memory lane. He motions me to a settee next to him and lights up a Marlboro in the old-fashioned way: with a matchbox and not a lighter.

'I came to this city before the Second World War,' he begins, 'I was born in East Bengal, what is now Bangladesh, but my father was working here. When I was three or four years old, my mother and I moved to Calcutta as well.

'I have been living here for more than seventy years now. The city has changed a lot; every city changes. I once met an American in America; he was a banker who had been a pilot during the Second World War. His memory of Calcutta was that of a beautiful city. I asked him, "Are you joking?" He said, "No, I remember it as a beautiful city."

'He must have found it beautiful because during the war, the Red Road, which runs along the Maidan, was used as a runway. While landing and taking off, he must have had a marvellous view of the river, the Maidan, the beautiful buildings, the botanical garden. He obviously did not go to the lanes of north Calcutta.

'I lived in north Calcutta, where there were huge palaces as well as slums. You could see the contrast. But now most of the slums have disappeared, making way for high rises. During the 1960s and '70s Calcutta was really dirty. There was a huge influx of refugees, there was no arrangement for sanitation, people were living on the pavements. Now Calcutta is expanding, many people have shifted, refugees are resettled. It is no longer as dirty as it used to be.

'But there is one thing about Calcutta,' he takes a long drag from the cigarette, 'If you spend two or three days here, you may not like the city. You might even hate it. But live here for a month and you will fall in love with it. You will discover the warmth of the people. You will know the real spirit of Calcutta.'

The phone rings. As Gangopadhyay is engaged by the caller, I look around. I suddenly notice that all along, nearly a dozen people in the room have been eagerly listening to his story in complete silence. They are leaning forward on their seats, chins resting on palms.

By the time he puts down the phone, the chain of thoughts is already broken. I resume the conversation by asking him about the time when he started writing poetry. Poetry, he has said in interviews, remains his first love, even though he makes his living out of writing prose.

'When I fell in love for the first time,' he replies with a laugh. The audience laughs too.

'I must have been fifteen or sixteen then. You write when your love is not fulfilled, when your heart is broken. The inspiration for writing comes from grief. What is supposed to be the very first poem written in our civilisation came from grief. It all began with two birds—one bird gets killed and the other bird is wailing over the sudden death of its partner. Hearing the bird's cries, Valmiki uttered two lines—that is supposed to be the first poetry. In personal life too, nothing can be sadder than losing your girlfriend.' There is laughter in the room again.

'In those days,' he continues, 'friends' sisters were our target.'

'And sisters' friends too?' I suggest.

'I didn't have a sister. For me it was always friends' sisters. The one I fell in love with happened to love poetry. I didn't know much about poetry then, but to impress her

I started reading and remembering poems. But the affair didn't last long, and then I started writing for myself.

'I sent a poem to *Desh* (the literary magazine of the Anandabazar group). Now when I think of it, it was a very weak poem, very bad poem. But it got published. I ran into the girl soon after, and she told me, "Look, *Desh* has just published a poem, and the poet's name is the same as yours."

'In college I started publishing a poetry magazine called *Krittibas*. I was nineteen then. The magazine still comes out as far as I know. Because of the magazine I came to know other poets: Shakti Chattopadhyay, Tarapada Roy, Sarat Kumar Mukhopadhayay. We soon became close friends. There was another person, Bhaskar Dutta, who never wrote a line of poetry but he was always a friend of poets. He went to England, lived there for thirty-six years, but stayed in touch with us.

'Those were wild days. We were all bohemians. We had no sense of time. We would drink, we would smoke ganja, we would eat whatever we could manage to get to eat, we would travel out of Calcutta together whenever we could.

'Shakti was the most daring of us. One evening he was engaged in an *adda* at Coffee House with a friend who had come from Chaibasa in Bihar. When the friend got up to leave because he had a train to catch, Shakti offered to accompany him to the station. And there, without a ticket, without informing anybody, Shakti also got into the train!

'He stayed there for three months. Then news came to us that he was in prison. We became worried and I went to look for him.'

'Was he in prison?' I ask.

'Prison? Oh yes, he was in a beautiful prison! When I found him, he was actually surrounded by four young girls, all beautiful.' Once again there is laughter in the room.

'The experiences later became *Aranyer Din Ratri*?'

'Yes, but in the film, Satyajit Ray changed the nuances of the original story. Ray made his characters upper-class, who travel in a car and stay in a forest bungalow. Whereas we were all from lower middle-class families; we could not afford a car and always travelled in a train, that too ticketless.

'During the making of the film, Satyajit Ray had asked me, "How does *mahua* (alcoholic drink made by fermenting flowers) taste?" I told him, "It is available in the tribal areas. Go taste it." He turned up his nose and said, "No, no, no, I can't drink that." I said, "If you don't drink it, how will you describe the taste?"

'And so he made a mistake in the scene where the characters drink. If you drink two or three glasses of *mahua*, you go euphoric; you start talking and singing. But in the film, the characters go glum.

'Then there is another scene, in which the four friends are walking back to the lodge after a drinking session, and they are singing and dancing on the road when a car passes by, its headlights shining on the men. In real life, we were walking on the road naked when this incident took place. The occupants of the car, seeing us in that state, had thought we were ghosts and sped away. Of course, Satyajit Ray didn't want to show his characters naked.'

'You all were naked?'

'Absolutely naked. It was a forest area, after all, and it was night. Since we were away from civilisation, we had decided to do away with civilisation: no newspapers, no shaving, and, that night, no clothes either.'

'Were you already friends with (the Beat poet) Allen Ginsberg by then?'

'Allen Ginsberg came later. He came to Calcutta in 1962, and stayed for eight months. Before setting out for India, he had met Buddhadeva Bose, who was the most famous Bengali writer at the time, in America; and Bose had told him that if he wanted to meet Bengali poets, he should go to Coffee House on College Street.

'So one afternoon we were sitting in Coffee House when we saw two strange-looking Americans walk in. Until then, we had seen Westerners only in suits, but these two wore kurta and pyjamas and were barefoot. They were Allen Ginsberg and (his companion) Peter Orlovsky.

'We became very close friends. He introduced us to LSD. But nobody in our group had the courage to take the pills, except Shakti and I.'

'How was the experience?'

'Great, absolutely great. For four hours we were in a trance, getting visions, beautiful visions. For Shakti the experience was a little different towards the end: he believed he was dying and he got a little scared. But in my case images from my childhood began flashing in my mind. I began recalling incidents that had taken place during the age of four or five—incidents that I had completely forgotten about.

'Later when I met Jack Kerouac (another Beat writer, who became a cult figure for his travel-based novel, *On The Road*) in America, he told me that if you take four pills of LSD at a time, you will be able to recall your existence even in your mother's womb.

'But I was very impressed by Ginsberg's erudition. He was a great scholar, though you could not tell that from his appearance. He looked shabby and he chose to stay in a cheap hotel near New Market. It was a small hotel, very dirty—it no longer exists. He would even advise us to live cheaply.

'He would say, "If you want to be a poet, you have to be a poet twenty-four hours, you must devote all your time and energy to poetry, you must learn to live as cheaply as possible, you must take up no other job."

'Shakti tried to do that for a while but I could not. My father had died and I had a family to support. I did several jobs at a time. In the morning I had a government job—a clerical job, in the evening I would work as the Sunday editor of a small newspaper called the *Janasevak*, and in between I gave tuitions. I was practically working almost all day. Still I would find time to meet friends, drink with them, travel with them, write poetry.

'After Ginsberg went back I met another poet, Paul Engle. He had come to India to shortlist young poets writing in vernacular languages, for the International Writing Program at the University of Iowa. He eventually chose me for the scholarship, and that raised a hue and cry. There were angry voices, as to why he had chosen me of all people? How was I to know why he had chosen me? May be he liked me because my face is round.'

Once again there is laughter in the room.

'When I went to America, in 1963, I was not sure about my future. I was living in a nice flat, I had a French girlfriend, and the scholarship I received was sufficient to pay for my liquor and also to send home some money. Yet I was not happy, I felt uncomfortable and restless.

'Then one morning, standing in front of the mirror, I asked myself, "Why do I feel restless?" The man in the mirror replied, "Your face is flush with happiness when you write a poem. And since you write in Bengali, go back to the people who understand Bengali."

'That was it. I decided to return, even though I could have stayed on. In those days migrating was not a problem; in fact all the poets who came for the program, except the ones who were married, stayed on in America.

'I returned to Calcutta in the end of 1964. I had no money, no job. I started writing prose, mostly newspaper columns. I took several pen names: Nil Lohit, Sanatan Pathak, Nil Upadhyaya.

'This went on for two or three years before the editor of *Desh* asked me to write a novel for their Puja edition. In Bengal, novels are usually serialised by a magazine or featured in their Puja number before they appear in the book form. I decided to take up the offer because I needed the money, but I had no idea how to write a novel.

'I suddenly remembered Jack Kerouac's advice. When I met him in America, he had told me, "Writing a novel is very easy. Just take a piece of paper and think of one day in your life. It could be, say, April 24, when you were waiting at the bus stop. Start your story from the bus stop, and as the bus moves, your story moves too." So I wrote a story called *Atma Prakash*.

'At the same time, I was continuing to publish *Krittibas*, the poetry magazine. But I seldom had the money to pay the printing press. Each time I ran into a debt, I would avoid going in the direction of that press.

'Once, I ran a bill of seven hundred rupees at one press, and the amount was simply too high for me to pay. I began avoiding the street on which the press was located.

'One morning, as I was getting down from a bus near New Market, I came face to face with the proprietor of the press. I began to tremble with fear. Where was I to get seven hundred rupees from?

'But the proprietor, who published a film magazine, called *Jalsa*, grabbed my hand and told me, "Don't be nervous. I am not taking you to the police station. Last Puja you wrote a novel for *Desh*, this Puja you write a novel for us. I won't pay you a penny for that, and in return you can forget about your dues."

'The thought that I was no longer required to pay him back the seven hundred rupees was exhilarating. I felt immensely grateful to him. That's when I wrote *Aranyer Din Ratri*. Satyajit Ray picked it up from *Jalsa* and made it into a movie. His producer paid me four thousand rupees. It was big money in those days—I got married with that money.

'Ray's next film, *Pratidwandi*, was also based on my novel. From a struggling poet I became a prose writer. All along my ambition had been to be a poet, publish three or four slim volumes of poetry at the most and maybe teach in a mofussil college. But these novels changed my life.'

The unmistakable smell of fish frying in mustard oil is now coming from the kitchen. For a Bengali, it is an assuring smell—a sign that everything is fine. The other people in the drawing room, who have been eagerly listening to his story, are slowly getting fidgety.

'What are you working on now?' I ask him, more as a way of letting him know that I won't take more of his time.

'I am getting ready to write something for next Puja. Then there is another story I have in mind—a new interpretation of Rama's character in the *Ramayana*. I like reading the Ramayana and the *Mahabharata*, and I must have read each of them about twenty times. Now it suddenly strikes me: Were Luv and Kush sons of Rama or Ravana?

'There are some clues in the original text which indicate that Sita got pregnant by Ravana when she was in his custody, which is why Rama was so angry and not willing to take her back.

'The story has relevance today because when a woman is raped, she bears the burden of guilt. The rapist, if convicted, goes to jail for a few years and comes out, but the woman is ostracized for the rest of her life. This does not happen in Western societies, but only in ours. Rama could have set an example by readily accepting Sita.'

'Do you think women are better off in Bengal, in the sense that Bengali women are known to be more assertive?'

'To an extent maybe, but that does not mean Bengalis don't ill-treat their women, even though they worship Durga and Kali. But yes, as a city, Calcutta is more permissive than others. The concept of living in, for example, was accepted in Calcutta long before it became fashionable. Bengalis are generally more tolerant about other people's ideas.'

'One last question: How do you compare yourself with Tagore, considered the greatest of Bengali writers?'

Suddenly there is silence in the room. The visitors once again lean forward, chins resting on palms.

Sunil Gangopadhyay replies, 'I may have written more number of pages than Tagore, but if you pick up any

Tagore work, not one page is below average. Some of his stories may appear dated, but not one page, not one line is below average. He was a great writer.

'My attitude towards writing has always been casual. I have always written in my own style, come what may. If people don't like what I write, I will stop writing; but as long as I write, I will write in my own style. I have never written to achieve greatness or immortality. I care two hoots for immortality.'

11

AT FOUR IN the afternoon, with the sun moving to a corner in the sky, Kalighat Road is peeling off its afternoon sluggishness and tuning into cricket. The match in Colombo has already begun. Sri Lanka and New Zealand are clashing in the first semi-final.

Business, too, is slowly picking up on the road, which is lined with shops selling items of worship, shops selling musical instruments, shops selling household needs such as umbrellas and steel trunks, hawkers selling vegetables—and women selling sex.

Prostitutes in garish red sarees, unconcerned about cricket, are seeking eye-contact with passersby in the hope of an approving glance. But hardly anyone turns his head, so used the locals are to the sight of them. Weary of what looks like an unending wait, some of the women withdraw into the privacy of crevices along the road for a smoke.

Apparently, it's all right to sell sex in the open, but not smoke. Which isn't that strange a distinction: sex is their means of earning a living; they are no different from the vegetable vendors squatting on the pavement, their wares spread out on display on jute cloths; but when it comes to smoking, they are like any Indian woman who, even if a habitual smoker, would avoid lighting up in a marketplace.

In Kalighat live Bengal's two most powerful women: Goddess Kali and Mamata Banerjee. They live a stone's throw from each other, their homes joined by the road where the prostitutes are standing. Three dramatically disparate female forms—the divine, derided and the deified—sharing space without conflict.

Such dazzling disparity easily defines the rest of Calcutta. Where else in the world can you still see buses and taxis sharing the road with trams and hand-pulled rickshaws? It is a different matter that most buses and the yellow Ambassador taxis are weather-beaten enough to look nearly a hundred years old themselves.

The taxi that had brought me to Kalighat was one such. The only thing that had looked new in the car was a sticker pasted on its windscreen. It bore the smiling face of the otherwise mercurial, frequently fiery, Mamata Banerjee.

Elections are in the air, and Mamata, after decades of political struggle, finally seems evenly poised against her enemies, the Communists, who have ruled West Bengal for nearly thirty-five years.

Mamata Banerjee is the only woman politician the state has known despite the celebrated contribution of its women to the freedom movement, and the fact that the female of the Bengali species is more deadly than the male.

You will not find characters like her in Tagore's plays or Satyajit Ray's films. Bengali women are expected to be ladylike: they can speak their minds behind the curtains but cannot take their anger to the streets. Mamata did precisely that.

She fought the Communists on the streets of Calcutta; then went on to fight with her own party, the Congress, accusing it of having become a stooge of the Communists; and by the age of forty-two, in 1997, had formed her own party, the Trinamool Congress, and become a political force to reckon with.

Since then every coalition wanting to rule India has gone begging to her for support. Mamata, in return, almost always got the plum railway ministry. What she eventually wants is the chief ministership of West Bengal, and she finally seems within striking distance.

The driver of the aged taxi was an elderly Bihari who had migrated to Calcutta way back in 1958, when he was only eighteen. He must have seen Calcutta evolve over the decades. I had asked him about Mamata's chances in the elections.

'How can I tell?' he'd replied disinterestedly, 'she may win, she may not, who knows?'

'But what is your hunch?'

'I think she will win this time. Communists have plundered Calcutta for the past thirty-five years. People have had enough of them.'

'Are you going to vote for her?'

'Let's see,' he dismissed my question. 'Where in Kalighat should I drop you?'

'At the temple.'

At the temple, whose origins predate British Calcutta, stood an army of *pandas*—the middlemen who are adept at arm-twisting you into emptying your wallet for a one-on-one meeting with the deity. They stood with the eagerness of a bride's family awaiting the arrival of the groom's party. Even before I could pay the taxi driver, they had begun walking towards me with the measured steps of a cat about to pounce on its prey.

Suddenly they were all over me, each promising a more fruitful audience with the goddess than the other. I ignored them, not even making eye contact, and walked straight towards the temple. They followed me like flies, upon which I paused and took my notebook out. I looked around leisurely and pretended to take notes. The ploy worked. They left me alone and went back to their positions while I quietly slipped into the temple.

Inside the sanctum sanctorum, Mother Kali stood like the creation of a child assigned by the crafts teacher to create an image of the goddess: the three red eyes and the long golden tongue protruding out of her lips seemed cut from art paper and pasted on a black face.

'Step in, step in,' the young priest urged me. 'You only have to pay two hundred rupees.'

'No, I am fine.'

'Just two hundred rupees. Not a paisa more. Mother will not disappoint you.'

'No, thank you. I am a journalist. I've come here to write.'

The priest immediately lost interest in me and ushered in two young girls who were going to write their exams and were anxious to propitiate the goddess.

I walked back to the sweetshop where I had deposited my shoes, wondering along the way: so *this* is the Kalighat temple the world talks about. And I stepped out on to Kalighat Road—straight into the noise of cricket.

The sound of commentary now keeps me company

like a shadow as I walk the length of the road, past the shops and the hawkers and the prostitutes.

The sight of so many women together, standing in the open to solicit customers, that too in a place as public as Kalighat, comes as a bit of a shock to me, perhaps because I am now accustomed to the ways of Chennai, where there are no designated red-light districts and where one gets to know about prostitution rackets only through newspapers.

I want to talk to these women, probably even have a smoke with them. I am sure they will have lots to tell, but no way can I bring myself to strike a conversation with them—certainly not in the open. Yet I am tempted to linger on, just to watch them go about their business. Am I being a voyeur?

I pause at a *paan* shop. It has a portable TV and a small crowd gathered around it. New Zealand, batting first, have just lost their second wicket for sixty-nine runs. I ask for directions to Mamata Banerjee's house. 'Keep walking straight,' the crowd guides me in unison.

Once Kalighat Road terminates, I enter a narrow lane called Harish Chatterji Street. On this street lives Mamata Banerjee, in a shanty that would go unnoticed but for the door-frame metal detector and paramilitary guards at the gate. A party worker has been stationed outside the gate to deal with visitors, mostly poor people coming with petitions.

The party worker scolds them: 'Who will sign on your petitions? Don't you know that all the leaders are out campaigning?'

The petitioners grin but persist, upon which the worker accepts the pieces of paper and tells them that he will pass these on to his bosses.

I ask the worker, a sunburned young man who wouldn't be more than thirty, if *Didi*—as Mamata is respectfully called by her followers—is going to win the elections. I expect to bring out the jingoist in him, and brace myself for a spirited speech about how Bengal is on the verge of a revolution that will see *Didi* stride home with an absolute majority.

But the man becomes thoughtful and, after a moment of silence, says mournfully: '*Dekha jaag. Jeta to ucheet*'—Let's see, there is no reason why she shouldn't win.

Such measured words. In any other part of the country, a lowly political worker like him would've considered his duty to enthusiastically declare that his leader was winning hands down, even though the truth may have been quite the opposite.

But a quintessentially Calcutta man, no matter what his occupation, likes to speak in enigmas—even in the most mundane of situations. He never lets go of an opportunity to bring out the poet-philosopher-satirist in him, be it in the corridors of power or on the aisle of a local train.

Ask him a simple question and you will seldom receive a simple reply—he will instead throw back at you something that is either profound or tongue-in-cheek, or even cheeky. To understand Calcutta, you not only need a good pair of eyes but also a healthy pair of ears.

But I must give the Trinamool worker the benefit of the doubt. Perhaps he is being genuinely modest—as modest as the house he is minding.

The shanty has always been Mamata's home and probably will always be. If she wins the elections, it will be the most important address in Calcutta.

Also if she wins, the city will witness change in

government for the first time in thirty-five years. Will that change Calcutta too?

I walk out of Harish Chatterjee Street, back into Kalighat Road, and once again walk past the prostitutes, past the *paan* shop where a small crowd is still gathered around the TV set, past lethargic policemen who are listening to the commentary on earphones.

A taxi approaches from the opposite direction; it is empty. I get in and ask the driver to take me to Dharmatala.

DHARMATALA IS ONE of the first neighbourhoods to come up in Clive's Calcutta, separated from the calm of the Maidan by the busy Chowringhee Road. I am going there this evening in search of Khalasitola, the country liquor bar where once upon a time, many a literary gem is said to have been conceived or composed in a state of intoxication. It seems to be the alcohol-serving version of Coffee House: I have recently read somewhere that you aren't Calcuttan enough if you haven't got drunk there.

I have never tasted country liquor, and so sitting in the taxi I brace for an unknown spirit burning my esophagus. I promise myself not to drink more than a glass, or maybe two.

The taxi drops me at Metro Cinema on Chowringhee Road. From there I turn into SN Banerjee Road and begin my search. I ask people for directions. Some haven't even heard of the place, others ask me to keep walking straight.

Further down the road, I ask a fruit-seller where Khalasitola is. Just when he begins explaining, a man who is hanging around the fruit stall joins in. He too begins giving directions. The two men get into an argument. The fruit-seller tells me I should take the first left, the other man tells me I should keep walking and turn left only after I spot tram tracks on the road.

A few paces ahead I enquire from another shopkeeper: he reacts as if I am asking for directions to a fictional place. Could Khalasitola be fictional—one of those places which may or may not have existed but which is now part of literary folklore?

What is very real at this hour—it is six-thirty—is the bustle on SN Banerjee Road. Traffic is moving slowly, noisily. The pavement is overrun by office-goers returning home. Sweet shops are doing brisk business. In Calcutta, you can usually guess the historical or social importance of a road by the number of sweet shops dotting it.

I pause at a small shop, called Anurag, where *samosas* have just been ladled out of oil. A human beehive is already formed around the shop—this must be the scene every evening—and it is a while before I catch the shopkeeper's eye.

I buy two *samosas* and a hundred grams of *jalebis* and eat them as I walk now at a leisurely pace down the road. I walk past open-air kitchens. Pavement-dwellers are cooking their humble meals over mud ovens. Soon they will eat and slither into the low tents they've pitched by the road. Inside the tents they will worry, argue, fight, love, make love, go to sleep—right under the noses of pedestrians and yet so far away from them.

So far, no one has been able to tell me where Khalasitola is. People I've asked either haven't heard of it or have been pointing me deeper into the road, and before long, SN Banerjee Road comes to an end.

I turn left. I am now on Acharya Jagadish Chandra Bose Road, still hoping to hear loud drunken—and perhaps literary—voices emanating from a rundown bar. No luck. Life seems to be normal on this road too: office-goers are hurrying home, shopkeepers are watching the match on TV, those not interested in cricket are engaged in *adda* at cigarette shops and tea stalls.

I turn left again and find myself standing outside a dental clinic: 'Dr Alexander Mao, BDS, FAGE, MIDA.' Dentistry has been one the respectable occupations of the Chinese settled in Calcutta. From Dr Mao's signboard I realise that I have now entered Lenin Sarani—or Lenin Road.

Khalasitola may just be somewhere around, who knows, but I am no longer interested. I've already walked a lot: SN Banerjee Road had turned out to be a long one. Moreover, the *samosas* and *jalebis* have killed my appetite for a drink. I make do with Thums Up at a roadside cigarette stall.

Thums Up has always been my favourite soft drink, right from childhood. Remember the jingle, *Happy days are here again*? The best part is that even thirty years on, Thums Up tastes just the same and it is a bonus when the shopkeeper uncaps the moisture-coated bottle for you—just like he did in the olden days when they didn't have cans or pet bottles.

As I slowly sip my Thums Up and smoke a cigarette, a muscular kurta-clad man, who seems fresh after a bath, comes over and playfully thumps the back of the shopkeeper.

'Looks like Sri Lanka are winning,' the shopkeeper tells him.

'Who cares,' the muscular man reaches for one of the jars on display and helps himself to a toffee.

'Tomorrow India are playing Pakistan in the second semi-final, I'm sure you will watch that,' the shopkeeper grins.

'Who cares,' says the muscular man. He then notices my presence and launches into a diatribe, addressed at no one in particular: 'Do you think I'm crazy to be watching the match tomorrow? So much hype for one bloody match! Switch on the TV, they are talking about it. Pick up the newspaper, they are talking about it. As if nothing else is happening in the world other than the bloody India-Pakistan match! These media people are the biggest culprits, *shob shuorer bachcha* (all children of pigs)!'

Then, as I leave, he delivers the parting shot: 'I pray to god, I pray to Mother Kali, that it rains heavily tomorrow and the pitch turns into slush!'

12

THE NEXT EVENING it rains heavily, all of a sudden—not in Mohali, where India and Pakistan are playing, but in Calcutta.

A cool breeze sweeps forcefully through the hall, bringing along with it a fine mist of rain, as I sit in front of the TV clutching a chilled can of beer. India are batting first, and Sachin Tendulkar has just got out after scoring eighty-five.

Suddenly, a prick of sadness: in a few days I would have spent a month in Calcutta and I will have to return. I've woven my life around the city during this time, as if I've always lived here, and now I hate the thought of uprooting myself from the rhythm.

But only the ones with roots can talk of being uprooted: I never had any to begin with.

In Kanpur, where I was born and lived until the age of twenty-three, I remained, at least culturally, a Bengali—an outsider. In Delhi, where I worked for seven years after leaving Kanpur, I was an outsider like everybody else in that city. In Chennai, which has been my home for over a decade now, I remain an outsider—sometimes a Bengali, sometimes a 'north Indian'. In Calcutta too, because I am a non-resident Bengali, I am an outsider.

But only in Calcutta, no matter what the city thinks of me, do I now feel some sense of belonging. The older you grow, the more precious the sounds and smells of childhood become—and Calcutta is full of them.

Kanpur, on the other hand, drifts away each year from being the city it used to be during my younger days. The faces I grew up with are either gone or look uncomfortably older, reminding me of my own mortality. Sights change—it is inevitable, but even the sounds and smells are no longer the same for me in Kanpur.

That's because my mother, who had kept much of the sounds and smells of my childhood alive—blowing of the conch shell, incense burning on coconut husk, *chochchori* cooking in the kitchen, the general chatter in Bengali—is now gone.

She died suddenly, at the age of fifty-nine, three years after I got married. As a possessive Bengali mother, she was keen that I always remain a son of Kanpur and never belong to Calcutta. But quite ironically, it is Calcutta that reminds me of her the most today and makes up for her absence in many ways. Here I will always be the child.

THE RAIN HAS long stopped. Crackers are beginning to burst. India have beaten Pakistan by twenty-nine runs.

I get another can of beer from the fridge and retire to my room. I tune into Radio One, the '100 per cent retro station'. The voice of Kishore Kumar, singing to the rhythm of RD Burman, bursts out of the speakers.

I had expected his voice. Radio channels in Calcutta, whenever they play Hindi songs, are usually partial towards Kishore Kumar and RD Burman—much to my gratification. To say I am a die-hard fan of these two men would be an understatement.

You may possess an impressive collection of songs of your idols and have the luxury of listening to them at will—even playing the same song several times in a row, but it is an altogether different sensation when the radio plays a song you love. It is a validation of your craze. You feel victorious.

Calcutta, despite being synonymous with the richness of Bengali music, acknowledges the timelessness of the Hindi songs left behind by Kishore Kumar and RD Burman—perhaps more than any Hindi-speaking city.

Listening to radio in Calcutta in 2011, therefore, feels almost the same as listening to radio in Kanpur in 1981. As if the thirty years never lapsed. Now you have vivacious radio jockeys, back then emotionless announcers—that's the only big difference.

The radio jockey, usually a young chirpy female voice, not only guides you through the show but also assures you, with her choice of songs, that yours is not the only heart that beats for Kishore Kumar and RD Burman.

One more sound, then, that binds me to Calcutta and makes it harder for me to leave.

13

TODAY IS THE FINAL. India will play Sri Lanka in Mumbai. But Calcutta, more than Mumbai, must be eagerly waiting for the match to begin. So what if Sourav Ganguly is not playing.

And so after a short walk at the Central Park and a heavy breakfast, I set out to see how the city is faring on the day of the most important match of World Cup 2011. I have no particular destination in mind, so when a taxi slows down at my waving, I ask the driver to take me to Park Street. It has been my default destination in Calcutta.

Only after I get into the taxi do I realise that I needed to go to Park Street anyway. Some days ago, acting on impulse, I had entered the shop of Barkat Ali & Sons, the tailors, and given measurements for a white shirt. Their old-fashioned signboard ('Established 1924') always caught my eye during my strolls on Park Street and I had wanted to get a shirt stitched there, just for the experience. The shirt is supposed to be ready today. It better be. Tomorrow is Sunday, when the shop is shut, and Monday I am back in Chennai.

The taxi driver turns out to be a gloomy young man. When I ask him if he was going to catch the match on TV, he waves his hand dismissively.

'But it is the final. Won't you watch?'

'If I sit down to watch the match, how will I earn my living? And if I don't earn my living, how will I eat?' he almost snaps at me.

The driver, as evident from his accent, is from Bihar. Most taxi drivers in Calcutta belong to Bihar. Some of them hail from eastern Uttar Pradesh. Very few Bengalis drive taxis, and getting into a taxi driven by one could also mean getting into a conversation that might threaten to last beyond the journey.

As we approach Park Circus, we find the traffic pausing for a tram that is snaking out of the local depot. I've never been inside a tram depot, for that matter I have not been inside a tram in a long, long time. I have only one memory of a tram ride, this must be sometime in the late 1970s, and all I remember is feeling suffocated by the crowds even though the tram moved with considerable speed on the Howrah Bridge.

I suddenly decide that I must have a look at the tram depot. I am not a Calcuttan, who takes the sight of a tram for granted. I live in Chennai, where tram rides are a distant memory. Therefore the depot, to me, is a living museum. Before the traffic can resume on Park Circus, I quickly pay the taxi driver and get out of his Ambassador.

Inside the depot, two trams, one behind the other, have been queued up for departure. Two more trams are parked in the shed. There are a couple of buses parked there as well. They, the trams and the buses, bear a common signage: CTC, or Calcutta Tramways Company.

CTC, now owned by the government of West Bengal, was formed in London in 1880, when horse-drawn trams began to run between Sealdah and Armenian Ghat, a distance of about three kilometres. A service had been started on an experimental basis on the same route seven years earlier but was scrapped within nine months due to lack of patronage. But with the setting up of CTC, the tram was formally introduced as a mode of public transport in colonial Calcutta. The horses pulled them at first, steam locomotives came next, but by the end of 1905, the trams were running on electricity—as they still do. From the early 1990s, the company started a bus service as well to reduce the losses it incurs from running trams.

Right in the centre of the depot, as big as a school playground, is placed a wooden cot on which about half a dozen men, in khaki uniforms, are lazing. The 'CTC' logo is embroidered on their pockets.

'Anyone of you drives a tram?' I ask them. They eye me suspiciously. When I introduce myself, space is made for me on the cot and a tram driver is placed next to me. His name is Uma Shankar Pandey, a wiry man of fifty-two who hails from Bihar. In about fifteen minutes, a tram driven by him will pull out of the Park Circus Depot and head for the Howrah Bridge.

'I came to Calcutta in 1981 to join the Calcutta Tramways Company,' Uma Shankar Pandey tells me, 'ever since then I have been driving trams. They first give you training for four months at Tollygunge, only then you can take the tram out on the roads.

'The tram works on the same mechanism as the suburban trains, only that the train has more coaches and the tram has only two. Otherwise everything is the same—power handle, air brake, compressor, motor.

'When I started driving trams in 1981, there were dedicated lanes for trams on the sides of the roads, which made life easier not only for us drivers but also for passengers. There were assigned halts and places for passengers to wait in and get on and off easily.

'Now there is nothing. About eight or nine years ago, or was it ten years ago, the state government uprooted the tracks and placed them on the centre of the roads. Now it has become very difficult for people to get on to trams and so the income has also come down. Many lines are also closed now. The Behala line is closed. South Calcutta's main line, which went up to Bhawanipore, is also closed.

'The company, in order to sell its property—tram depots are prime property—is slowly closing down routes and reducing the number of trams. If the company had its way, all the depots would have been sold to builders by now. There are seven depots left now across Calcutta. But each time it tries to sell depot land, some union or the other rises in protest and the sale gets stalled. That is how we are surviving.

'Life on the road is not at all easy for us. The government has literally handed over the roads of central Calcutta to autorickshaws, which are all owned by *mastaans*—goons. The autorickshaws follow no rules and hinder traffic movement—their drivers neither listen to the police nor to the public. They have a free run of the road. They are a big nuisance not just for trams but also other vehicles.

'The police will readily seize licences of other vehicles that are at fault, but will never touch an autorickshaw driver. That is because they know that the autorickshaw driver enjoys the patronage of either a *mastaan* or a senior police officer.

'Because of the unruly ways of the autorickshaw drivers, the speed of the trams has slowed down. Of course, there is much more traffic on the road today than there ever used to be. In 1981, it would take only half an hour to reach Howrah Bridge from Park Circus. Today it takes an hour and a half.

'Had the British still been around, they would have installed a seat in the driver's cabin if they saw that a driver has to keep standing for four or five hours. In the cabin we have no protection from the heat or cold or rain. Since we are surrounded by electrical circuits, there is always a risk of us getting an electrical shock during rains or trapped in a fire due to short-circuit. You can say that Mother Kali is keeping us alive. The company does not seem to care for us.

'In the 1950s, when the government had hiked the fare by just one paisa, the communists had burnt eighteen trams across Calcutta. Eighteen trams, can you imagine? But the same communists, once they came to power, have been hiking the fares and nobody questions them.'

'What's the fare from Park Circus to Howrah Bridge?' I ask him.

'Rs 4.50 for first-class and Rs 4 for second-class,' says Pandey, 'the first-class car has fans and the second-class car does not, otherwise there is no difference between the two classes. But the new tram cars are made of plastic and glass, and it can get very hot inside. We sweat profusely.

'To tell you the truth, the new trams are nothing but refurbished versions of the old trams—they have removed the steel and replaced it with plastic. The steel, which was of best quality, has gone to the homes of the bosses.

'There is so much corruption, so much nepotism—you will be surprised if you hear the stories. Most of the officers are related to some communist politician or the other. They draw salaries just to come to office and comb their hair.

'The tram is such a comfortable and cheap mode of transport. Women, children and the elderly find it very convenient because the floor is very low. But those in power seem to be bent on doing away with trams. They seem to be in a hurry to sell depot lands to the builders.

'We are poor people. We have no say in what's going on, we can only raise our voices. And if the bosses hear us saying anything that is not to their liking, they will promptly transfer us from one depot to another. That's all they can do. They can't take away our jobs.'

Uma Shankar Pandey looks at his watch and gets up from the cot. All this while he was being an angry employee of Calcutta Tramways Company, but now duty beckons him. He shakes my hand and walks up to the tram that has been queued up for departure. Not a single passenger yet, even though Park Circus lies in the heart of the city.

Pandey climbs onto the driver's cabin and sets the tram into motion. The conductor for the first-class car, who has been smoking a cigarette, takes quick drags before he puts it out and hops onto the moving tram. I have for long wanted to take a tram ride someday. Why not today, since I am even familiar with the driver? I run behind the tram and get into the first-class car and take a seat by the window.

The first sensation that strikes me is the vibration in the wooden seat caused by the movement of the tram. It feels like sitting on a sheet of iron that is being dragged on a metalled road. The sensation makes me uneasy at first but I soon get used to it and look around. 'This car is yours. Please take care,' says one sign. Another warns against pickpockets. Yet another advises passengers to 'kindly tender the exact fare.' I then look out.

Travelling in a tram from Park Circus to Howrah Bridge is a lot like taking a tour of a dilapidated library where new books stopped arriving sometime in the 1970s. The shelves groan under the weight of dust-coated hardbound books ranging from the twentieth century back to the eighteenth. The pages have long yellowed, many of them so brittle that they might crumble into pieces at the slightest touch. If smells can translate into visuals, then the sights you encounter during the tram journey can be described in just one word: musty.

The tram is today the slowest vehicle on road, because of which, despite its size, it no longer commands the respect of other vehicles. They crowd or cross its path as and when they please: the onus is on the tram driver to stay slow and calm.

On Lenin Sarani, an autorickshaw wanting to cross the road noses its way into the small gap between our tram and the bus ahead. But having nosed its way in, the autorickshaw is unable to move further because the street it wants to get into is already clogged with vehicles. As a result, it ends up blocking the path of our tram. An ugly war of words breaks out between Pandey and the autorickshaw driver.

Pandey wants the autorickshaw to back out to let his tram pass. Nothing doing, retorts the autorickshaw driver, he will clear the path only when he finds passage into the street. The angry exchange continues for several minutes, and the autorickshaw driver—who looks no less dangerous than a *mastaan* himself—emerges from his vehicle to sort out poor Pandey.

By now the first-class car of the tram has gathered about twenty passengers, and as soon as they see the autorickshaw driver menacingly approach the tram, they spring up from their seats in Pandey's defence. Finding public anger pitted against him, the autorickshaw driver backs out. But he remains defiant and refuses to reverse his vehicle to let the tram pass. He stubbornly waits till he finds his way into the street and only then our tram resumes its onward journey.

For many years now, the tram has been a sight for me on Calcutta's roads, like an artifact meant to be watched from a distance; and now, for a change, I am inside it, watching the city from its window. To enjoy a tram ride, you need to have a lot of time if not patience, because often you will find pedestrians moving faster than the tram. But then, the tram was meant for simpler, slower times—when the buildings flanking its routes were not crumbling but brand new and splendid, when Calcutta was a city of palaces, when the tram was the fastest mode of public transport.

After the halt at Barabazar, which predates Charnock's Calcutta, I am the only passenger left in Pandey's tram. The conductor occupies a corner seat and lights up a cigarette and smokes it peacefully as the tram trundles towards Howrah Bridge. The cigarette, I am sure, costs more than the tram fare from Park Circus to Howrah Bridge—the brand I smoke certainly does. That should give you an idea of how cheap tram travel is today, though I am not sure if a cigarette was more expensive than a tram ticket in the olden days when the average middle-class Bengali couldn't do without both.

Trams no longer ply on the Howrah Bridge. In 1993, fifty years after it was opened to public, the cantilever bridge was found to be not strong enough to withstand continued movement of trams. Ever since then, trams have been terminating close to the bridge. I alight at the final stop, shake hands with Pandey one more time, and walk towards Calcutta's most famous landmark. All my life

I have seen the bridge either in pictures or from a distance, or travelled on it in a car or taxi, but now for the first time I was going to make physical contact with it.

Climbing the steps leading to the bridge, I notice a signboard from which I learn two things: that the bridge is officially called—not surprisingly—Rabindra Setu, and that it is maintained by the Calcutta Port Trust.

The first thing that strikes me, as soon as I begin my walk, is that the maze of steel girders, which gives Howrah Bridge its distinct look, does not serve as the protective railing as you imagine it to when you view the bridge from a distance. The intricate steelwork actually hangs like a ceiling over the bridge: if you ignore looking at what is above your head, the Howrah Bridge could well be just other Indian bridge bound by rib-high railings. But then, it is the steelwork that makes Howrah Bridge what it is— an engineering marvel. Before it was built—the construction began in 1936 and took seven years—Calcutta was connected to Howrah with a pontoon bridge.

There is something else about this bridge apart from the engineering: energy. You encounter a torrent of load-bearers coming your way as soon as you step onto the bridge. These two-legged trucks, mostly sturdy Bihari men, keep up the cargo movement between the Howrah Station and the various warehouses that dot old Calcutta. Since balancing heavy load on the head calls for concentration, the load-bearers, as they trot along, either look straight ahead or have their gaze fixed on the pavement. Even the slightest distraction can topple them and cause damage to the goods they are ferrying. That would be an undignified and a heart-rending sight: a poor man, who carries loads for a living and takes pride in his efficiency, taking a tumble and losing control of goods in his custody. Fortunately, I haven't seen such a thing happen before and I don't see it happening now as the coolies, clad in dhotis or lungis, hurry past me.

I am perhaps the only pedestrian who is not crossing the river in a hurry. Even the river does not seem to be in a hurry. From the height, the steamers too appear to be moving in slow motion. I can also see the Vidyasagar Bridge, downriver, which was built during the 1980s but whose construction had taken twice the time.

I pull out my phone and take pictures. I click the load-bearers, I click the river, I click the other bridge. Suddenly a voice from behind: *'Ekhane chhobi tola nishedh kintu'* — Photography is prohibited here.

It is a traffic cop, seated on a chair placed on the sidewalk, warning me. The warning is of the benign sort. What he means is that it doesn't matter that I have taken some pictures, but that I should not take any more. I offer him an apologetic smile and walk on. A few metres down I come across a DVD-seller. On a table he has spread out dozens of DVDs — all pornographic. Breasts of various ethnicities from across the world are on display, in the open, on India's busiest bridge.

'Rs 60 each,' he tells me. 'Buy two for Rs 100.'

I come out of the other end of the bridge, the Howrah Station side, and notice that the deodorant billboard — 'When the match ends, your game begins' — is still in place. Today is the last match — it would have begun by now — and the users of the deodorant have one final opportunity to test its seductive powers on their women.

I now walk all the way back to the Calcutta side, climb down the bridge and stroll into Strand, where the warehouses, dating back to the British days, are concentrated. Trucks are parked. Load-bearers are milling about the place. Many of them are circled around what appears to be a wholesale ginger shop, where the TV is on. Sri Lanka are batting first.

I find a taxi back to Park Street, which has practically emptied out. Small crowds have gathered outside shops that have their TV sets facing the street. I spot only one man in the entire length of the street who is not concerned about the cricket and is focusing on his work—a boot polisher.

Barkat Ali & Sons, which was supposed to deliver my white shirt today, is shut. 'Have they closed for lunch?' I ask the cigarette-seller on the pavement.

'No, they have closed for the day. They closed at one o' clock.'

'Why?'

'The match,' he laughs.

I tear a page from my notebook, write an angry note and hand it over to him. 'Pass it on if you see somebody from the shop,' I tell him and take a taxi back home.

INDIA HAVE JUST begun batting when I settle in front of a TV. I happen to be at the same relative's house in Beleghata, where I had watched the match between India and South Africa.

This evening the relative appears somewhat subdued. He is certainly not as animated as he had been in the previous game. 'You know,' he takes a sip from his drink, 'I got a call from a friend this afternoon. He told me this match is fixed. He said Sri Lanka would deliberately lose and in return get a large sum of money from India. I don't know how far that is true, but I have lost all interest in this game.'

He then grabs my arm and tells me, 'Come, let's go and get some biryani from Shiraz. That's our dinner tonight.'

Leaving the other guests behind in front of the TV, we drive down to Park Street. Since the roads are empty, we are back in no time, carrying ten packets of the famous Shiraz biryani along with a bucket of Kentucky Fried Chicken. India are 114 for three wickets. The target is 275 runs—a distant dream at the moment. Dhoni comes out to bat.

'Why has he come to bat now?' the relative asks, 'Doesn't Yuvraj Singh bat at no. 5?'

'Maybe he wants to show us some magic,' replies one of the guests. There is laughter in the room. The chicken is passed around and more drinks are poured.

Dhoni begins hitting the ball. The women in the room begin to cheer. The Indian team is four runs short of victory, with eleven balls to spare, when Dhoni hits a six and lifts the World Cup for India. As the Indian team rushes to the ground in jubilation, our host remarks mournfully: '*Era to sob Souraver-ee toyri kora chhele!*'— These boys have been groomed by Sourav, after all.

Crackers begin to burst. Celebratory motorcycle processions are out on the street. The room fills with the aroma of biryani from Shiraz.

14

'DHONIT', SCREAMS THE front-page headline of the *Telegraph*, informing readers that finally Dhoni had done it—winning the World Cup for India after twenty-eight years. The lead piece is written by Kapil Dev, the captain who had first won it in 1983.

And so the carnival, which saw players from fourteen countries playing for their national pride, has ended.

In a few days will begin another carnival—the Indian Premier League or IPL—when a number of these players, setting aside their respective national identities, will regroup under teams pompously named after various Indian cities to play for money.

For example, the Sri Lankan captain Kumar Sangakkara. Only last night, he was India's principal foe. But in the IPL, he is going to lead Team Hyderabad. So the same Hyderabadis who had wanted him to lose last night will root for him during the IPL season, which drags on for two months.

Thanks to IPL, cricket fans in India no longer have fixed loyalties. That's half the fun gone out of the game. Though many who would like to believe that the fun has only begun, with the explosive batting and aggressive bowling one is treated to in a twenty-over per side tournament such as the IPL—patriotic sentiments put aside.

I turn the pages. Very little, other than cricket, seems to have happened around the country, if this morning's paper is anything to go by. There are large—and lively—pictures of hip Calcuttans, including celebrities, watching the match on TV and, subsequently, celebrating.

I come across a report about two newborns in a Calcutta hospital, a boy and a girl, whose respective parents were confident—even as the final was underway in Mumbai—that the arrival of the babies would bring good luck to Team India.

'Baby Boy Gupta and Baby Girl Jaiswal may not know each other when they are old enough to understand the significance of their birthday,' the report concludes, 'But in cricket-crazy India, they will always share a common bond—of being the chosen ones.'

In the Letters to the Editor column, however, I find concerns other than cricket being expressed. One reader from Howrah has written: 'Sir—People often smoke while they drive. This is as dangerous as talking on the cell phone while driving, particularly in the case of two-wheelers. The burning ash motorcyclists let out into the air can get into the eyes of riders of two-wheelers coming behind them. This can sometimes even lead to accidents. I wonder why the traffic police are indifferent to this problem. I have never heard of drivers being punished for smoking, even though this is dangerous and smoking in public places is a cognisable offence.'

The letter writer's concerns are unlikely to be addressed anytime soon in this city.

I glance through the classified ads—hoping to find something odd, something typically Calcutta—when I notice an insertion: *For spot dating/close relation with broad minded friends/housewife with privacy (Govt. Regd), contact*—a number is given.

I sit up. Almost every widely-circulated newspaper in the country carries its share of classified ads that sell sex in the name of massage parlours and friendship clubs, but this one catches my eye because of the supposed government registration.

I have never come across a sex-selling agency invoking the name of the government. I must find out more. Who knows, this could be my chance to meet a housewife, without the help of a pimp and with the assurance of the government. I call up the number.

'Where are you calling from, sir?' a young woman's voice answers the phone.

'Salt Lake.'

'Come over, sir. Our office is near Rabindra Sarobar metro station.'

'But that's far.'

'Where far, sir? Just get into a taxi at Salt Lake, won't take you more than forty-five minutes.'

'Forty-five minutes? That's a long time.'

'Sir, today is Sunday, there won't be much traffic. You will be here in thirty minutes. Please come over, sir.'

'Let me think about it.'

I hang up. The thought of a long taxi ride on a Sunday morning—my last Sunday in the city before I return, that too without knowing what's really in store for me at the spot-dating agency—is suddenly not very appealing.

I would rather have another cup of tea, read some more cricket stories in the *Telegraph*, and go to Central Park for a long walk before returning home for lunch. Unnati, the cook, is already grating onions to prepare mutton curry.

The phone rings.

'Sir, it's me. We just spoke.'

'Yes, tell me.'

'*Chole aashoon na*, sir,' she pleads—Come over, sir.

'But I can't come that far.'

'We are not *that* far from Salt Lake, sir. *Chole aashoon, chole aashoon.*'

'All right.'

'Call us when you reach Rabindra Sarobar station. We will guide you.'

Her voice is persuasive not in a sleazy way, but in a manner that is official yet friendly—the one that reminds you about paying your phone bills or credit card dues.

I have a quick shower and get dressed. As soon as I reach for the door, my mother-in-law intercepts me.

'*Kothaye cholle shokal-shokal?*' she asks—Where are you off to so early in the day?

'To gather material for my book.'

'Tell me one thing, why do you always wear black or grey?'

'That is because I like these colours, *ma*.'

'Why don't you wear bright colours? My *jethamoshai*—he was a great man, he had a great personality . . .'

'Yes, I know, *ma*.'

'He liked to wear bright colours.'

'Yes, you have told me about it.'

'Next time when you go shopping, get yourself some bright T-shirts. I will give you the money.'

'Sure.'

'When will you be back?'

'I should be back for lunch, hopefully.'

ON REACHING RABINDRA SAROBAR station I call up the number again. The same woman answers, but this time transfers the call to a male voice.

'Walk straight,' the male voice gives directions, 'take the second left, keep walking, you will soon find a bank. Opposite the bank you will see a *paan* shop. Wait at the shop. And yes, what colour shirt are you wearing?'

'A black T-shirt.'

'Fine, wait at the shop. Someone will meet you there.'

I do as asked.

At the *paan* shop I am met by a young man—he must be barely twenty—who asks me to follow him. I walk behind him rather nervously: this seems more like an undercover operation than a government-registered business. Soon we are climbing the stairs of a residential complex.

The spot-dating office is on the first floor. It is an office in the real sense.

As soon as I enter, I find two young women seated at a small desk. They are dressed in ill-fitting salwars and kurtas, and look rather impoverished. They are stationed there to answer the calls that are pouring in after the ad appeared in this morning's *Telegraph*.

I hear them explain repeatedly to the callers, 'We don't provide prostitutes, sir. We are in the friendship business. Come over, sir. *Chole aashoon*.'

It was one of these women who had spoken to me and persuaded me to come all the way, but I am now unable to tell which. They are both busy answering calls and don't even notice my arrival.

I am greeted, instead, by a formally-dressed man who extends his hand and introduces himself as the manager. He shows me into his cubicle, asks me to be seated, and pushes a form towards me. 'You need to fill this up first,' he says affably.

My form asks for my name, age, height, weight, address and phone numbers. As I write these down, he regards me from across the table.

'*Kothay thhaken?*' he suddenly asks me—Where do you live?

'Why, in Calcutta.'

'But are you a resident of Calcutta?'

'No,' I tell the truth, 'I live in Chennai. I am visiting my mother-in-law.'

'We provide services even in Chennai. We have contacts in all cities.'

'Really?'

'Yes. Housewife, airhostess, college girl—whatever you want.'

'I see. It is interesting that you have government registration. I noticed that in the ad.'

'We are registered as a club, a friendship club. There are only two such clubs in the whole of Calcutta that have government registration, we are one of them.'

'So you have competition.'

'Competition?' he laughs, 'There is no competition in this line of work. Business is always good for everybody— even during recession.'

'I am sure.'

'*Cha khaaben?*' he asks—Will you have tea?

As I sip sugary tea from a tiny disposable cup, he asks me: 'So, what do you do in Chennai?'

'I have a small business,' I suddenly decide to lie, not wanting to put him on guard by giving out my real profession. 'Printing business.'

'Very good. So what are you looking for?'

'Meaning?'

'I mean what type of woman? Housewife?'

'That's right.'

'Very well, the deal will cost you Rs 3,000.'

'But I cannot spare more than Rs 1,500 at the moment. That's the truth.'

That is indeed the truth. A month in Calcutta has depleted my cash reserves; and considering that I have been technically unemployed during this period (which means no salary to look forward to), I do not want to spend a lot on a deal I am not even sure will fructify.

'Rs 1,500? That's too less,' the manager tells me, 'You won't find a woman of your standard with that money.'

'But that's all I can spare for now, trust me.'

'That may be so, but it is important for us to find you someone of your standard. You have a certain standard, don't you? We can't fix you up with just about anybody.' He looks genuinely concerned.

'In that case, I will come back some other time.'

'Please wait for a while. Let me see what I can do.'

He rests his chin on his knuckles and gazes down at the table. A minute passes. He picks up the intercom and speaks softly. Soon an assistant, also clad in formals, emerges from behind me and hands me a slip. It has the name of a woman—'Mousumi Chatterjee'—and her mobile number.

'She lives alone in Shyambazar,' the manager says, 'her husband works in Muscat, and her son lives in a hostel.'

The assistant dials the number and hands over the phone to me, 'Here, speak to her.'

The woman I speak to sounds like any cultured Bengali woman: courteous, confident and articulate. She makes polite enquiries and asks me to call her from my phone so that she can recognise my number later.

When I call her, she asks me: 'Are you familiar with the five-way intersection at Shyambazar?'

'No.'

'No problem. Get into a taxi and ask to be dropped at the five-way intersection. All taxi drivers know the place. Near the intersection is a Kali Bari. Once you reach the

Kali Bari, call me. I will come and pick you up from there.'

As I hang up, the manager smiles. 'So, will you please make the payment now?'

I hand him three five-hundred rupee notes and ask him, 'Do I have to pay her something?'

'Absolutely nothing,' he says and hands me a receipt ('N.B. *In any circumstances, money is not refundable*'). The receipt carries a customer care number, functional on weekdays, 11 am to 2 pm.

As I get up to leave, he shakes my hand once again and says: 'Please come again.'

Soon the taxi is racing—from south Calcutta to north, and so is my heart. Is it a good idea to be visiting an unknown woman in her flat, even though all I want is a chat with her? How is she going to react if I tell her that all I want is a chat? What if something untoward happens?

At the same time, a moral dilemma is staring me in the face: what if Mrs Chatterjee turns out to be irresistible?

KALI BARI, THE home of Kali, is central to the Bengali's existence.

Any Bengali settlement—no matter how self-sufficient with factories, banks, post-offices, schools, colleges, shops, playgrounds—is incomplete without a Kali Bari.

Even outside Bengal, nearly every city that has a sizeable Bengali population boasts of a Kali Bari, which not only serves as a temple to the dark goddess but also as a cultural hub of Bengalis living in that city.

Calcutta, where Kali is omnipresent, has several of them. I am now standing in front of the one near the five-way intersection at Shyambazar. It sits rather inconspicuously among the row of shops that line the road. Pedestrians passing by pause for a moment or two to bow before the deity with their hands folded.

I call up Mrs Chatterjee to announce my arrival. She says she will come and pick me up soon. How soon, she doesn't indicate. Until then, I am supposed to wait in front of the Kali Bari.

I stand in front of the temple, and right in front of me is a fruit stall. The fruit-seller, a jovial young man, is arranging his wares into heaps. He has just begun his day even though it is well past noon. I soon get to know why he is late today.

The evening before, he had wanted to stay home to watch the World Cup final, but his father insisted that he must open the stall and do business as usual. To stay connected with the match, the fruit-seller had brought along an old transistor radio from home and placed it on top of the heap of apples, so that not only he but even hangers-on and passersby could listen to the commentary. The moment India won the Cup, people who had been listening to the commentary on his transistor radio burst crackers in celebration. Since all this had happened close to midnight, it had not been possible for him to wake up early enough and open the stall on time.

I hear him repeat the story to almost every known face that comes up to greet him. He tells each of them how glad he was that he had not stayed home to watch the match and had instead brought the transistor radio along: '*Oi bhabey* enjoy *ta ke bhaaga bhaagi korlam aar ki*'— This way I could share the enjoyment with others.

Even as I listen to the fruit-seller, I have an eye on the pavement. Every woman walking in my direction is Mrs

Chatterjee until she has walked past me without giving me a second glance. At times I tell myself, 'I hope she is the one', and at times, 'Hope she's not the one.'

Thirty minutes pass, no sign of her yet. I call her again.

'I feel so bad I've kept you waiting,' she tells me, 'but something has come up, you see. Can you please wait for some more time?'

I walk up and down the pavement to kill time. One moment, the fragrance of incense and flowers from the temple; another moment, the stench from a butcher's shop a few metres down; I alternate between smells. Each time the walk makes me even more impatient, I return to my position behind the fruit stall.

I want to leave now. It has been more than an hour since I arrived in Shyambazar. By now the fruit-seller and other shopkeepers have started throwing questioning glances at me. But what if Mrs Chatterjee calls the moment I get into a taxi?

I decide to call her one last time. Her phone rings for a long time and when she finally answers my call, she offers the same syrupy Bengali apology: 'Aamar khoob kharap lagchhe, jaanen to—I feel so terrible, you know. But I will take another hour at least.'

Maybe she is busy telling her story to someone else.

I am angry and at the same time relieved. I cross the road and get into a taxi. Thinking of the time wasted and the money spent, I pull out the receipt from my pocket to call the customer-care number but realise that it does not function on weekends.

I redial the spot-dating agency's number instead. I am greeted by the same female voice that had persuaded me into making this journey in the first place. The woman is apologetic. 'We have never had such complaints about Mousumi madam, sir,' she tells me, 'She must be really caught up in something. Why don't you come back tomorrow, sir?'

'But I'm leaving tomorrow.'

'Not to worry, sir,' she assures me, 'when you return to Calcutta you can avail the same service—for free.'

Sitting in the taxi, I replay the entire morning in my head. Only one voice stands out now: that of the fruit-seller. I will always remember his words: '*Ei bhabey* enjoy *ta ke bhaaga bhaagi korlam*'—This way I could share the enjoyment with others.

He may not know English, but he knows the word 'enjoy' and the art of sharing enjoyment. He is a true child of Calcutta.

15

THE SAME EVENING I return to Park Street, for one last outing before I leave for Chennai.

I will return to Calcutta again, but I am not sure when, so I have come here to take a good look at the signboards that I have come to associate the city with: Oxford Bookstore; Music World; Flurys; Mocambo; Peter Cat; Trincas; Bar-B-Q; Moulin Rouge; Oasis; Magnolia; Olypub; AN John (hairdressers); Barkat Ali & Sons (the tailors).

During the one month that I've stayed in Calcutta, I have bought numerous books from Oxford, eaten at most of these restaurants, had my hair cut at AN John, got a shirt stitched at Barkat Ali & Sons (the shirt was delivered home this afternoon, with a small note of apology, even as I was waiting for Mrs Chatterjee at Shyambazar). If I also include the tram ride, I can say I have lived in pre-Independence Calcutta without even travelling back in time.

This evening I am also meeting Sajal Mitra at Oxford Bookstore. Sajal is about my age, runs a family business that takes him across continents, and loves visiting bookshops. Once upon a time I knew him only as a relative of my wife, but now we are good friends and go out together for a drink whenever I am in Calcutta. He was with me that night at Trincas when the idea for this book took root. Oxford is always our meeting point; only after reaching there do we decide where to head next.

Sajal is already at the bookshop when I walk in. I desist from buying any more books; I have bought nearly every book that had caught my fancy over the past one month. Sajal buys Thomas Friedman's *The World is Flat*.

Sajal should know whether the world is flat or round because he is forever travelling. One day he is in Indonesia, another day in Brazil; in between he would have squeezed in trips to Istanbul and Johannesburg. His company, which dates back to 1938, offers laboratory testing for minerals and metals imported by international firms; and as the world shrinks, his horizon expands.

Sajal and I are now going to Shobhabazar, in north Calcutta. We have decided to take a ferry across the river—something neither of us has ever done before. Sajal sends his car away, for he does not want to keep his driver waiting for an uncertain period, and we get into a taxi.

On the way, he tells me about something that happened to him in China just a week ago. He was at the airport in one of the smaller Chinese cities when his bag, containing his passport and money, went missing from the restroom.

He had placed it on the floor, against the wall, before using the urinal, but when he had turned back to claim it, the bag was gone.

So did he manage to get home? That's another story—the kind which makes evenings with Sajal enjoyable, and often enlightening. Not that he is the talkative kind—he is anything but talkative, and that makes you take him seriously.

As the taxi ploughs its way into north Calcutta, I silently wonder about the cruel irony of life: Sajal is not a writer but he gets to travel around the world, whereas I am the one who likes to write about places but who is forever desk-bound for the lack of enough money or leave—or the courage of Sunil Gangopadhyay.

SHOBHABAZAR, NAMED AFTER a Bengali merchant whose ancestors had made Sutanuti a thriving textiles market much before the arrival of Job Charnock, is one of the oldest existing neighbourhoods of Calcutta and—as expected of old neighbourhoods—congested, chaotic and noisy.

But the riverside of Shobhabazar is wrapped in contemplative silence, insulated from the noise and chaos, as Sajal and I wait on the pier for the next boat. We have bought tickets, costing five rupees each, to travel across the river to the Howrah Station.

The ferry will originate from Baghbazar, come downstream to collect passengers from Shobhabazar, make another halt at Ahiritola—thus covering the entire length of what is geographically north Calcutta, or old Calcutta—before going across the river to the Howrah Station.

It is 7.15 pm now and the river has dissolved into

darkness, distinguishable because of the lights on the opposite bank reflecting on its surface. It being a Sunday, there are not too many people waiting along with us for the ferry. Somewhere close to where we are standing now—the precise location is not known—Job Charnock had dropped anchor some 16,000 Sundays ago.

Even though the river had played a pivotal role in the founding of Calcutta, it wasn't until late 1965 that ferries began to run between Calcutta and Howrah. The service was started by the River Steam Navigation Company, which had been running a cargo service between Calcutta and Assam for nearly a century till then. Its steamers would sail to Assam with textiles, machinery and fertilisers, and return to Calcutta with tea, jute, wax and oil. Even after Bengal was partitioned in 1947, when much of the river route came under the newly-created East Pakistan, the company's steamers kept up the movement of cargo between Calcutta and Assam. But in September 1965, when India went to war against Pakistan, Indian boats were banned from East Pakistan and those already in Pakistani waters were seized.

The company, which boasted of a fleet of sixty-two steamers at the time, lost fifteen of them—their cargoes included—to Pakistan. Of the remaining forty-seven, twenty-three were held up in Assam and twenty-four in Calcutta. Since the company's directors did not want the boats to idle, the ones trapped in Assam began to ply within Assam, while the ones stranded in Calcutta were pressed into service across the Hooghly. Thus began the Calcutta-Howrah ferry service, a war boon, on 22 November 1965.

Until then, the thousands who lived in Howrah but worked in Calcutta, and the thousands who lived in

Calcutta but worked in Howrah, relied solely on the Howrah Bridge to cross over. The bridge, twenty-two years old at the time, was already groaning under the weight of the expanding population and the need for another bridge was beginning to be felt. The ferry service became a hit and was soon taken over by the government.

Our boat arrives. We step aboard to join about fifty other passengers travelling from Baghbazar. They are seated on the wooden benches of the launch and are wearing grim expressions. For them, the ferry ride seems no more exciting than a bus ride on a clogged road—it's just another mode of getting home.

Sajal and I choose to stand against the railing, and we watch the Shobhabazar ghat recede rapidly as the ferry gets back into the middle of the river to continue its journey downstream. Suddenly, the Howrah Bridge comes into view, shining as if made of gold. To watch the iconic bridge bathed in powerful yellow lights, that too from the middle of the river where the pleasant river breeze is now kissing us—this should be one of the most exhilarating moments of my stay in Calcutta.

Until a few seconds ago, the bridge was not visible at all, but now it is, in its full glory—a confirmation that Shobhabazar, located in the erstwhile village of Sutanuti, indeed sits on the bend of the river, which is why Charnock thought it made an ideal site to build a settlement.

The boat has barely picked up speed when it slows down and turns towards the bank to make the halt at Ahiritola ghat, where many passengers step off and many others step in. It once again lumbers towards the bridge, goes right under it, and deposits us across the river—at the Howrah Station. The ride from Shobhabazar, including the halt at Ahiritola ghat, has lasted barely twenty minutes. The same distance, when covered by road, is likely to take twice the time.

We walk down the pier, surrender our tickets to a *bidi*-smoking man guarding the entrance to the Howrah Station, and step into its bustle. In doing so, we trample upon a carpet of used tickets.

Howrah Station, like any railway station in India, thrives on chaos: hurrying passengers, haggling porters, impatient trolley-pushers, indifferent staff, whining beggars, shouting vendors. This is what you see on the surface. Scratch it a bit and you will find an underbelly, far removed from the romance of the railways—a parallel universe of thieves, pickpockets, pimps and other characters who are considered despicable but are humans all the same.

This red-brick station, one of the oldest and the busiest in the country, must be holding in its bosom a million unsavoury—and sometimes heartrending—stories that would only reiterate the timeless link between deprivation and crime. But this is not the time to look for such stories—not when you are romancing Calcutta.

Sajal and I have tea at one of the stalls outside the station. As we sip on the tea and survey the chaos, quite glad that we are not part of it, Sajal plucks an anecdote from a recent trip to Australia.

Taking the train out of Brisbane one night, he had found himself sitting next to an extraordinarily beefy man who turned out to be a bouncer hired by the railways to deal with unruly teenagers returning home after drinking all night. The bouncer, finding a patient listener in Sajal, began to pour his heart out. He lamented how he not only had to deal with tough college boys but also rein in teenaged girls acting under the influence of alcohol. One night, he had to control a drunken girl who, when challenged by her friends, had dropped her clothes and streaked through the coach. On another night, he had to arrest a girl who, responding to a similar challenge, had defecated inside the coach. His was an unenviable job, the bouncer had complained. As the journey wore on, he had become comfortable enough with Sajal to make a confession: he despised Indians. When Sajal had asked him why, he narrated an incident. One night, he—the bouncer—was on duty in the same train along with two fellow bouncers, both Indians, when drunken behaviour by local students nearly caused a riot. The Indian bouncers, finding themselves outnumbered by hefty Australian youth, had fled the scene, leaving their Australian colleague behind to deal with the nasty situation. Ever since, he hated Indians.

'Can't blame him for hating Indians, can we?' I ask Sajal, as we walk back to the ferry ghat at the station.

'No, we can't,' he says, 'I can't imagine Indians who go there to make quick money putting their lives at risk, that too for an Australian.'

We buy tickets for the return journey to Shobhabazar and get into a waiting steamer. As we go under the Howrah Bridge once again, we decide to get off at Ahiritola ghat, the first halt, and walk along the river for a while before deciding what to do next.

We are now walking on one of the oldest pathways of Calcutta, moving—in the seventeenth century geography—from the village of Sutanuti to the village of Kalikata. We could well be walking on the footprints of Charnock, for he may well have landed where we have landed just now, at the Ahiritola ghat, which is not far from the Shobhabazar ghat.

Charnock must have lived somewhere close by as well. The location of his residence, just like the exact location of his landing, is not known. What is known is that he lived in a thatched house, which, a couple of years after his death in 1693, accidentally caught fire one night and got burned down. The house was rebuilt with bricks, but the cost of the reconstruction—Rs 400 at the time—had exceeded the East India Company's expectations. Moreover, it was turning out to be far from the factory, which had just been set up in adjacent Kalikata. The Company, therefore, decided to auction the renovated house, which was sold for Rs 575. A speck of history lost in the sands of time.

We would have walked barely a couple of hundred metres on the riverside road when we hit a stretch that is brightly lit by neon lights, is noisy and smells of fresh flowers. *Mehbooba mehbooba*, the famous dance number from *Sholay*, is blaring from loudspeakers. We stroll through the noise of music, wondering if we are in the midst of roadside festivity. To our left is a row of stalls selling garlands, snacks and items for religious rituals; to our right, where the river is, stands a dharmashala, a temple and yet another building which Sajal instantly recognises as the Nimtala ghat—the famous cremation ground.

'Are you sure this is Nimtala ghat?' I ask Sajal. I had, for some reason, imagined it to be a desolate, jungle-like place by the river, where jackals howled and mysterious-looking ascetics roamed. It's by the river all right, but I hadn't expected to be in the midst of an urban jungle, bathed in neon lights and throbbing to the beats of *Mehbooba, mehbooba*.

'Of course it is,' replies Sajal, 'we came here to cremate my father just three years ago. You want to take a look inside?'

We step into the building, which could pass off as a modern-day temple from the outside, and find ourselves in an airless hall where two flower-bedecked bodies lie on the floor, awaiting their turn to be wheeled into cave-like passages that lead to the electric furnaces. Relatives are seated on benches along the wall—weary, expressionless and forced to hear the dance number from *Sholay*. One of the bodies has its face covered—perhaps an accident victim. The other body is that of an old man, who seems asleep rather than dead. A young woman is seated next to him on the floor, affectionately stroking his face as if he were still alive. Perhaps she was the favourite granddaughter, who now has only a few more minutes left to feel the deceased man in flesh.

We walk across the hall, past the two bodies, and emerge out of the rear door to a terrace overlooking the river. Here there are several pits meant to hold pyres but it appears they have not been used in a long time. Calcuttans seem to prefer electric cremation which, compared to the traditional method, not only takes lesser time but is also easier on emotions.

In one corner of the cremation ground is a monument under whose canopy street-children are playing. It turns out that Tagore was cremated at this spot seventy years ago. I try to imagine the scene: the body of India's best-known poet, the world's most-revered Bengali, sage-like in appearance, placed by India's most-revered river, amid a sea of mourners—the confluence of dignity, devotion and death. In reality, I learn later, the scene had been anything but dignified. The crowds had plucked the poet's hairs during the funeral procession and had descended on the pyre, looking for relics, even before the body could fully turn into ashes.

We walk back into the crematorium hall, where the young girl is still sitting by the old man's body and stroking his face, and step out onto the road. Another dance number is now playing on the loudspeakers, and as we resume our walk, we notice the source of the music. Right next to the crematorium, a temporary shrine has been erected by the road, where a bunch of children from a nearby slum are dancing wildly in front of a collage of pictures showing various gods. The gods happen to be the members of Indian cricket team that won the World Cup last night. Adults reeking of alcohol are cheering the children.

Receiving the dead is a way of life for residents of Nimtala. The arrival of bodies means nothing to them — it certainly does not come in the way of celebrating a happy occasion such as India's victory in cricket. A few steps ahead, outside a roadside saloon, a young man is getting his hair washed with beer. A small crowd watches with curiosity as the barber slowly empties the bottle of beer over his client's head. The exercise appears to be a first for both, the barber as well as the young client, because both are laughing.

'Maybe we could go to a nice place and have some beer?' Sajal asks me. His suggestion, I am certain, is not prompted by the sight of beer but because the crematorium is not an ideal place to wind up an evening. It reminds you of things you would rather not think of.

'Do you have a place in mind?' I ask him.

'No.'

'Let's go to Floatel,' I suggest, suddenly remembering the floating hotel off Dalhousie Square. 'You will like it.'

Theoretically, Nimtala to Floatel is one long walk along the river—a distance of about two miles. But these two miles, dominated by the Howrah Bridge, are a documentary-maker's delight rather than a walker's paradise. On this stretch lies the core of Calcutta, sitting on three hundred years of history, lined by once-magnificent colonial-era buildings that have attained timelessness in their various stages of dereliction, packed with crowds and cargoes.

We look for a taxi, but are unable to find one. We eventually get out of Nimtala in an autorickshaw, which we share with several other passengers. Sajal sits next to the driver. The autorickshaw drops us at Central Avenue, the nearest arterial road, from where we take a taxi to Floatel.

Sitting eighty feet above the river, cut off from the noise of Calcutta, we clink our glasses. What a coincidence that I should find myself at Floatel on my first as well as final evening during this trip to Calcutta, seated on the lap of the Hooghly, midway between the two iconic bridges. I am at the same table too—the Howrah Bridge to my right, the Vidyasagar Bridge to my left—only this time I feel a little proprietary about the city.

'See the bridges? I ask Sajal.

'Don't they look beautiful when lit up? It doesn't feel we are in Calcutta.'

'You know, just beyond the Howrah Bridge, where we took the steamer from, used to be the village of Sutanuti. And this place, where we are right now, used to be the village of Kalikata. And there, the Vidyasagar Bridge, that was where the village of Gobindapur used to be. The three villages were leased by the East India Company and together they became Calcutta.'

'I knew about the three villages,' says Sajal, 'but I did not know about their locations.'

'Even I did not. But now I do.'

SUMMER

SUMMER

1

RETURNING AFTER A year, I find some things have changed in Calcutta.

A larger-than-life portrait of Mamata Banerjee now adorns a hoarding outside the airport. Wearing a smile and her hands folded in greeting, the new chief minister is welcoming visitors to the city.

Rajarhat Road, leading from the airport to Salt Lake via New Town, is now dotted with brand-new tri-headed streetlamps, a part of Mamata's plan to beautify Calcutta into another London. The radio in the car, tuned in to 98.3 FM, is repeatedly broadcasting her greetings to Calcuttans in between songs of Kishore Kumar: today happens to be *Poila Baisakh*, the Bengali New Year's Day. In the vast expanse surrounding Rajarhat Road, more cranes are at work and more high-rises nearing completion. Inside the city, metro rail bridges remain frozen in their various states of incompletion. And at home, Badan Singh, the one-eyed watchman, is not there to carry my bags up.

All these years, Badan Singh would be waiting at the gate for my arrival and insist on carrying my bags despite my protests. I would relent because my bags are never very heavy. It would feel good, I must admit, to be climbing the stairs without any weight on your shoulders—a luxury that I do not enjoy in my lift-less flat in Chennai. But this morning, for the first time since I got married, I feel a little less pampered in Calcutta.

Badan Singh has quit after twenty-five years of loyal service. He had been like a member of the family, the only person in this world my mother-in-law could blindly trust the house keys with. But none of this had mattered to him when he decided to leave, unaware of the retirement benefits that awaited him. Unnati, the cook, who was fond of Badan Singh and called him *dadu*, explains to me why he left.

Badan Singh had apparently gone to see a doctor one evening recently, and the doctor, a talkative Bengali, had asked him how much he earned. When Badan Singh stated his monthly salary, the doctor is said to have exclaimed: 'Even a dog would earn more than you!'

Badan Singh, suddenly realising that he was grossly underpaid, told my mother-in-law that he was leaving for Bihar for good, but had actually taken up another job in the neighbourhood. He had not asked for a raise because he knew it was pointless. My mother-in-law, even though she had set aside one lakh rupees for his retirement, was not the one to give out-of-turn hikes. Having been a government employee herself most of her life, she functioned like the government when it came to her own employees.

My mother-in-law, however, does not buy the cook's story that the loyal Badan Singh had deserted her for a better-paying job. She wants to believe that he has indeed gone back to Bihar. '*Lok ta khaarap chhilo na,*' she says— He wasn't a bad sort.

Badan Singh ceases to be the subject of discussion once lunch is served. Lunch is a lavish spread—since today happens to be the Bengali New Year's Day—but almost entirely non-vegetarian. There's fish even in the *daal* and cabbage curry.

The cook, since I hadn't come to Calcutta for a year, had forgotten that I am not very fond of fish and meat. She is deeply embarrassed now, after having toiled for hours in the kitchen.

'You eat only *rui* fish, don't you?' my mother-in-law asks me.

'That's right. I don't like any other fish.'

'The *daal* and the cabbage curry have *rui* fish only, then why can't you have them?'

'I can eat *rui*, fried or in the form of curry. But I do not like the idea of fish in *daal* or vegetables.'

'That is strange. Had your mother been alive, I would have told her point-blank that she hadn't taught her son anything about the art of eating.'

'You cannot teach such things, *ma*. It is all about one's temperament. I have never been particularly fond of meat or fish.'

'No, you need to be taught from childhood, only then you learn.'

'I don't think so,' I tell her, in English.

'But I think so,' she tells me, in English.

I begin to enjoy my rice with *shukto*—a healthy vegetable stew dominated by slices of bitter gourd and raw banana—with the juice of an entire lemon squeezed over it. My mother-in-law, as usual, begins telling me about her childhood and about her illustrious *jethamoshai*, the army officer-turned-philanthropist.

After lunch, I settle in bed with the *Telegraph* and realise that the changes I find in my life in Calcutta are trivial compared to those faced by its citizens under the rule of a quixotic chief minister.

The lead story in the paper is about the arrest of two *bhadraloks*—a Jadavpur University professor, fifty-two, and a retired engineer, seventy-two—for forwarding online a cartoon that lampooned the chief minister. The newspaper has reproduced the offending cartoon, which is not only innocuous but also in good taste: it merely parodies a dialogue from Satyajit Ray's famous film *Sonar Kella* to poke fun of the temperamental Mamata.

Shortly before their arrest, the professor had also been beaten up by a mob of Trinamool Congress workers. The two men were released on bail after they had spent a night in the lock-up and been charged with outraging the modesty of a woman—in this case, the chief minister of West Bengal.

Paribartan—change—had been Mamata Banerjee's war cry during the state elections a year ago, when she won a landslide victory, ending thirty-four years of Communist rule in West Bengal. Barely five feet tall and always clad in rubber *chappals*, Mamata had finally achieved what the mighty Congress, once her parent party, could not in three-and-a-half decades. In Biblical terms, she was the David who felled Goliath.

While the Communists had accepted their defeat with exemplary grace, Mamata, even after assuming power, remained a street fighter. Having thrived on politics of criticism for several decades, she has come to believe that criticism is solely her preserve and is unwilling to be at the receiving end. She has never lived in a glass house before to know that if you continuously throw stones at others, you must expect at least a stone or two in return if not a fusillade. And this wasn't even a stone, but an innocuous political joke. She has four more years to go.

THE SAME EVENING on Park Street, I notice the first visible signs of *paribartan*. I find the railings on the sidewalks painted blue, the colour of Mamata Banerjee's party. During my previous visit, they had been green.

I also find a paramilitary post, fortified by sandbags, right on the traffic intersection outside Oxford Bookstore. The men at the post are dressed in khaki fatigues and they are young and heavily armed. Their presence makes my favourite place in Calcutta resemble a war zone. Two months before, the city had been shaken by a rape case. A woman visiting one of the nightclubs at the Park Hotel had been offered a ride back home by a man she had befriended there, and allegedly raped at gunpoint in his car by several men. The woman had filed a police complaint only a few days after the incident, saying she needed time to recover from the shock.

Mamata Banerjee had called the episode '*sajano ghotona*'—a fabricated story, aimed at maligning her government. A Member of Parliament belonging to her party, also a woman, had gone a step ahead by saying that it wasn't rape but a 'deal gone sour.' The insensitive nature of their remarks kept television channels busy and overshadowed the real issue: safety of women.

In the end, the rape case left scars on Park Street—in the form of the paramilitary post—and took a toll on Calcutta's celebrated nightlife. All pubs and discotheques must now shut by eleven-thirty. So far, Calcutta had been the only Indian city where one could party into the small hours without fear, unlike in other cities where police would be clamping down on late-night revelries.

I still remember that night at Venom, a popular discotheque on Camac Street, where during Durga Puja a few years ago, my wife and I and her friends drank and danced till three in the morning. As we made for the exit, sweaty and tired, we walked past young women who were still walking in, smelling of expensive perfumes. I had felt proud of Calcutta. Things have changed—and how soon.

2

LATER IN THE evening, we—my mother-in-law, my wife and I—attend a dinner party thrown by Asit *babu*, a family friend, who lives a couple of streets away in the same block. Throwing a dinner party every *Poila Baisakh* is a ritual he has been following without fail ever since he came to live in Salt Lake a couple of decades ago. The invitees are mostly Bengali families living in the block: they all probably bear in mind that they don't have to cook on the evening of *Poila Baisakh* because they would be invited for the now-institutionalised dinner party thrown by Asit *babu*.

The party, I discover, isn't the kind where guests make small talk over drinks before descending on a buffet spread, but like a traditional wedding feast where guests are being straightaway led to the tables so that they can get on with the business of eating without feeling obliged to mingle around and make small talk. They are being indulged by obedient bearers, under the supervision of the host himself.

Asit *babu*, when he spots us, takes me aside and tells me in mock-warning, 'Dare you eat right now. Let your wife and mother-in-law eat and go home, you and I are going to have some Black Label.'

And so, after about an hour, when the last batch of his guests sits down to eat, Asit *babu*, who is nearly my father's age, grabs me by the arm and leads me out of the dining area into a room that has a low ceiling and is dimly lit. Another guest, an elderly gentleman, accompanies us.

Asit *babu* switches on the air-conditioner and pours our drinks. Cigarettes are lit.

'How do you like the room, *jamai*?' he asks me. He calls me *jamai*—son-in-law—because my father-in-law was a good friend of his.

'The ideal place to drink,' I tell him.

He looks pleased. 'Every evening, no matter how late, I escape to this room for at least half an hour. I sit here, have a drink, talk to myself—it's like meditation for me. What is the use of all the wealth if I cannot earn a few moments of peace for myself?'

The elderly gentleman and I nod in agreement.

'How many people did you call for the dinner?' I ask Asit *babu*.

He leans back on the sofa and takes a long drag from his cigarette. 'I asked the caterer to prepare food for 500 people.'

'500? That's almost as big as a wedding reception.'

'Asit Basak's *Poila Baisakh* dinner is no less than a wedding reception, *jamai*. Are you even aware of this evening's menu? It will make your mouth water.'

'What all do we have?'

'You did not even notice what people were eating? There is chicken curry, there is *bhetki* fish, there is *ilish* fish, there is prawn curry, what more do you want?'

The menu, far from making my mouth water, begins to kill my appetite. I had agreed to stay back for the drinks because I had assumed there would be mutton and *rui* fish. I quickly set the cravings to the vegetarian mode and concentrate on the drink.

The first round of drinks gets over in no time and the elderly gentleman, who is clearly not a seasoned drinker, begins to nag Asit *babu*, 'When are we eating? It is eleven-thirty, almost midnight.'

'What is the hurry? *Jamai* has come home for the first time, let me take care of him.'

Asit *babu* gets up to make the second round of drinks. As he comes over to hand my glass, he puts a hand on my shoulder and looks into my eyes. 'You know, *jamai*,' he tells me, 'when I came to Calcutta from East Bengal, I had no money in my pocket. Absolutely zero money. I saw so much hardship, you can't imagine. One day, I wanted to borrow ten rupees from a person, just ten rupees, but you know what that person did to me? He thumbed his nose at me.

'That was the day I told myself that I will be rich one day. Today I am drinking Black Label. I drink nothing but Black Label,' he raises his glass.

Then, still looking into my eyes, he suddenly breaks into a song: '*Aamake aamar moton thhakte dao, aami nijey ke nijer moton guchhiye niyechhi*'—Let me live the way I want to, I have sorted my life out.

It's a very popular song, from a recent Bengali film called *Autograph*, and I had not expected a man my father's age, who should be more at ease with the lines of Tagore, to burst into a filmy song without warning, that too right on my face.

Returning to his seat, Asit *babu* continues: 'You know, *jamai*, when I was poor, I had only one ambition in life:

that I should have a big house and a big car, and whenever I would come home from work, a guard should open the gates and salute me.

'Today I have a big house, two cars, there is a guard too who salutes me. I also got a national award for running a successful small-scale industry. I received the award from the prime minister himself.

'I have achieved all this through hard work. Nothing comes easy, *jamai*, nothing. You have to earn it. No one helps you.' And once again, without warning, breaks into the song: '*Aamake aamar moton thhakte dao, aami nijey ke nijer moton guchhiye niyechhi.*'

'When are we eating? It's almost midnight,' the elderly gentleman is getting restless.

'You can afford to eat late tonight. What is the hurry? Don't you see *jamai* and me are having a discussion? We are going to have one more drink after this.'

'One more drink? No, no, no. It's almost midnight!'

'Quiet!' Asit *babu* mock-admonishes him. I feel sorry for the elderly gentleman: he must be not only habituated to eating on time but also finding it difficult to keep his salivary glands in check ever since Asit *babu* bragged about the menu.

Soon Asit *babu* gets up to pour more drinks. He has been insisting on making the drinks himself. When he comes over to hand my glass, he says, '*Jamai*, do you see that lamp?'

He is pointing to a lamp on the bar table. It resembles a soothsayer's crystal.

'Yes, it is beautiful,' I tell him.

'You know, whenever I am alone in this room, I don't switch on the other lights. I only keep that lamp on. I play with its lights. I see the lights assume different shapes. I talk to the lights.'

The door bursts open and Asit *babu*'s wife barges in. She is livid at the sight of three men drinking in a smoke-filled room. 'Guests are leaving and they are looking for you,' she scolds him, 'and here you are, drinking!' She launches into a long rebuke.

Asit *babu*, red-eyed by now, silently absorbs his wife's outpourings. When she finally demands an explanation, as to why he suddenly went missing from the dinner, he looks deep into her eyes for several moments and then breaks into his favourite song: *Aamake aamar moton thhakte dao, aami nijey ke nijer moton guchhiye niyechhi*. He does a little dance as he sings.

'Disgusting!' she fumes, marching out.

Asit *babu* shuts the door and makes a gesture of relief by throwing an invisible blanket off his shoulders. 'Now that she is gone,' he announces, 'we can drink some more.'

'No, no, no. No way! We need to eat, it's almost midnight,' the elderly gentleman is now raising his voice.

The truth is it is well past midnight. By the time we eat it is one-thirty. Fortunately, Asit *babu* is too drunk to notice that I haven't touched any of the delicacies he had boasted about—delicacies that any true Bengali would die for.

THE NEXT MORNING I am woken up by my mother-in-law's heavy voice. I open my eyes to find her standing at the window by my bed. With her forehead pressed against the grille, she is calling out, 'Prodeep! O Prodeep!'

Pradeep is the new watchman, who now lives in the room vacated by Badan Singh. He is only a part-time watchman though. His primary job is that of a driver, for a Marwari family living a few houses away. The rest of the day, he serves as our watchman.

He is responsible for, among other things, opening and closing the tap to the overhead water tank and cleaning our car. Occasionally, he drives our car as well. He gets paid a little more than Badan Singh and is entitled to the same perks, which includes the morning tea.

Pradeep is a young man, barely into his twenties, someone I can order around. I send him to buy *samosas*, *rossogollas* and sweet curd. To me, the sweets and savouries—and not meticulously-prepared fish dishes—define the taste of Calcutta.

3

I TAKE MY cup of tea to the balcony, where I sit with that morning's newspaper, eagerly awaiting the watchman's return. The *Telegraph* has expressed concern about Mamata's political machinery increasingly misusing the power of the police to deal with dissent: it says that the arrest of the professor and the retired engineer was only the tip of the iceberg. The social media, the paper points out, is already abuzz with comments that compare Mamata's rule to Stalinism.

As a not-so-interested spectator of Bengal's politics, I had been surprised by Mamata Banerjee's landslide in the elections. I had not expected West Bengal to vote out Buddhadeb Bhattacharjee, a *bhadralok* to the boot, who during the latter part of his long stint as chief minister was slapping restrictions on general strikes—*bandhs*—and laying the red carpet for private investors.

But in his eagerness to wash West Bengal's taint of being a business-unfriendly state, he had probably forgotten that he belonged to the same Marxist government whose sole mission once upon a time was to take away excess land from the rich and distribute it among the peasants. And so, when he sought to take away land from the peasants and hand it over to the rich at subsidised rates to set up industry, there was a backlash.

In any other state, such a move by the government would have gone unnoticed and even earned laurels for the chief minister for being pro-industry and therefore pro-development, but in West Bengal, for long a communist state, the poor suddenly began to see the government as a land-grabber than a land-giver. There were violent protests at Nandigram, where an Indonesian group proposed to set up a petrochemical hub, and at Singur, where Tata Motors proposed to set up a car factory.

Mamata Banerjee, seizing on the anger of the peasants, became the new Marx in Bengal. Her relentless protests not only drove the two projects out of the state but also drove the Communist coalition—led by the CPM, which stands for Communist Party of India (Marxist)—out of power. She has barely completed a year as chief minister and is already being compared with Stalin, the highly-feared dictatorial face of communism.

Her biggest flaw is that she leads a party that fancies itself to be a cadre-based party like the CPM, but has neither an ideology nor the discipline. To make matters worse, thuggish lower-level functionaries of the party have become a law unto themselves in their respective neighbourhoods.

Even the arrest of the Jadavpur University professor and

his elderly neighbour had been triggered by lowly Trinamool Congress leaders, who exploited Mamata's sensitivity to criticism so that they could be in her good books. What's worrying is that they had succeeded in their misdemeanor.

Sitting in the balcony, as I await the return of the watchman from the sweet shop, I notice our next-door neighbour taking a walk on his terrace. Until last summer, he had been one of the most powerful men in the whole of West Bengal, not just Calcutta.

Asim Dasgupta, the neighbour, was the finance minister of the state for almost a quarter of a century before the Communists were voted out. Power always sat lightly not only on his shoulders but also on the walls of his house, which is modest compared to many other houses in Salt Lake. It used to be as quiet when he was a minister as it is now. The only change I notice is that the two police constables occupying a wooden booth outside his house now look relaxed: earlier they would eye every passerby with suspicion.

For a moment I consider seeking an appointment with him from the balcony, but better sense prevails and I call him on the phone a little later—once he has finished his walk and I have had my breakfast. He asks me to come over right away.

Asim Dasgupta is one of the most impeccable *bhadraloks* I have ever come across: soft-spoken, erudite, courteous, and cultured. I first met him during my wedding, and subsequently a couple of times at his home: I found him personally answering calls on the land phone—I saw no secretary or assistant—and patiently dealing with the callers. Often the caller would be someone seeking a favour, as would be evident from his polite but firm reply, 'I cannot go outside the law to help you, but if your grievance is genuine, I will see what I can do.'

I always found it hard to imagine him making angry speeches during election campaigns—which a politician is usually required to—and wondered why a *bhadralok* such as him should choose to be in politics, which is not the cleanest of professions. But this is Bengal, where most communist ministers have been thorough *bhadralok*s who placed their party above the power they personally wielded as ministers, and who muddied their hands in politics only because of their commitment to an ideology.

Politics does not interest me, even though I have done my stint as a political reporter, and the subject of finance baffles me—so what am I going to talk to him about? I am going to talk to him about himself, the man behind the long-time minister: who is he, what is he, and how is he, especially after the defeat in the elections.

'I was born in Calcutta in 1945,' Asim Dasgupta tells me his story. 'We were twins, my brother Atis and I. My father participated in the militant nationalist movement and after Independence joined the civil service. My mother was a teacher. She was a brilliant student, and was with the Left movement right from her student days. Both of them had spent time in jails. So there were two political influences for me, militant nationalist and leftist.

'My early memories go back to the early 1950's when teachers sat down in protest outside the Raj Bhavan on a winter night. Since my mother was among the protestors, my father had also gone there, and we brothers could not sleep at night. But in the morning when our parents came back, we were in our own way quite proud of them.

'I got into Presidency College in 1960 to do my honours in economics. I also started participating in student politics. I joined the Students' Federation of India, which was then Students' Federation. I must also mention here that comrade Buddhadeb Bhattacharjee and I were in the same batch in Presidency College.

'What drew you to the Students' Federation?'

'You see, like I said, I was and even now I am interested in militant nationalism. The nationalist movement had two streams. One was the non-violent tradition which believed in getting independence through discussions; unfortunately that eventually led to independence through partition. The other was the militant nationalist tradition (the path chosen by Subhas Chandra Bose, who raised an army to drive out the British)—in Bengal that tradition was always stronger—and on matters of principle that appealed to me more.

'Let me tell you something. In the 1950's, Clement Atlee (who was the British prime minister when India became independent) was passing through Calcutta and he stayed at the Raj Bhavan. During dinner, the governor, Phani Bhushan Chakraborty, asked Atlee why the British had left India in such a hurry. Atlee replied that the British had left because Subhas Bose's campaign was leading to an uprising in the Indian army and the navy, and that Gandhi had a minimal role in their withdrawal. The governor mentioned this conversation in a book that he wrote later on.

'The militant nationalist movement later on merged with the socialist movement in Bengal. Most of the nationalist leaders, when they returned from jail in Andaman after independence, joined the Communist Party of India. The Students' Federation had both these appeals, nationalist and socialist. Incidentally, Subhash Bose was the leader of Students' Federation at one point of time. Even today, the Forward Bloc (the party founded by Bose) is a very important constituent of the Left front.

'Coming back to my college days, I graduated in 1964 and got admitted to the Masters course in Calcutta University. I had lost my father in 1963, and my brother and I, to back up the family income, had taken up teaching in schools. I was also receiving scholarship so that had helped.

'Now in Masters, I stood first in first-class. I was awarded several gold medals—I am unable to recall how many. Immediately after the results were out I was taken in as a lecturer in Calcutta University. This was 1967. I taught for three years, after which I applied for leave from the university because—I feel a little reticent to mention this—I had got admission into both MIT (Massachusetts Institute of Technology) and Harvard.

'MIT was really number one in economics and I chose to do my PhD there. I was also lucky to get the Woodrow Wilson Fellowship. When I was there, I also taught briefly at the Boston University, in its College of Business Administration, and was adjudged the best teacher.

'My thesis topic was "Income distribution and capital formation and growth in developing economies with special reference to India." It was a mathematical model and I proved that there is no conflict between equity and growth. Not only is there no conflict, in fact it is a movement towards equity that fosters a growth process that is most sustainable.'

'How would you explain this to the layman?'

'Let's take an economy of only three people, A, B, and C. Suppose A has a monthly income of Rs 8000, while B and C have monthly incomes of Rs 4000 each, then, crudely speaking, the gross domestic product (GDP) of that economy would be 8000+4000+4000=Rs 16000. Now assume a growth process where A's income increases substantially from Rs 8000 to Rs 28000, while the incomes of B and C drop to Rs 2000 each. The GDP would be 28000+2000+2000= Rs 32000, which is just double the GDP of the previous situation, but socially it would be very unequal. Even if the income of B and C becomes zero, you still have the GDP growing but the situation becomes even more socially unacceptable. A becomes very powerful and he monopolises. This kind of growth is now a matter of concern even in Western economies.

'In my thesis I showed that if we move the other way, where you redistribute land a bit—better still if you can do it radically—and put a ceiling on land-holding, we can achieve a growth that is socially sustainable. If anyone holds land beyond a limit, the government will distribute the excess land among the landless and poor farmers and help them with irrigation, seeds and fertilisers. This will ease the monopolistic control of the big farmers. There will be more competition in the system. People will have little more income. This is what I proved in my thesis—and this is what we did in West Bengal.

'You know, very big farmers sometimes leave the land fallow for a very interesting reason. Because he is also very often a moneylender, he does not want the poor to become prosperous because then he would suffer on the money-lending side. But small farmers, with their own family labour, will go in for second crop and sometimes even a third crop.

'The model worked. In 1977, when the Left Front came to power, West Bengal was a rice-deficit state, but today it is the largest producer of rice in the country. West Bengal, not to everyone's knowledge, is also the highest producer of vegetables. The overall effect was that there was a sharp decline in the number of people living below poverty line, from 61 to 21 per cent. If you could travel to the districts you would appreciate it.

'I have been told that—I have not checked it myself—the thesis of mine is now one of the most intensively-read theses in the MIT library.'

'When did you join politics?'

'When I came back in 1975, I had offers from several American organisations but I declined. I said I will go back and start teaching at the Calcutta University and try to apply what I had learned in MIT. In 1977, the Left Front came to power in West Bengal. I became a member of the CPM around that time.'

'When exactly did you join the party?'

'That is confidential information, but around that time.'

'You came back in 1975, so sometime between 1975 and 1977?'

'Sometime between 1977 and 1980. In our party before you become a member you have to be an auxiliary member. You are tested by the party, then you become a full-time member.

'My first interaction with the Left Front government was in 1977. Dr Ashok Mitra was our finance minister. He had taught us briefly at the Calcutta University, so in that sense he was my ex-teacher also. He invited me to write what is known as the economic review. Major states always publish it. It is like the economic survey of the government of India, with a good statistical appendix.

'So I wrote the economic review for 1977–78. I wrote it myself, A to Z, in a very short period of time, eight weeks I think. For some reason the review got an acclaim I was not bargaining for, and then the request came that I should keep writing it, which I did for five years or so. To my surprise I was made a member of several committees and also the State Planning Board. I was touring all the districts of West Bengal. Apart from Calcutta there are eighteen districts, the number was a little less back then.'

'Were you still teaching full-time at the university?'

'Yes, I would teach throughout the week and on weekends go out to the districts. That's where I really got to know real economics. Later I introduced a course on development management at the university and made dissertation a compulsory part of the degree—dissertation based on real-life experience in rural and urban areas.

'In the winter of 1986, I was asked by the party, particularly comrade Jyoti Basu, to stand in the election from a constituency called Khardah, about 30 km from Calcutta, in North 24 Parganas. During this time I was also made a member of the state committee of CPM.

'The election results were in our favour. Comrade Jyoti Basu told me, "You are going to be a member in the cabinet. You may have to hold the portfolios of finance, planning and also excise. The swearing-in ceremony will be held in a week's time, so be mentally prepared." He also told me that I had to present my budget as soon as possible. So you see, even minutes before I did not know that I had to hold this responsibility. I was able to present a full budget in one month's time, because as a member of the Planning Board I knew about the functioning of the government both at the state and the district levels—I was lucky to have that exposure and experience.'

'How did your family react to your joining politics? Did they resist?'

'I think my wife may be able to answer this question better because I lost my mother some years ago. But when I was given charge of the ministerial portfolio, I made one request to my party; to let me keep on teaching. I said I will take half day off and keep on teaching one general class and one special class at the Calcutta University. The request was granted by the party and also formally by the government. That was one thing that was bothering me, that if I was cut off from teaching, I could not have endured that.

'But my mother was only glad that I was participating in politics. I also had full support from my wife. She is an ex-student of mine and she had joined the Reserve Bank of India (RBI) after completing her Masters, I think, in 1970. She was doing her daily chores, working in RBI and bringing up our two daughters, all at the same time.

'In Bengal, in those days, people who joined politics were slightly different from what you saw in other states. We joined by sacrificing something, either career or something else.

'You might have noted that I maintain a modest lifestyle. This house was built with the help of a housing loan my wife got from the RBI. She will be able to tell you better.' He calls out to his wife, Syamali.

'He has a few questions where your presence is relevant,' he tells her. 'One is that when I joined politics, was there any resistance from home?'

Mrs Dasgupta tells me, 'I always gave preference to what he wanted to do. But I also wanted that he should continue teaching because you have no idea how much he likes to teach, how much he loves his students.'

I ask her, 'What was his first salary as a minister?'

Mr Dasgupta replies, 'With the permission of comrade Jyoti Basu, I had fixed the salary of ministers at Rs 2,500 per month. That was my first salary.'

'No, it was Rs 1,800 at first,' Mrs Dasgupta corrects him, 'later you were bringing home Rs 2,250. Your last drawn salary was Rs 7,500, with Rs 50 deducted as professional tax.'

Mr Dasgupta says, 'All the ministers earned the same amount, except the chief minister, who always got Rs 250 more. Had I stayed on in the profession (of teaching) I would have earned Rs 40,000 a month.'

Mrs Dasgupta says, 'We did have some financial difficulties after we built this house, because the bank had started making deductions to recover the loan.'

'How much money did you need to build this house?' I ask her.

'It cost us two lakh and eighteen thousand rupees.'

'We repaid the loan over many years,' says Mr Dasgupta, 'but our needs are little, so we could manage.'

'That's right,' Mrs Dasgupta says, 'he has no addictions, no wants, he is fine with whatever he has.'

'What did the children have to say?' I ask them.

Mrs Dasgupta says, 'They were very young when he became a minister. They didn't realise it. They went to a Bengali-medium government school, where the monthly fee was Rs 12 a month, so we hardly had to spend anything on their education.'

Mr Dasgupta says, 'We had told them not to tell anyone that their father is a minister. My wife shops for groceries herself, and for many years the people at the market did not know she is my wife. Later when they came to know, they would tell her, "You must be having a lot of money."'

Mrs Dasgupta says, 'The other day I was bargaining for something at the market and the shopkeeper said, "Why do you need to bargain? Your husband has so much money!"'

I ask Mr Dasgupta, 'You mentioned a twin brother, Atis. Where is he?'

He replies, 'I studied economics, he studied history. He retired as the dean of social sciences at the Indian Statistical Institute, and then became the director of the State Archives. He quit last year when the new government came. These days he writes poetry.'

Mrs Dasgupta excuses herself, she needs to go out. As she gets up, Mr Dasgupta tells her to leave behind some money for him because he too needs to go out in some time.

I ask Mr Dasgupta: 'Isn't a simple lifestyle common to all Left ministers?'

'When we joined the party, most of the comrades led very simple lives, even now they do. There have been, I must say, some deviations and the party has started taking corrective steps. But compared to any other party we like to think that our deviations may be the least. But wherever there have been deviations, people of West Bengal did not like it.'

'Can you give me an example?'

'I will refrain from mentioning any names, but the percentage of deviations would not be significant.'

'The deviations were in terms of lifestyle?'

'Yes, but more important than that is how you relate to people. People expect certain standards from Left politicians. You have to remain modest even if people criticise you. A state government has limited powers, not all demands of the public can be fulfilled quickly. You have to make the common man understand that. He will make the same demand ten times, he will criticise you, but you have to listen to him patiently and explain that you are trying your best to do what he wants you to do.

'Now you may like to ask why we lost the elections. You see, West Bengal is a state where the land-man ratio is the most adverse. It has the highest population density as per the 2011 census. Therefore, if you reverse the ratio, land availability per population becomes the lowest here, even lower than Kerala. Setting up a small industry is not a problem, because you hardly need any space. Setting up even a medium-scale industry is not a problem. In fact, out of the 2,541 new industries that were set up after 1991, when the Left Front government announced a new industrial policy, 72 per cent were medium-scale industries. The remaining 28 per cent were all large-scale industries, for which we needed land. But we never had any problem negotiating with farmers except for two cases.

'One was Nandigram (the site for the petrochemical hub), the other was Singur (the site for Tata Motors' car factory). Our own self-analysis is that we should have been much more patient in negotiating with the farmers. That lack of patience was not correct. It was through that loophole that all the other forces got combined. Along with that the deviations, the behaviour of a section of our party representatives, primarily at the medium and lower levels ... People of West Bengal do not accept arrogance. In my view arrogance by itself is against democracy and any Left movement has to be democratic. You have to be democratic first, then Left.'

'Was that all, or was there a general fatigue since you had been ruling for thirty-four years?'

'There has not been a single instance in our country where an elected state government has been in power for this long. There has not been any elected government anywhere in the world to last this long. The new generations that have come in have not seen the previous (Congress) regime. In rural areas, where there was oppression by the zamindars, people still remember but not always. So even if you are not alienated by the incumbent government, sometimes you think, "All right, let us have change." It was a change for the sake of change. The slogan of our opponent was change—*paribartan*. But I am told that people are now wondering what kind of a change was that, and apparently there is a wind of change against that change.'

'But it is often said the Left Front government was responsible for the decline of Calcutta—how one industry after another moved out of Bengal because of trade unionism.'

'Let me give you a complete picture. Bengal, for all its contribution to the freedom movement, ended up getting partitioned and more than one crore refugees came to this side of the border. The population of West Bengal is now nine crores, but if you go back to 1947 it was half the number.

'Secondly, West Bengal was a premier industrial state of India until it received a huge blow in 1958, long before the Left Front came to power in the state, when the Central government announced the freight equalisation policy.'

(The quixotic policy, which remained in force until

1993, was intended to facilitate equal growth of heavy industry across the country, but it only ended up severely hurting the interests of mineral-rich states including West Bengal, Bihar and Orissa. As per the policy, an industrialist could set up, for example, a steel factory anywhere in India and not necessarily near the source of iron ore deposits—the extra cost of transporting the mineral from the mines to his factory was going to be borne by the Central government. It made the location of mines virtually mobile).

'Once the policy was announced,' says Dasgupta, 'West Bengal lost the locational advantage it enjoyed because of its physical proximity to mineral deposits. But at the same time (since the policy pertained to minerals), the cotton-growing states in western India retained their locational advantage and continued to prosper. Not that I have a problem with that, but the freight equalisation policy seemed to be selective.

'If you were to draw a curve of the industrial index in West Bengal—I did that in my economic review—you would find the curve falling significantly after the introduction of the policy and hitting its nadir in 1970–71, when Congress was still in power in the state. Then it started picking up in the mid-1980s and picked up even further once the policy was abolished.'

'But hasn't trade unionism been detrimental to the image of Calcutta? It is said to have led to the closure of a number of industries.'

'A study was conducted by the Labour Commissioner when the Congress was in power in the state, because those were the days of strikes and *gheraos*, and it was found that the closure of factories had nothing to do with the labour agitation. The factories closed down or moved out purely because of financial reasons. Comrade Jyoti

Basu would tell trade union leaders, "You have to think of the industry, survival and growth, and along with that you have to think of your interests also." He would never encourage any trade union activities which disregarded industrial growth.'

'The general perception is that Bengalis are not hardworking, they only love to talk, but at the same time they don't like it when someone from outside, say Marwaris, come to their city and work hard and prosper.'

'I will not mention any particular community, but the original businessmen in Calcutta were the Basaks and Sils—they were Bengalis. They were so powerful that the East India Company used to borrow money from them, but the British did not want the locals to assert themselves so much, that is why they encouraged the other groups to come in. In the districts, Bengali businessmen are just as agile.

'There was a professional study carried out by the Bengal Chamber of Commerce—because this has been the general view that Bengalis do not work, etc.—and they found out that productivity wise, the average output of Bengali workers was higher than the national average.

'A Bengali worker is very laborious. He will always deliver the goods. If you take him into confidence, he will even go out of his way to do your work. But if you try to bring in feudal norms, he will not.'

4

THERE IS A famous song, sung by the singer-composer-filmmaker Anjan Dutt, so famous that he used its catch line as the title of one of his films:

Paaraye dhukle thyang khnora kore debo
bolechhe paarar dada ra
onno paara diye jachchhi tai
Ranjana aami aar aasbona
Ranjana aami aar aasbona ...

In these lines—I am translating it loosely—a boy is telling the girl he is in love with: 'The toughies in your locality have threatened to break my legs if I step in there again, so I am taking another road. I will never step into your neighbourhood again, Ranjana. Never again, Ranjana.'

The song underscores the power that the neighbourhood toughie, or *paarar dada*, wields in Calcutta. *Paara* means neighbourhood, and *dada*, even though it literally means 'elder brother', stands for a ruffian or toughie in this context. Every neighbourhood has a dozen or two *dadas*: they would have all grown up in the locality and know the lanes like the back of their hand. Every evening, they congregate at a designated spot for *adda* and other forms of recreation.

A typical *paarar dada* is usually the combination of a good samaritan, moral policeman, social worker, arbitrator, extortionist, goon and a politician. If you are nice to him, he is the most useful man to have around—he will go out of his way to help you in times of need; but if you choose to ignore him or rub him the wrong way, he will be a perennial thorn in the flesh.

One sultry evening I find myself in the company of a *dada* who belongs to the Amherst Street *paara* and who enjoys the patronage of Mamata Banerjee's Trinamool Congress. He is thirty-eight years old, scrawny and unkempt, with a face that seems incapable of a smile. We meet at a tea stall, a stone's throw from the houses of Raja Ram Mohun Roy and Ishwar Chandra Vidyasagar.

The meeting has been facilitated by a book-binder living in the area, who takes care of the *dada*'s financial needs from time to time not only because he comes in handy during difficult situations but also because the *dada* ensures the safety of his three grown-up daughters. That's one thing about the *dada*s: they are fiercely protective of the young women in their area and can go to any length to save them from harm.

'I never had a woman in my family,' Tapan Barik, the *dada*, tells me, 'I was very young when my mother died, too young to even have any memories of her. I was brought up by my father, who was employed in a shop.

'Had my mother been alive or if I had an elder sister, I may not have joined this line. But I grew up without the love and care of a woman. I had no one to put sense into my head or stop me from falling into bad company.

'My father would only get angry and beat me up whenever he found me in the company of boys who he considered good for nothing. At times, as punishment, he would not give me food. The good-for-nothing boys would then feed me, and soon I became one of them.

'Today there are about twenty *dada*s like me in this neighbourhood. We all report to a bigger *dada*, who is far senior to us in age and experience—nothing ever happens in this area without his knowledge or permission. He in turn reports to a well-known Trinamool Congress politician. I am sorry I cannot name either of them.'

'Did you not go to school?'

'I did, but I only studied up to the ninth standard. It wasn't as if my father could not afford to educate me—we were not exactly poor—it was just that I had no interest in studies.

'After dropping out of school I started hanging around with those boys. I would play street football with them. I would also run errands for the *dada*s of that time, and earn some pocket money from them.

'When I was eighteen or nineteen, I became a worker of the Congress party. One of the *dada*s—the one who is our boss today—was a Congress politician at the time. He would assign me to gather people for public meetings, stick posters and paint slogans on the walls. This brought me a small but steady income. I no longer had to depend on my father.

'But let me tell you one thing: I would have become a Congress worker even if our *dada* had not belonged to that party. Like any other patriotic Indian, I too grew up in awe of the *tirangaa*'—the Indian tricolour—'and only the Congress party had the three colours in its flag. I felt it was my duty to serve the party.

'Later, when Mamata*di* broke away from the Congress to form the Trinamool Congress, she retained the tricolour in her party flag and I was only too glad to follow our *dada* into her party.

'By forming a new party, she gave a new lease of life to the Congress in Bengal. Until then, there was no discipline in the Congress: every politician considered himself to be the leader of the party. But now the leadership is centralised, more like the CPM.

'By this time I had graduated from sticking posters to settling quarrels in the neighbourhood. If a tenant complained to us that he was being harassed by his landlord, a group of boys would go to the landlord's house and ask him to behave. If he listened to us, well and good, or else we would keep going back to him, at times drunk in the nights, and create a scene outside his house.

'Most decent people comply once you start creating a scene outside their house, though occasionally you need to beat people up or threaten them with weapons.

'Similarly, if a landlord complained to us that his tenant was refusing to vacate, we would make life difficult for the tenant. We *dada*s are always on the side of the party that is genuinely aggrieved. And we know who is genuinely aggrieved and who is not, because we know this neighbourhood inside out.

'It is our job to keep an eye on the neighbourhood. We know exactly what goes on in each house, because our boys are everywhere. Nothing remains hidden from us. If a property is being sold, we immediately get to know about it and we take a 2 per cent cut from the buyer as well as the seller.

'These days, many people are selling their houses to promoters to build flats, because they find it difficult to maintain old houses. In such cases, we take a 2 per cent commission from the seller, but we don't take any commission from the promoter because we make money by supplying him construction material. Any promoter coming to our *paara* will have to buy construction material through us—he cannot purchase them directly.

'Another source of our income is the donations we collect during Kali Puja. We collect money from every single household, every shop, every business; we make them pay according to their capacities. Some of the money is spent in celebrating Kali Puja, the remaining we keep.'

'How do you divide the money you make?'

'For every deal or collection, our *dada* keeps 40 per cent and distributes the remaining 60 per cent among us.'

'What about your *dada*'s *dada*, the senior Trinamul Congress leader, does he not make anything?'

'He doesn't bother with each and every deal.'

'What is the biggest amount you have made so far—personally?'

Tapan thinks for a few moments and says, 'Rs 30,000. I made that money through honest means (he uses the word *sat path*, the path of truth).'

'How?'

'A man wanted to sell his house, and he had asked me to find a buyer. I found him a buyer and charged a 2 per cent brokerage fee from the buyer as well as the seller.'

'And tell me about an incident that you will never forget.'

'This happened during the elections in 1998 I think. I had hurled a bomb near a polling booth in Amherst Street.'

'You threw a bomb? Were people killed?'

'We hurl bombs not to kill people, but only to scare them. So I threw a bomb that afternoon, unfortunately the policemen on duty saw me before I could escape and they chased me. I kept running till I reached College Street, where I climbed up the roof of a hostel, and from the roof jumped on to the lane behind. I landed on my chest, hitting the edge of the footpath. Clutching my chest, I ran again till I escaped the police. I had to remain in hiding for two months. I had to take painkillers for a long time before the pain in my rib cage subsided. I can never forget that afternoon.'

'How often did you hurl bombs?'

'Whenever I was ordered to. I have hurled bombs, burned buses, beaten people up—you need to do all kinds of things in this line of work.'

'Have you ever killed anyone?'

'Such a situation never arose. Most people get frightened when they see a gun in your hand.'

'Have you ever used a gun?'

'No, but I have carried it, to threaten people.'

'Have you ever been to jail?'

'I have been caught by the police many times, but I never had to go to jail because as soon as I would be taken to the police station, our *dada*'s *dada* would call the police officer on duty and ask him to let me go.'

'Do you ever regret being in this line?'

'Of course, who likes to be in this line, but as I said, I had no one to guide me. Now I am thirty-eight, I am not educated. Who will give me a job? Who will marry me?'

'What is the future you see for yourself?'

'It is all very uncertain. The rate at which flats are coming up in place of the old houses, the whole face of the neighbourhood will change in a few years' time. People living in flats don't care for *dada*s like us; they live as a self-sufficient community.

'And these new boys'—he means the younger crop of *dada*s—'are no good. *Aamra bomb o chhurechhi, football o khelechhi* (we have thrown bombs, and at the same time played football). But these boys neither have the courage to throw bombs nor the stamina to play football. They are only interested in two things, *mobile aar meye* (buying mobile phones and getting girlfriends).'

'Did you ever have a girlfriend?'

'Yes, I was twenty-two or twenty-three then. There was this girl who lived in the adjoining *paara*. She loved me too. We saw each other for two years.'

'Then what happened?'

'Then she got married and went away.'

'Her parents married her off?'

'No, no, she married on her own. She had an affair with me but married someone else. She was not a nice girl.'

'Have you heard the song, *Ranjana aami aar aasbona* . . .'

'Who hasn't? It is a famous Anjan Dutt song.'

'The song, I am sure you must know, is about a boy giving up on the girl he fancies because the *dada*s of her *paara* have threatened to break his legs if they spot him near her house again. So no one threatened to break your legs when you went to see this girl in another *paara*?'

'No, *dada*s make such threats only if a boy pesters a girl against her wishes. But this girl liked me; she loved me for two years.' Tapan Barik, the *dada*, suddenly looks skyward. I realise he is trying to contain his tears.

5

IT'S DIFFICULT TO tell whether the notice at Mother Teresa's home speaks poorly of Calcutta or highly of the Missionaries of Charity, the religious order she set up in 1950 that continues her work:

PLEASE BEWARE!

WE HAVE HAD REPORTS OF THEFTS OF SHOES, MONEY AND CAMERAS IN THIS AREA.

KEEP YOUR PERSONAL BELONGINGS WITH YOU AT ALL TIMES.

YOU DO NOT NEED TO REMOVE YOUR SHOES TO ENTER MOTHER'S TOMB. ALTHOUGH THE TOMB IS A SACRED PLACE, WE ARE CONCERNED ABOUT THE LOSS OF SHOES AND THE DISTRESS CAUSED. THEREFORE WE URGE YOU TO KEEP YOUR SHOES WITH YOU.

THE MISSIONARIES OF CHARITY ARE NOT RESPONSIBLE FOR THE LOSS OR DAMAGE OF ANY POSSESSIONS.

GOD BLESS YOU.

I arrive at Mother House—where Mother Teresa lived most of her life and died—shortly after noon, unaware that it shuts for visitors between twelve and three. I ring a metal bell. The sister who opens the door refuses to let me in and asks me to come back at three.

I can come back at three, or come back another day, but having come all the way and missed the closing time by only a few minutes, I am not inclined to leave without pushing my luck. I plead with the sister, but she is firm. From her accent I can tell she is from Kerala, and I make one last-ditch attempt: 'I've come all the way from Madras.' It works.

She says she can allow me into Mother Teresa's tomb and the museum, but she cannot let me see Mother Teresa's room during non-visiting hours. 'And no pictures, please,' she tells me.

The tomb is in a hall large enough to be the drawing room of an upper middle-class Bengali home, its windows opening to the busy AJC Bose Road. The windows are open, their lower halves curtained, exposing the hall to the fury of Calcutta traffic. But the calm inside seems to be absorbing the sound outside.

Mother House is not conspicuous by its presence in a city that boasts of charming, although crumbling, buildings. Watching the traffic from the window, I wonder how many passersby must be aware that here lived Mother Teresa, whose fame in the West made Calcutta a byword for poverty.

No one, of course, likes to think of her as someone whose popularity only sullied Calcutta's image. On the contrary, anyone suggesting that she picked up the dying from the streets only to save her own soul is frowned upon.

But Mother Teresa has had her share of critics too. Like fame, criticism too came mostly from across the seas. If there was a Malcolm Muggeridge, whose 1969 documentary about her work, *Something Beautiful for God*, propelled her to global celebrity, there has also been a Christopher Hitchens, whose book *The Missionary Position* mercilessly questioned her motives behind helping the poorest of the poor. According to Hitchens, she was not interested in providing medical treatment to the poor—which she could easily afford, given the enormous funds at her disposal—but in promoting a cult based on death and suffering.

Criticism and praise—and now her pending sainthood—notwithstanding, one question remains unexamined: How much did Mother Teresa, feted by the world for picking the dying from the streets of Calcutta, matter to Calcutta? One thing is certain, though. In Calcutta, even five Mother Teresas together cannot surpass the admiration its people reserve for the poet who wasn't a saint but certainly looked like one: Rabindranath Tagore.

There can, however, be little doubt that her work—and the celebrity it earned her—inspired generations of world citizens, Indians included, to lend a helping hand to the poor. Doing-something-for-the-poor became fashionable, especially after Indian beauties, while competing in international pageants, began naming Mother Teresa as their role model.

Mother House is the headquarters of the Missionaries of Charity. Mother Teresa lived here from 1953 until she died on 5 September 1997, just five days after Princess Diana, her most famous admirer, was killed in a car crash. Fresh marigold flowers have been arranged on her grave to say: A CLEAN HEART CAN SEE GOD.

The museum next-room gives an account of her final hours:

'On her last day, Mother Teresa received visitors, met with her sisters and signed letters. To her spiritual children, she wrote a last message: "Be only all for Jesus through Mary." She expressed a great urgency to finish her work. In pain from the day before, she was overheard asking, "What is Jesus asking of me?"

'In the evening, Mother Teresa's back and chest pain intensified. At around 8 pm, she began to struggle: "I can't breathe." As she gasped, she looked at the crown of thorns and touched the crucifix on the wall. The sisters rushed to her side. Her doctor was called. A power failure made it impossible to give her oxygen.

'The Parish priest anointed her. With her lips she followed the prayers of the sisters around her, while in the chapel the novices prayed. In the end, Mother Teresa opened her eyes wide, closed them and sighed.

'The death certificate noted her "going home" at 9.30 pm.'

From September 7 to 13, her body rested in St Thomas' Church, next to Loreto House off Park Street, so that mourners could pay their last respects. She was buried in Mother House and given a state funeral. *The New York Times* reported on September 14:

> Mother Teresa was buried yesterday in Calcutta, India, after a funeral largely closed to the poor she had devoted her life to helping.
>
> In six hours of ceremonies that began with a military escort from a quiet convent church and ended with a Gurkha rifle salute over her tomb, the nun was honoured with both pomp and sorrow by her city, her adopted country and the world.
>
> The crowds that assembled to see her cortege pass were far smaller than expected and far more decorous than usual in India. Largely for security reasons, the military insisted on barring many of the poor.

The exhibits in the museum include the torch that was used in her room during the power cut on her final night, syringes and needles that had been used for her blood tests, a tube that had been inserted down her throat to her lungs when she was very sick, her rosaries, blanket, sweater, metal buckets, wheelchair, toothbrush, toothpaste (Pentodont and Colgate Gel) and a bunch of business cards she had received from visitors (the card on top of the bunch belonged to 'Dr N Janardhan Rao, Secunderabad').

Seeing the exhibits I feel a little sad. Mother Teresa died when she was eighty-seven. Of those eighty-seven years, she had spent sixty-five in Calcutta; and of the sixty-five, nearly fifty were spent picking up the dying from its streets.

Even if she had ulterior religious motives behind her work—such as saving her own soul or aiming to become a saint—so what? She at least rescued emaciated and disfigured humans from the humiliation of dying on the street and made sure that they had a roof over their heads in their last days. Maybe her brief did not entail nursing a destitute back to health but ensuring that he did not get devoured by dogs and vultures once he died.

On my way out, I profusely thank the sister who had let me in and ask for directions to Nirmal Hriday, the home for the dying destitute, where it all began. She tells me that I should have no problem finding the place: it is right next to the Kalighat temple. I walk out and hail a taxi.

Nirmal Hriday is indeed next to the temple, right on Kalighat Road that connects the home of Kali with the home of Mamata Banerjee—the road that is lined by prostitutes throughout the day. I have walked on this road before on more than one occasion, but never realised that Nirmal Hriday, which had earned Mother Teresa the Nobel Prize, is located right here. Nobody had ever told me, nor had I ever asked.

When you are a visitor to Calcutta, the last thing you would ask for is directions to the home of the dying destitute, unless you have been assigned to write about it or are a volunteer seeking to cleanse your soul. As someone writing about Calcutta, I should have known where all Mother Teresa's centres are located. But then, I have always associated her with the poor, and never with Calcutta, even though the city has more than its share of poor.

When I think of Calcutta, it is not Mother Teresa's image that first springs to my mind—it's either Park Street (incidentally renamed Mother Teresa Sarani, but to little effect), or the Howrah Bridge, or the tram. Though for many Westerners, who come all the way to volunteer for the Missionaries of Charity, Calcutta—and often India—begins and ends with Nirmal Hriday. They carry back horrific tales, as if the entire city is Nirmal Hriday multiplied by a thousand. Whereas to the lay Indian visitor, long used to the sight of poverty, Nirmal Hriday—the clean heart—may not even register its presence.

Nirmal Hriday turns out to be a former dharamshala that was built in 1929 in memory of the well-known Marwari businessman Ramchander Goenka by his three sons. He was the great-grandfather of Ram Prasad Goenka, or RPG, the 'takeover king' of Calcutta: remember HMV cassettes becoming RPG cassettes one fine morning? In 1952, the dharamshala was handed over by the Corporation of Calcutta to the newly-established Missionaries of Charity.

Here too, visitors are not allowed between twelve and three, and since it is only two o' clock, a watchman is guarding the entrance. He is having a difficult time preventing two small groups of persistent women from entering.

One group of women has come to adopt a child, and the guard tells them that they need to go to Shishu Bhawan, the orphanage run by the Missionaries of Charity on AJC Road, a stone's throw from Mother House. They had come expecting to see newborn babies, and now when the watchman is sending them away, they are reluctant to leave.

The other group of women happens to be related to an elderly man who went missing the night before from his home in a nearby slum, and they have heard that he was brought to Nirmal Hriday. The women want to go in to see if he is really there, but the watchman is not letting them in. 'Come back after three, I cannot allow you in now,' he tells them rudely.

I tell the watchman I am a journalist, and he lets me in very reluctantly, after I promise him that I will watch the functioning of the home from a distance and not be a hindrance to people going about their jobs.

As I step in, I mentally prepare myself to be swallowed into a world of gloom, where the poorest of poor could be seen surrendering to death, without a fight but with dignity. I have seen the ill, I have seen the dead, but I have never seen the dying.

Once inside, however, I find myself suppressing a grin. The inmates are sprawled on beds that have blue sheets and blue pillow covers. So distracting is the blue that you nearly miss the emaciated men. And they are all clearly amused that a white man is at their beck and call.

Calcutta remains a British city at heart and retains great respect for the sahib—pronounced *shaheb* in Bengali—which literally means master. Since the British had been the masters of Calcutta for nearly two-and-a-half centuries, *shaheb* became a generic word for British men and—by extension—all white men. The inmates, who must have grown up listening to stories about India being ruled by *shaheb*s, are now being attended to by one.

The white man in question, a sprightly muscular volunteer, is promptly responding to their needs. Someone needs water, someone needs food, someone needs to be placed in a more comfortable position—the volunteer is responding to their calls as quickly as possible. He is conversing with them in sign language, most of the time giving them the thumbs up.

The inmates are of varying ages and build, and display varying degrees of physical suffering. What unifies them is their shabbiness. They are all evidently poor and have been picked up from the streets. But none of them appears to be in a tearing hurry to meet his or her maker. They all look eager to get away from the prison of care to the freedom of the streets.

Only one inmate, an old man, who doesn't seem impressed by the foreigner's service, seeks to reach out to me by repeatedly making a sound with his throat. As if he has something to tell me. I cannot go over to him because I am a trespasser until the clock strikes three. Could he, by any chance, be the same man who had disappeared from his home the night before and whom the group of women has been trying to trace?

I spot an aged desk in a corner, and cannot resist walking over to it. On it is a sheet of yellowed paper, encased in glass. It contains handwritten data. In 1952, the year Nirmal Hriday opened—it had opened in August—as many as 446 destitute were admitted, of which 226 died and 165 were discharged. In 1953, the number of admissions was 1,180, of which 645 died and 420 were discharged. On this sheet, entries have been made, in Mother Teresa's handwriting, up to the year 1961, when 1,249 were admitted, of which 552 died and 632 were discharged.

I ask a nurse passing by whether figures are available for the period after 1961. At first she does not understand my question, and when she finally does—at least it looks like she has understood—she shrugs and tells me that she has no idea.

'Is there someone who keeps a record of admissions?'

'No idea.'

'Whom can I find out from, whether a record is still being maintained?'

'No idea.'

After I let her go, much to her relief, I return to the yellowed paper. I like looking at old documents, the ones handwritten with fountain pens. It suddenly strikes me that the number of deaths and the number of discharges, for nearly every given year, do not add up to the number of admissions. Each year, a few dozen inmates have remained unaccounted for. So what happened to them—did they go absconding from Nirmal Hriday, or were they traced and taken away by their families? I don't see anyone to put this question to—certainly not anyone who can answer it with some authority.

On my way out, I ask the watchman—who is now affable because I haven't done anything to put his job at risk—about the functioning of Nirmal Hriday.

'If our workers find someone sick or dying abandoned on the road,' he says, 'they bring that person here. If a person dies, we arrange for cremation depending on their religion. It is not difficult to determine a person's religion.

'But if a person recovers, we drop him at the very spot he had been picked up from. It is not our job to find out where he lives and drop him home. And if an inmate happens to be visited by his family, we discharge him right away because we care only for abandoned people, and not for people who have families,' the watchman tells me matter-of-factly.

'How many dying people are brought here each day?' I ask him.

'That is difficult to say, but our capacity is about 120

beds. We have twenty-five full-time workers and eight nurses, including a foreigner nurse. Besides, there are foreigners who come as volunteers every day. We also have a doctor who comes twice a week.'

'The doctor comes only twice a week?'

'Yes, only twice a week.'

As I shake the watchman's hand and step onto Kalighat Road, I find myself wondering: 'Is this it?'

I came to Nirmal Hriday expecting to be struck by suffering and compassion as enormous as Mother Teresa's reputation. But what I just visited was only a dharamshala, where pilgrims often happen to spend their final nights on earth.

6

IT IS JULY when I come back again to Calcutta, and walking down from College Street to Sealdah, make a startling discovery.

Fish is as integral to a Bengali meal as Tagore is to Bengal, but what I didn't know was that most of the fish that Calcuttans eat, especially the popular *rui* and *katla*, comes not from Bengal but from distant Andhra Pradesh.

'A Bengali kitchen cannot function without the trucks coming from Andhra Pradesh,' says Topu, a talkative fish-dealer at the whole-sale fish market in Baithakkhana, one of the oldest fish markets in the city. 'Andhra Pradesh sends us sixteen items in all. Fish, eggs, cabbage, cauliflower, tomato, capsicum, beans, raw jackfruit, tamarind, raw mango, drumsticks, even rice. Do they add up to sixteen?'

'Not yet.'

'I am not able to recall the remaining items, but I know for a fact that Andhra Pradesh sends us sixteen food items in all.'

'Tell me about the fish. How much fish do you receive from there every day?'

'At least five trucks come to our market every morning. Each truck carries 125 crates, and each crate holds 40 or 45 kg of fish. Now calculate.'

'That adds up to about 28,000 kg.'

'Absolutely correct. Now this is the figure for our market alone. In all, seventy to eighty trucks carrying fish come to the city every morning. Now calculate, and you will get an idea how much fish comes from Andhra Pradesh.'

'That adds up to four-and-a-half lakh kg daily.'

'Absolutely correct. We also get fish from Bangladesh, Digha, Diamond Harbour and Orissa, but the quantity is not as significant.'

'I find this difficult to believe,' I share my surprise with him. 'I always thought Calcutta got its fish from the river and the ponds.'

'Let's not get into that subject,' Topu tells me, 'then our conversation will become political.'

'Why do you say so?'

'West Bengal was the biggest fish-producer once upon a time. But Jyoti Basu filled up Salt Lake and built a township on it.'

'Jyoti Basu? I thought Salt Lake was Dr B.C. Roy's creation?'

'What difference does it make? All politicians are the same. Now look at Mamata Banerjee, is she any different?'

Another fish-dealer, who has been listening to our

conversation, interrupts Topu, 'She wants to turn Calcutta into another London. I say it would be easier to turn London into another Calcutta.'

7

FIVE-THIRTY IN THE morning. The sky is overcast. The roads are wet. On the pavements a chunk of Calcutta's population is stirring awake—a new day, new challenges staring them in the face. The labourers—robots of flesh and blood—are already on their feet, transporting load in two-wheeled carts. Their feet move fast, as if someone's life depends on their pace, but their eyes are long dead.

I sight many more human robots and human trucks on the Howrah Bridge, on my way to the Howrah Station. Unknown to them, they have been the stars in films that portray Calcutta as a pitiable, chaotic city. This morning, my wife and I are escaping that Calcutta, even if for a couple of days, by boarding the Ganadevta Express to Shantiniketan—the abode of peace, the land of Tagore.

The train leaves on the dot at 6.05 am and soon it leaves behind the trappings of a modern city to emerge into the timeless Indian landscape of lush green fields. Since Bolpur station, where we need to alight to get to Shantiniketan, is two and a half hours away, I plan to get some sleep, but a salesman in our coach begins his performance.

'Do you see this Parker roller-ball pen?' he is asking the passengers, 'This will cost you Rs 260 in the market. Why does it cost that much? That is because it is endorsed by Amitabh Bachchan. Now look at this pen'—he holds up another pen—'this is as good as a Parker, writes just as well, and I am here to sell it to you for only Rs 120. Why does it cost less? Because for this pen, I am the endorser, I am the seller. Now look at this Swiss knife set. In the market you won't get it for less than Rs 3000. But I am here to sell it to you for Rs 250. Yes, Rs 250 only. And this lock you see, it sounds an alarm as soon as ...'

The salesman is a mobile shop. His arms and shoulders are laden with knick-knacks that he is out to sell: from pens to card-holders, Swiss knife sets to manicure sets, umbrellas to locks. As far as physical appearances go, he cuts an utterly unimpressive figure: he must be about fifty, he is bald and dark, and he is wearing clothes that could do with a wash. Yet the persuasive quality of his speech makes him comparable to a top executive making a power-point presentation to boast about the health of his company.

While he speaks, passengers look up from the pages of *Ananda Bazar Patrika* and *Bartaman* to listen to him, even though they may not have the slightest intention of purchasing his wares. But by the time he finishes his presentation, lasting nearly twenty minutes, many of them begin to show interest.

'Pen *ta ektu dekhi*'—Let me take a look at the pen.

'Lock *ta koto bolle?*'—How much did you say the lock was for?

'*Chhata ta bhalo hobey to?*'—Is your umbrella any good?

Soon the salesman is collecting money. He has been able to sell five pens, three locks (with inbuilt alarm), two umbrellas, and two Swiss knife sets—all in a span of thirty minutes. He has many more coaches of the train to cover.

As he walks across the vestibule and disappears into the next coach, I wonder: why don't companies looking for a turnaround in their fortunes ever think of hiring the services of a salesman peddling his wares in the trains of Bengal? The trains are his Harvard, and he just might do a better job than a CEO who has actually been there. Tagore, who remains India's tallest poet, hardly went to school.

An old, blind baul singer now takes the salesman's place. He is accompanied by an assistant who goes around the coach with a begging bowl. The singer plucks at his *ektara* and sings a song about some never-achievable what-ifs: what if the sky was land, what if ants were oxen, what if leaves were money ... I place a ten-rupee note in the bowl.

Shantiniketan is about thirty minutes from Bolpur station on a cycle-rickshaw. It is a hamlet that is slowly, but surely, metamorphosing into a town. Resorts have started opening for the comfort of tourists who have Shantiniketan on their to-do list while visiting Bengal. The one where we are booked is right on the main road: a not-so-old bungalow with spacious lawns, transformed into a profitable business. Since this is off season, we seem to be the only guests.

It begins to rain as soon as we check in, so we order room service. Lunch turns out to be most gratifying because it includes *postor bora*, patties made from poppy seeds, something that I have never had ever since I left home—my Kanpur home—nearly two decades ago. They could have well been prepared by my mother, only that here I have to pay for them. It is painful to pay, that too a steep price, for dishes that you take, or once took, for granted. At the same time, you are willing to shell out any amount to reclaim the taste from the days left long behind.

After lunch we lie on the bed and watch the rain pouring, exactly what Tagore would have experienced, seated on an easy chair, a little over a kilometre away from where we are, about a hundred monsoons ago. For him the sight inspired poetry, for us it induces sleep.

SILENCE IS INDEED the sound of Shantiniketan. Those who have been coming here, or living here, for many years may not agree though: they are likely to complain about the place not being what it used to be. But a first-timer like me couldn't have asked for more peace.

This peace was originally discovered not by Rabindranath Tagore, but his father, the saintly Debendra, when he happened to rest under a tree while travelling through the area. In 1862, he acquired seven acres of land around the tree to build a retreat for meditation, which he named Shantiniketan.

It was in the winter of 1901 that Rabindranath, forty years old at the time and already an author of twenty-one books, set up an open-air school here with five students, one of them being his own son Rathindranath. Rabindranath hated classrooms, and wanted his students to be one with nature while imbibing lessons in English, Sanskrit and Mathematics. The school, which he called Brahmacharya Ashram, grew over the decades into Viswa-Bharati, the university he founded with the help of the money that came with the Nobel Prize. The hamlet became famous to the world as Shantiniketan.

The two-and-a-half days we have here melt away in no time and I wish we could have stayed longer and had more *postor bora*. We have eaten well, slept well, and have managed to do whatever tourists must do during their visits to Shantiniketan—which includes spending some time on the banks of a miniature river called Kopai; pausing at a small railway station called Prantik; having lunch at Bonolokkhi, a nature-conserving farmhouse that also functions as a restaurant serving homely Bengali meals; and, of course, a tour of the Viswa-Bharati campus, which includes the various houses where Tagore worked and lived.

Tagore, I've read somewhere, got restless if he lived in one house for too long and got another one built. In Shantiniketan he lived in five different houses, not too far from each other, but each architecturally different. None of them is grand or reeks of opulence: they are all minimalistic in design and décor, just as a poet's house should be, but at the same time bear the aura of a great mind.

In between the buildings, displayed in a glass case, stood Tagore's car—a black Humber, registration number 'WBA 8689'. In 1938, when he was seventy-seven and no longer finding it easy to walk around the campus, his son Rathindranath bought him a pair of Humbers from a dealer on Park Street—one car was stationed at Shantiniketan and another at Jorasanko, the family home in north Calcutta. Rabindranath loved his car, but could use it for barely three years because he died in 1941, in Calcutta.

We moved around Shantiniketan mostly on cycle-rickshaws, still the only mode of public transport in the abode of peace. From the market outside the campus—it looked more like a village market—I bought myself an ochre-coloured *kurta*, just to feel Shantiniketan long after I had left it. I also bought, from what appeared to be the only non-academic bookshop in the university town, a copy of Jean-Paul Sartre's *Nausea*. I knew I might never get down to reading the book, but I also knew its pages would long outlive the fabric of the *kurta*. Since I usually sign my name and write the date on every new book that I buy, I would always remember that I first visited Shantiniketan in July 2012.

8

TAGORE IS CREDITED with composing the national anthem of not only India but also Bangladesh. But Bangladesh, even though it adopted Tagore's lyrics and tune as its national anthem, chose to crown Kazi Nazrul Islam as its national poet, and in doing so, handed him the dignity he long deserved. Nazrul, imported from Calcutta by the newborn nation during the fag end of his life, died like a king in Dhaka and remains buried there. Only that he may not have realised that he spent his final years as a king: for much of his life he remained stricken by a rare mental dysfunction that had also robbed him of his speech.

Nazrul, born in 1899, is Bengal's best known poet-composer after Tagore. The collection of his songs, just like Tagore's, is an institution in itself. There are scholars and singers who specialise in Nazrul *geeti*, just as many others specialise in Rabindra Sangeet. Unlike Tagore's poetry, which often celebrated nature's beauty, Nazrul's verses frequently bore the spirit of rebellion; unlike Tagore, who remained productive until he died at the age of eighty, Nazrul was hit by mental dysfunction when he had barely reached his forties and remained afflicted by the condition until he died at the age of seventy-seven; unlike

Tagore, who had material comforts at his disposal, Nazrul often grappled with penury even after he had earned fame as a poet. Tagore was affectionate towards him. When Nazrul went on a hunger strike in jail after being arrested on charges of sedition, Tagore sent him a telegram: 'Give up hunger-strike, our literature claims you.' Nazrul revered Tagore and wrote two poems in tribute when the senior poet died in August 1941. By then Nazrul's wife was already paralysed waist-down and he was neck-deep in debt. In a matter of months he lost his mind as well as his speech and had to be taken care of by his disabled wife.

Nazrul's wife, Pramila, was a Hindu. He gave his two sons Hindu names while retaining the title Kazi (the muezzin): Kazi Sabyasachi and Kazi Aniruddha. He was a fiercely secular Muslim who even wrote Hindu songs in the praise of Goddess Kali, and one wonders whether he would have accepted Bangladesh's invitation to become its national poet had he had control over his senses. The Islamic Bangladesh took him away because he was a Muslim, and now, nearly three decades after his death, he has been resurrected on the roads of Calcutta because he was a Muslim.

Chief minister Mamata Banerjee, forever anxious to keep the Muslim voter on her side, has ensured that the face of a young and handsome Nazrul, accompanied by a few lines of his poetry, features on billboards adorning a number of bus-stops across Calcutta. Those lines invariably happen to be from the poems he wrote in honour of Tagore: she clearly intends to kill two birds with one stone.

This is the same Calcutta where Nazrul, once a fiery poet and journalist, spent three decades of his life as a living corpse. In 1942, when he was struck by mental illness, Tagore had just died, and by 1972, when Bangladesh took Nazrul away, Kishore Kumar had become India's favourite singer after the success of *Aradhana*. How India had moved on during these three decades. Nazrul, however, remained confined in modest, rented homes across Calcutta, remembered from time to time by well-wishers who were eager to get him treated. In 1953 they even sent him and his family to Vienna, but doctors there pronounced his condition to be incurable and Nazrul was brought back to Calcutta. His well-wishers, even his sons, decided to move on with their own lives. That very year, Nazrul's younger son Kazi Aniruddha, who was beginning to gain popularity by playing the tunes of popular Hindi songs on the electric Hawaiian guitar, brought home a girl, all of eighteen, whom he had married some months earlier at a marriage registrar's office, unknown at least to the girl's parents.

The girl, Kalyani, is now seventy-six; the oldest surviving member of Nazrul's family in India. Another branch of the family—the family of Nazrul's elder son Sabyasachi, who became famous as an *abritti*, or recitation, artiste— lives in Bangladesh.

Sabyasachi, even though his wife and children settled in Dhaka along with Nazrul, worked mostly out of Calcutta and died here. He remains buried next to his younger brother Aniruddha at the graveyard in Gobra. Aniruddha was the first to die, in 1974, at the age of forty-three; Sabyasachi died in 1979, at the age of fifty. Their father lived the longest, dying in Dhaka in 1976, at the age of seventy-seven.

Kalyani today lives in her father's home—the home

where she grew up—in Dorjipara in north Calcutta. She earns her living by teaching Nazrul *geeti* in a few schools and also to students who come to her home to learn. She is attractive and graceful, and looks years younger than seventy-six. It is easy to imagine how beautiful she must have been when Nazrul's guitarist-son fell in love with her.

'I know Nazrul is an interesting character to write about,' she tells me the afternoon I call on her. 'Being his daughter-in-law, if I talk about him, people will assume what I say is correct. But honestly I don't know much about his childhood, I saw him only after my marriage, some sixty years ago.

'We all know that he was born in Churulia (near Burdwan) and was a bright student with a strong creative streak, but beyond that there is very little known about his childhood. I did consult some books to check the facts, *kintu sobai khichuri pakachhe* (people are cooking their own stories). They have contradictory information.'

'Would you like to recall how you became a part of the family?'

'Sure, I love to reminisce. I find it very romantic actually. You see, I am from a Hindu family. My father was an engineer with the Damodar Valley Corporation and I was the only child. I had a happy, carefree childhood with my cousins. Music was an important part of our growing-up years. We learned music at home and even had an orchestra. I played the tabla. Our next-door neighbour was Anandabala Devi. She was what you call a treasure-house of Nazrul songs. It was through her that I first learned about Nazrul's music.

'I first met Kazi Aniruddha when I was sixteen. This

must have been around 1950. We had gone for a family holiday to Ranchi and he was there with his band. They used to call themselves SABS (Sujit Nath, Aniruddha, Batuk Nandi and Shibnath Chatterjee). Only later I came to know that they were in Ranchi mainly to see *baba* (Nazrul), who was admitted in the mental asylum there at the time.

'They were staying in a hotel next to ours and we could hear them play all night. My cousin knew Batuk Nandi and through him I got to meet Aniruddha, who was a heartthrob of our times. He had recently recorded, on guitar, the tunes of two famous Hindi songs that had just been released: *Suhani raat dhal chuki* and *Ajeeb dastaan hai yeh*. I asked him for his autograph, and also asked him if he could give me the lyrics for these songs. He said he would.

'After we had boarded the train to Calcutta—we were returning in the same train—he handed me an envelope saying it contained the lyrics that I wanted. But the envelope was too thick to have only the lyrics, so I waited until everyone slept and opened it in the toilet. It was a long letter. *Train dulchhilo, aamiyo dulchhilam* (The train was swaying, so was my mind).

'Everything between us was said through letters. There was the telephone too, but there were always people around so I hardly talked to him on the phone. Also I had nothing to say really, I was yet to understand what was happening. Remember, he was a Muslim and I was a Hindu. It was through his letters that I first learned about his family and its condition.

'Around the same time, I took admission in the Oriental College. The idea was to get out of the house. We would meet sometimes, but most of the conversation continued to happen through letters. By the time I completed my graduation, my family had found out about our meetings and I was confined to home. They started looking for a suitable match for me. My father had even taken me to the anti-rowdy department of the police so that the officers could put some sense into my head, but it was too late. I was almost eighteen and we had already registered the marriage.

'I had a chance to leave with my husband when he was taking *baba* to Vienna for treatment, but considering my family's reputation, I did not. Back then it was not an everyday thing for a girl to leave home. But I had to leave suddenly when my mother-in-law got sick one day. My father was away on official work that day, so I wrote a note for my mother and quietly left the house to stay with my husband.

'They lived at 16, Rajendra Lala Street in Maniktala. The ground floor of the house was a *khatal* (cowshed). The landlord, Nagen Pehelwan, lived on the first floor and we on the second. We had four small rooms and an open space. There was no bathroom and no running water. One of *baba*'s servants, who lived close by, would get us water in buckets. *Ma* (Nazrul's wife Pramila) was paralysed and bedridden. She lived in the largest room. From her cot she could look straight into *baba*'s room and keep an eye on him.

'*Ma* was an amazing woman and very beautiful too. Lying on the bed, she would chop vegetables and even cook if the stove was brought close to the bed. I never felt for a moment that I was living among people who weren't well. *Baba* was also very handsome, it was impossible to look at him and say he was unwell. He was mostly lost in his own world, looking out of the window, smiling to himself. He would also look at the newspaper for hours, it would appear as if he was reading it, and at times he would fold the newspaper and keep it under his pillow.'

'Could he recognise anyone?'

'I am sure he did. He seemed happy to see his sons, to listen to music. He even reacted to birthday songs sung to him. He tried to talk but could only enunciate sounds. When I first met him, he kept looking at me and then at his son, as if trying to gather what was happening. '

'So he could not talk at all?'

'No, he could only make sounds. But he understood everything, just that you had to talk to him very slowly like you talk to children. I once went into his room to get his autograph—I was crazy about collecting autographs—and he did not want to sign. He resisted, even made angry noises, but after a lot of cajoling he wrote: *Kazi Nazrul Islam judiey galo* (Kazi Nazrul Islam is overwhelmed). I still have that paper with me.'

'How many members were there in the family?'

'There were five of us: *ma*, *baba*, my brother-in-law, my husband and I. After the birth of Anirban, my elder son, we felt the need for a bigger house and started to look for one. Finding a decent house was a struggle. People did not want to rent their houses to us. Some said they would not let out their house to Muslims, others said they would not let it out to a madman. Finally, my husband found out about some new houses that had come up in Paikpara, and we took a house there.

'*Baba* never had much of physical trouble; he enjoyed his walks, he was particularly fond of cars and loved going for drives. He was not happy if we had guests, although he could not talk, he would show his displeasure through gestures. I could go on telling you the stories from the time.

'Once, in the Paikpara house, my husband threw his cigarette without putting it out. The curtain and the mattress of *baba's* room caught fire. By the time we got to know, the room was full of smoke. *Ma* was screaming, and *baba* was sitting on a burning mattress, unscathed.

'*Ma* had very high tolerance for pain and hardship. Even though she was bedridden, she took care of *baba* all along. They were never separate even for a day. When she died, in 1962, *baba* kept staring at her body trying to understand what had happened. By then my brother-in-law had married and was living with his wife and children on CIT Road. One day, soon after *ma* died, my brother-in-law came over to take *baba* away. He wanted *baba* to stay with him for some time. But *baba* simply refused to go. He stood near *ma's* empty cot and made angry sounds, as if saying, "Where is she? I will not go anywhere without her." Finally my husband told him, "*Baba*, we are going to see *ma*." Only then he agreed to leave, like a sulking child. I will never forget that scene.' I see tears well up in Kalyani's eyes.

'One day, in early 1972, we got a call from the office of Sheikh sahib (Sheikh Mujibur Rahman, the first president of independent Bangladesh). He wanted to celebrate *baba's* birthday there and recognise his contribution to literature. We had no idea that *baba* would be made to stay there. But they treated him like a king.'

'Who all went with him to Dhaka?'

'Initially, all of us had gone. Shiekh sahib asked all of

us to settle in Dhaka, but we, my husband and I, excused ourselves on the pretext of our children's education. Our sons were studying in Ramakrishna Mission in Narendrapur. Moreover, in India you could live the way you pleased, but there one had to be very careful. But my brother-in-law's family chose to settle there. They were given the citizenship, a house and all possible amenities.

'My husband died all of a sudden in 1974, a couple of years after *baba* moved. He was only forty-three, and I was thirty-nine. My daughter was only seven and sons were around thirteen and sixteen. I was not prepared for it. I could not even afford to stay on in that house, and moved in here.

'My husband's life as an artiste was very tragic. He learned to play the guitar from Sujit Nath, who was the one to introduce Hawaiian guitar in India, and began to play with him. It was not easy to play tunes of Indian songs on a Hawaiian guitar, but together they accomplished that. *Baba's* rising medical expenses however, forced him to stop his classes.

'Although Sujit Nath was a friend, my husband did not want to learn without paying the fee. He would say, "Only when I pay, will he be interested in teaching and I will be willing to learn." So he learned and practised at home. I have seen it all my life: this family has always had a very strong sense of self-respect. My husband and his brother were always very careful not to use *baba's* name to promote their work.

'Until my husband was alive, I would go with him to all his shows, I would assist him, sometimes I even sang. I had also recorded a few songs just before his death. But after his passing away I suddenly had nothing to do.

'I began singing on my own shortly after *baba*'s death, when I was invited to sing at a function on his birth anniversary. There were two others singers at the function, and at the end of the programme while they were given thick envelopes, the organiser paid me only thirty rupees saying that he had to pawn his watch to get me the money. That evening I travelled in a bus for the first time and continue to do so until today. Not that I cannot afford a car—my sons have two cars each—but I have got used to this life.'

'What about your children?'

'My elder son Anirbaan was always interested in art, his teachers at Narendrapur had advised us to let him pursue fine arts. I hardly had the money to afford their academics, how could I think of arts? But he got a scholarship and got into the Art College on his own. He has always been a very hardworking boy. As a child he would tell his siblings: if you want a cycle, you will have to dream of getting a scooter, only then will you get a cycle. He is a famous artist now and has dedicated some of his works to *baba*. His wife is an engineer.

'Arindam, my younger son, was influenced by his father and began playing the guitar. It started as a hobby but he now plays professionally. He had to struggle a little in the beginning, but is doing fairly well for himself now. His wife is into business.

'Both my sons are married to Hindu girls. Both my daughters-in-law had left home to get married. One of them did not have the age proof and we were almost arrested, as her parents alleged that we had kidnapped their minor daughter. Every marriage in the family has a story attached to it. I can go on talking about them until evening.

'And your daughter?'

'Her name is Anindita. She also married a Hindu. She did a Montessori course and teaches in Naba Nalanda. She also sang with me for sometime. For the past few years now, she has also been anchoring the news on Tara channel. As far as my children are concerned, I have no worries now. When they were younger, it was quite a struggle to fulfil their needs.

'How old are your children now?'

'Anirban should be fifty-two, and Arindam about fifty. Anindita must be around forty-five. These days I often forget their birthdays. What to do, I am ageing.'

'Coming back to the days when you lived in the Nazrul household, did you come across a lot of manuscripts?'

'*Baba* hardly kept a record of his work. His music and poetry were all over the place. In fact, until the sixties, there was no such thing as Nazrul music. It was only in the late sixties that they realised his work could be compiled into what they now call Nazrul *geeti*.

'*Baba* did start working on notations for his songs before he fell ill, and it was Kamal Das Gupta, a close friend of his, who was primarily responsible for putting most of his songs together. Kamal Das Gupta, according to me, was the finest music director of his time. He got married to Feroza *di* (the singer Feroza Begum), and in 1967 moved to Bangladesh (then East Pakistan) with her and converted to Islam. There, Feroza *di* cashed in on her husband's name and became famous as a singer of Nazrul's songs.'

'When your father-in-law died, were you in Calcutta?'

'Yes, that is an interesting story. All the stories I have are interesting, actually (she laughs). We had been hearing of his deteriorating health. One day we got to know he had passed away. We needed to go to Dhaka but we did not have visas and it was a holiday. My brother-in-law said visas would be arranged there. The aircraft, however, developed some snag and we could reach Dhaka only in the evening. By then *baba* had been buried. I returned with some soil from his grave and took it to Churulia, where *ma* is buried, and sprinkled it over her grave.'

'Are you in touch with your brother-in-law's family in Dhaka?'

'Yes, we are. But you know the two families are different. I will tell you something, you write it the way you like: they forget the essence of Nazrul's work and get into the Hindu-Muslim stuff. Time was when my brother-in-law's wife worshipped Shiva. We did puja at home with all the rituals: plucking flowers, making sandalwood paste, it was so much fun. But after they relocated and converted, they forgot all about it—that is not nice.

'We have always been a liberal family. Durga Puja was big in our house. When my mother-in-law passed away, we followed both the traditions: she was taken away as a Hindu bride, with *shakha* and *sindoor* (white bangles and vermillion), and during the burial they followed Islamic customs. We still visit the graves of my husband and brother-in-law in Gobra.

'My brother-in-law never really lived in Dhaka. He worked here and mostly lived here. Towards the end he was almost a broken man. His wife has two daughters and a son. The younger daughter now lives in Calcutta, married to a Marwari.'

'So how is the royalty divided?'

'After my husband's death, I got to know that according

to Islamic law, if the son dies before the father, his family is not entitled to anything from the father's legacy. We told the lawyers that it was not an ordinary case and that Nazrul was not an ordinary Muslim. It was then decided that the royalty would be divided between my brother-in-law and me. But these days hardly any money comes by way of royalty.

'Mamata Banerjee is now proposing to set up Kazi Nazrul Islam Academy. It was supposed to be set up in Indira Bhavan (which served as Jyoti Basu's home, in Salt Lake), but now they plan to set it up in New Town. The idea is good, and I can only hope it will start functioning while I am still alive.

'I try to keep myself busy. I do everything on my own: shopping for groceries, cooking, teaching Nazrul's songs in various schools. Every Monday I go to a school near the airport, Tuesday to Sealdah, Wednesday to Gol Park, Friday I am at home, Saturday I go to a school in Paikpara. I don't need to work, but when I can, why not?

'I am also looking at selling this house. It simply has too many tenants: most of them no longer live here but at the same time do not want to give up their possession because they pay ridiculously low rents. Someone pays Rs 88 a month, another pays Rs 102 a month, and so on. It is better to sell the property and let the new landlord deal with the tenants. At my age I cannot fight with them.

'Once I sell this house, I will buy another house in north Calcutta. I don't want to move away from north Calcutta because most of my students live here. I have to think of their convenience, after all. Once I retire, my children can decide where they want to keep me, but as of now I have no plans to retire.'

And so: while Tagore lives on in Shantiniketan and Jorasanko, celebrated and feted round the year, the memories of Kazi Nazrul Islam flicker in aged and nondescript houses such as this—a house that may no longer be around in a few years from now.

9

'HAVE YOU HEARD of Tagore?' I ask the boy who must be about five years old.

He looks at me quizzically.

'Rabindranath Tagore? Have you heard of him?' I repeat my question.

He shakes his head and shyly withdraws. He is perhaps too young to remember the names of people other than those he sees often or who interest him.

I beckon his elder brother, a boy of ten, and repeat the question. He too shakes his head.

'Rabindranath Tagore? That man with a long, grey beard? You never heard of him?' I persist.

'No,' he says.

'But you must have seen his pictures, a man with a long, grey beard?'

'I don't know.'

'Have you heard of Salman Khan?'

The boy nods with a smile.

The two boys, who study in an elite English-medium school in south Calcutta, happen to be the sons of a friend of mine, a prosperous chartered accountant. I am sitting in his house in Jodhpur Park on a drizzly evening, along with a small group of his friends, drinking expensive Darjeeling tea and munching on chicken sausages. The house has a handsome teak bookshelf, laden with books about economics and world history, but no Tagore. Just because you are a Bengali does not mean you should have read Tagore or should know all about him—there are many Bengalis who would not have read a line of him but still revere him—but it is surprising when a boy as old as ten, living in a city where the poet exists in the soil and the air, has not even heard of him. Irrespective of what grown-ups would like to believe, a generation that will grow up without Tagore may have finally been born in Calcutta.

'Salman Khan is quite popular in Calcutta, isn't he?' I ask my friend.

'He is very popular with the younger crowd,' the reply comes from another guest, a woman.

I ask her, 'Do you have children?'

'I have a daughter, she is thirteen.'

'Is she a fan of Salman Khan?'

'No way, she does not like Salman Khan or Shah Rukh Khan. Her tastes are different, she likes meaningful movies.'

'Really? Who is her favourite actor then?'

'Aamir Khan,' she replies with pride.

I wonder: when the two boys of my friend and the daughter of this woman grow up, and when they too have children and their children grow up, what would Calcutta look and feel like?

10

LONG BEFORE CALCUTTA there was Chitpur Road.

Chitpur was a village that sat north of Sutanuti, and was famous for the Chitteswari temple, said to have been built centuries ago by a notorious bandit called Chitey but restored by the local zamindar in the early years of the seventeenth century. Soon a pathway began to connect this temple to another that was located eight miles south: the Kalighat temple.

The pathway, infested with bandits and wild animals, ran almost parallel to the river, in close proximity to the villages nestled on its banks. For these villages, the pathway served as the eastern boundary and the river the western.

With the merger of these villages into Calcutta, the pathway became the cultural spine of the newborn city. As time wore on, different segments of the eight-mile stretch came to be known by different names—Russa Road, Chowringhee Road, Bentinck Street and Chitpur Road.

Chitpur Road is the oldest and the longest segment, originating from Chitpur and leading up to Dalhousie Square, thus covering the entire length of north Calcutta. Officially it is now Rabindra Sarani—after its most famous resident, Tagore, who was born on this stretch in Jorasanko—but the old name remains on the signboards of most shops.

On this road came up, almost a century before Tagore was born, several occupation-specific settlements to service the city: Ahiritola for *ahirs*, or cowherds; Kasaitola for *kasais*, or butchers; Kumartuli for *kumhars*, or potters; and so on. Most of these settlements have transformed beyond recognition, some of them, such as Ahiritola, retain their names, but Kumartuli continues to thrive as a potters' settlement, producing idols for the numerous festivals Calcutta likes to celebrate.

Durga Puja, the biggest of the festivals, is three months away. The lay Calcuttan may not have started looking at the calendar yet because there are *still* three more months to go, but the idol-makers of Kumartuli—as I find late one afternoon—already have their eyes on the calendar because there are *only* three more months to go. There are far too many idols to be worked on, and the idol of Durga is not the easiest to make.

The goddess must have ten hands, and she must be shown riding a lion and slaying the buffalo-demon. Moreover, she must be presented along with her four children—Lakshmi, Saraswati, Kartik and Ganesh—even though the children play no role in the combat.

The idols are made of bamboo sticks and straw—the bamboo sticks serve as the skeleton and the straw as the flesh. Once the basic structure is ready, it is given a skin of *entel maati*, a sticky variety of clay procured from the bed of the Hooghly. Once the skin dries up, it is beautified with a coat of *bele maati*, a finer variety of clay which also comes from the bed of the river.

Idols under construction dot the pavement of the Kumartuli stretch of Chitpur Road, but most of the workshops are concentrated on the narrow Banamali Sarkar Street, which branches off the historic road and snakes down to the river. These workshops look small from outside but most of them are cavernous and can hold more than a dozen Durga idols each.

In one such workshop, Ganesh Pal, wearing nothing but a checked *lungi*, is busy fashioning a buffalo-demon from straw. The demon is several feet taller than Pal, and even though the image is in its crudest form and yet to get a head, it looks very real and menacing.

Pal is adding more straw to parts he wants to show as muscular, and removing from those that need to look leaner. He keeps adding and subtracting until he is satisfied with the contours of the demon's gym-fit body. 'I have been making idols from the age of eleven.'

'How old are you now?' I ask him.

'I am not sure, but well past fifty. I have grandchildren now.'

'Where are you from?'

'I am from Nadia. Almost all the artisans who are employed in the workshops of Kumartuli are from Nadia. Some of them are from Burdwan.'

'So you come to Kumartuli this time of the year?'

'No, we work here round the year. Here idols are made round the year for some festival or the other. But we keep going back home every now and then, Nadia is not very far.'

'How long does it take you to make an idol?'

'A Durga idol takes ten days. The four other idols (of the goddess' children) take another fifteen days. So it takes twenty-five days to make one set of idols.'

'And how many sets do you make every Puja?'

'All these are made by me,' he points to four large Durga idols in the shed that are complete and waiting to be painted. 'I end up making more than twenty sets every year. But I don't make them alone, my employer provides me with two helpers.'

'How much does your employer pay you?'

'He pays me just about enough,' he says, *'kaaj chole jaaye'*—I am able to scrape through.

'And during Puja, do you visit the pandals in Calcutta to see your creations on display?'

'Not at all. During Puja I am always back home in Nadia. I catch up on my sleep or play with my grandchildren. I have been making Durga idols for so long that Puja no longer fascinates me. I would rather spend that time sleeping.'

AS I WALK the length of Banamali Sarkar Street, walking past idols of Durga that are in different stages of completion, I hear the beats of the *dhaak*, the Bengal drum, which is played only during Puja and on no other occasion. The sound is playing in my head. The real sound of Kumartuli, at this hour, is that of a nervous silence. The artisans are anxious to finish their work on time.

Soon I am standing by the river, its waters darkening in the rapidly fading light. Near me is a pile of black clay. A country boat arrives, stopping a few metres from the ghat. Three vest-clad men get off the boat and wade through the river, carrying huge sacks on their back. They empty their sacks on the pile, raising its height. From this mound, clay will be scooped and taken to the idol-making workshops. Two more clay-laden boats arrive.

So it's all still done with hands: someone digs the soil from the riverbed, someone rows the boat, someone makes the idols. All this hard work only for five days of festivities in autumn, after which the idols will be consigned to the river and the clay will dissolve and return to where it belongs.

AUTUMN

AUTUMN

1

THE FESTIVAL IS invariably preceded by its fragrance.

When the flowers of *chhatim*, devil's tree, begin to drench the nights with their sharp, seductive scent, you know Goddess Durga and her four children are on their way to a pandal near your home.

Then there's the sweet smell of *shiuli*, the celebrated autumn flower, which also blooms at night and lies scattered around the tree by sunrise. The sighting of the white-and-saffron trinkets strewn on the ground is often a signal to check with the tailor whether the blouses are ready. For Bengali families, the countdown to Durga Puja usually begins with the first flowering of the *shiuli*, even though the precise date for the commencement of the five-day festival varies every year, depending on the positions of the sun and the moon.

The fortnight when the sun moves from the northern to the southern hemisphere, when autumn sets in, is considered inauspicious by Hindus; it is the fortnight when they appease the souls of their ancestors through rituals conducted on the banks of a river, most preferably the Ganga. The fortnight ends on a new moon day, called Mahalaya, which marks the descent of the goddess from her husband's abode to earth.

On Mahalaya, righteous Bengali families wake up at four in the morning and tune their radio sets to listen to

Mahishasura Mardini (Slayer of the Buffalo-Demon), a collection of hymns and songs that was recorded by All India Radio many decades ago and continues to be broadcast to this day. Even though the programme drags on for close to two hours, its message to the Bengali can be summed up in four words: Let the festivities begin.

Mahalaya is also when the artisans of Kumartuli, having raced against time in the preceding weeks to complete the idols, finally paint the goddess' eyes. I took the first flight out of Chennai this morning so that I could catch at least a couple of pairs of eyes being painted. But when I arrive at Kumartuli at three in the afternoon, I find the idol-makers still in a tearing hurry. A lion is having its mane attached here, a swan is getting its beak painted there, a demon is being painted blue elsewhere, tempers are running high everywhere. Considering that Kumartuli produces nearly 5,000 sets of Durga idols every year, of varying sizes and intricacies, last-minute frenzy is part of the business.

Finally, in one workshop, an elderly artisan, his chest bare and ribs showing, climbs up a stool and begins painting the eyes of a Durga. He is a picture of patience and concentration—even though a crowd of visitors has expensive cameras trained on him—as he sets about bringing the flawless clay face to life by giving it the most perfect pair of eyes. Only an artisan—and not even god—can create a perfect pair of eyes, and he accomplishes it in about forty minutes.

'She has eyes like Ma Durga'—that's how the beauty of a Bengali woman is often described. This afternoon I saw those eyes being made. I move away once the artisan begins painting the third eye of the goddess: I want to peep into some more workshops before the sun sets. A third eye, embedded on the forehead, will make even the most dizzying of human beauties look grotesque; but a third eye on the forehead of Durga doesn't take away from her beauty. She is a celestial beauty, after all, and her devotees are long accustomed to seeing her with that extra eye, which only adds to her divine persona.

Walking through the narrow lanes of Kumartuli, I realise that the artisans still have a long night or two ahead: many idols are awaiting finishing touches. From time to time, I am forced to step aside and squeeze myself against the wall as crowds suddenly erupt from the workshops with great force, carrying away idols that have been completed.

Every neighbourhood in Calcutta sends a small army of able-bodied youth to get the idols from Kumartuli to the pandal, and the boys carry out the duty with great pride and joy. Exactly ten days later they would be bringing back the same idols for immersion in the river.

The riverside, meanwhile, is calm, untouched by the frenetic activity taking place a few yards away. I buy a clay-cup of tea and settle on the steps of the ghat. Across the river, smoke is rising out of a factory chimney. Other than the bustle of the Howrah Station, I know almost nothing about life on the opposite bank. What if Charnock had chosen to drop anchor on that end?

AS I HEAD home, my taxi trails an open truck carrying idols of Durga and her children. The goddess' gaze is fixed on my taxi. About half-a-dozen young men escorting the gods to their pandal are perched on the side rails of the truck. They are all smoking and drinking cheap rum from plastic glasses. Since the traffic is moving slowly—this is the busy Chittaranjan Avenue—I watch them finish an entire bottle of rum, in full public glare. They know that the gods are idols of clay until the priest consecrates them on *sashti*, the sixth day from Mahalaya, when Durga Puja formally begins.

2

AS A LITTLE boy growing up on the pavements of Kumartuli, he would scrape dried-up colour from clay pots left behind by artisans so that he could paint the idols made by him. Today he lives in a skyscraper, in a luxury apartment complex on the Eastern Metropolitan Bypass, from where he can see much of Calcutta. The rise of Sanatan Dinda, one of the most celebrated artists of present-day Calcutta, has been literal. He is only forty-one.

One of the walls of his drawing room bears a prominent scribble, in Bengali: *Je bhalobaashe, shey dewaale lekhe!*'—Those who love, write on walls! Another wall bears a quote, in English: 'Youth has no age—Pablo Picasso.' Scribbling on walls, says Dinda, is a childhood habit; and just as old habits die hard, old mannerisms too don't fade away easily with fame. Notwithstanding his arty appearance that includes a ponytail, he remains a quintessential Kumartuli boy: unpretentious and rustic.

'If only you had told me a little earlier that you guys are coming, I would have prepared *maangsho bhaat* (mutton curry and rice),' he is almost shouting at the journalist-friend who has brought me to see him. A Sufi qawwali of Nusrat Fateh Ali Khan plays in the background.

'But there is still some food on the table, simple

food though, in case you haven't had lunch,' he urges us to eat.

'We are fine,' I tell him, 'We just had lunch.'

'Then let us have some tea. But you must come sometime for the *maangsho bhaat*.'

Soon a boy brings us tea. Cigarettes are lit up. Sanatan Dinda tells me, 'I was born in Kumartuli. My father ran a *muri* (puffed rice) shop there, he still runs the shop. As a child I would make clay dolls. That was my first love. I would go all over the place looking for clay pots used by artisans to mix colour, and scrape the residue to paint my dolls. Since drawing paper was too expensive for us, I painted on old newspapers.

'Poverty and property, I have seen both. We were not always poor. Our ancestral home is in Midnapore, in a village called Rabidaspur. My grandfather was a zamindar who once owned eighty *bighas* of land. He had two sons. He died when my father was just seven days old, and my grandmother died when my father was nine months old. My father and his elder brother were brought up by relatives and neighbours.

'My father, when he was eleven, came to Calcutta to work in a *muri* shop, the one that he runs now. His elder brother stayed back in Midnapore, but most of the land was lost when the communists came to power and began redistributing land.

'My father, from being a helper in the *muri* shop, went on to become one of the biggest suppliers of *muri* in Calcutta. When I was a little boy, I would have my evening snack in a gold bowl, with a silver spoon. We had 1,200 guests at my *annaprashan* and I got so many gold rings as gifts that I learnt to count using those.

'But a series of unfortunate events quickly changed our fate: seven boats carrying my father's consignment sank; there was a robbery in the train my father was travelling in; there was a robbery at home one afternoon while we were away and we lost everything including utensils. We had to cook in earthen pots and eat on leaf-plates. We were suddenly poor.

'We were a big family—father, mother, five elder sisters and I. At that time, I could not even dream of going to an art college. My father just wanted me to finish middle school and join my uncle's fish business in Howrah or work in a lathe factory close by.

'I first joined a drawing school when I was in the fourth standard. It was a small school in the neighbourhood. That's where I met my first teacher, Gopinath Roy, who is a sculptor now. He taught me the grammar of art. Before that I would draw, paint and make idols on my own.

'I was also very fond of writing on walls using *alta*. Such was my demand during elections that I would end up doing twelve to fourteen walls a night. I was among the highest paid wall-writers, getting forty rupees for a 100-ft wall. This was about thirty years ago, when I was eleven or twelve.

'I also went for numerous art competitions and almost always won the first prize. As prizes I got colours and drawing books, which was the biggest reason for me to participate. In one of the competitions, I won Maxim Gorky's *Amar Chhelebela* (My Childhood). The book had a deep impact on me.

'I was in the seventh standard when I joined a cultural club in Baghbazar. They used to give free training in music but I joined it for Samir Bhattacharjee, who was the art teacher there. I consider him my mentor. All through the week I would learn music and on Sundays learn drawing from him. I could not carry on for very long since I had no money to pay the fees, three rupees at the time.

'Samir Bhattacharjee asked me to come back, got me brushes, paints, books and in return asked me to train the younger kids at the club. It was at his home that I got exposed to magazines like *Desh* and *Ananda Mela*. I began to read the art critics of *Desh*.

'When I was in the eighth standard, I earned Rs 185 for helping with decorations at the local puja. I spent all that money buying second-hand books from a puja stall in Baghbazar. I remember carrying home the bundle of books on my head.

'I became a voracious reader. Maxim Gorky's *Maa* (*Mother*), Nikolai Ostrovsky's *Ispat* (*How the Steel Was Tempered*), John Reed's *Dunia Kaanpanor Das Din* (*Ten Days That Shook the World*), Lenin's biography, short stories by Tolstoy and Maupassant—I read them all. I also used to paint the illustrations from these books.

'Since I spent all my time painting and reading stories, I never had the time to study. I was very, very bad in academics. But to get into the Government Arts College I had to pass middle school. That is when two teachers, who taught us music and drama at the cultural club, took up the responsibility to get me through middle school. They would teach me daily outside the gate of the club.

'After middle school I went to the arts college. I wanted to learn sculpture, but it was cost intensive: I would have had to buy stone, bronze, and equipment. With painting, however, I was confident of doing well even if I just drew on a newspaper with charcoal. I passed first class first.

'Like many other art students, I also wanted to join the Ananda Bazaar group as an illustrator. But in October 1992, just three months after I left college, I had an exhibition of my works at the Academy of Fine Arts. It was a group exhibition, in which two other artists also participated, and the theme was "On Human Predicament".

'Some foreigners, who had casually strolled into the hall, bought six of my twelve paintings. I made Rs 38,000, all of which I spent in buying paints, brushes and canvas. I always wanted to integrate painting with sculpture, two-dimensional with three-dimensional. I had done some of it in Kumartuli, but I began working on it seriously now.

'A few months later, in an exhibition at the Birla Art Academy, I exhibited a huge three-dimensional painting. Mr Harsh Goenka of the RPG group noticed it and contacted me. He came to my house, which was also my studio, and bought all my paintings, a truck full of them, for Rs 63,000. A few days later (his younger brother) Mr Sanjiv Goenka called me to do a mural at the Victoria House, the headquarters of CESC (Calcutta Electric Supply Corporation, run by Sanjiv Goenka). Soon after Mr Harsh Goenka called me again and asked me to do a wall at CEAT House in Bombay.

'I never had to look back after that. I am indebted to many people who have helped me at various stages of my life. *Kintu aamar jeebon ta struggle-phuggle kichhu noi* (But I don't want to glorify my journey as a struggle). I simply did whatever was required of me; I would not have survived without that.

'Struggle, poverty, grief, despair—these words do not exist in my dictionary. One just has to keep working hard. Success doesn't come to you accidentally. I have achieved success step by step. It has been a natural progression.

'Despite the success I have enjoyed, my parents continue to live in the same old house in Kumartuli. My father, even though he is eighty now and can barely see, hear and walk steadily, continues to run the *muri* shop. He is a true businessman. He says, "If I do not run the shop, what will I eat?" I am proud to be his son.

'I lived in Kumartuli for the first twenty-one years of my life, and in Hathibagan, where I moved to after college, for another eighteen years. The houses in both these places bear my stamp: their walls have my paintings, my sketches, my scribbling—lines from my favourite poets, quotes from my favourite writers. Now I live a lavish life in this expensive flat and although I have been writing and painting on the walls here also, it does not feel the same.'

3

FOUR DAYS TO go for *sashti*, which means I have as many days to go around Calcutta before pandal-hoppers take over the roads and before everything shuts down except places offering food and entertainment.

The celebratory mood has already gripped the city. Shopping malls resemble gardens in full bloom. Radio jockeys are in a state of excitement. Puja-related hoardings loom over thoroughfares, my favourite being the advertisement for a particular brand of mustard oil, which shows the goddess and her children dining the traditional Bengali way: seated in a circle on the floor.

The thoroughfares, meanwhile, are dotted with pandals. Even the narrowest of streets boasts of a pandal or two. To have your own pandal is an assertion of your existence in the city. When residents of a neighbourhood, no matter how humble it may be, pool in resources to celebrate their own puja, it's their way of saying, 'We too matter.'

But Durga Puja was not always a public event in Bengal. Until late eighteenth century, it was celebrated only in the courtyards of the wealthy and the powerful. In 1790, in a riverside village called Guptipara, 75 km north of Calcutta, twelve young men who had been barred from participating in the local landlord's puja raised money and held a public puja for the first time. The practice caught on and such pujas came to be known as *barowaari*, the fusion of *baro* (twelve) and *yaar* (friends).

Much later, as nationalist sentiments began to pick up, the term *barowaari* was changed to *sarbajaneen* (for everyone) and celebrations began to spread to nooks and corners of Bengal, certainly of Calcutta, as an assertion of native identity.

This afternoon I have come to Shobhabazar Rajbari, one of the oldest existing palatial houses of Calcutta, where in a grand altar that overlooks a rectangular courtyard, an artisan is fixing hair on the heads of the goddess and her two daughters. Another artisan is getting ready to drape the divine ladies in elegant saris. The male gods, Kartik and Ganesh, have already been groomed. The altar is witnessing this exercise for the 256th autumn in a row.

Durga Puja was first celebrated in Shobhabazar Rajbari in 1757, when Robert Clive won Bengal in the Battle of Plassey. It is not incidental that the two events—the maiden puja celebrations at the house and Clive's victory at Plassey—took place in the same year. If anything, the events are strongly linked, the link being Raja Nabakrishna Deb (1733–97), the owner of the palatial property.

Raja Nabakrishna Deb, even though the title prefixed

to his name may suggest so, was not born into a royal family. He began his career as a lowly tutor, teaching Persian to Warren Hastings, himself a humble clerk with the East India Company at the time. He was soon making himself useful to the foreign traders as an interpreter-cum-middleman.

In 1757, when Robert Clive was all set to fight the Nawab of Bengal at Plassey, Nabakrishna was part of Clive's local machinery that worked behind the scenes to ensure that the battle remained one-sided. Once the battle was won, through treachery rather than military might, Nabakrishna was rewarded handsomely for his services. Overnight he became Calcutta's wealthiest landlord and went on to get himself the title of a raja.

This palatial house, to be later known as Shobhabazar Rajbari, was one of the first properties to be acquired by Nabakrishna after Clive's victory, and he had the grand altar constructed in just three months so that he could host a lavish Durga Puja that autumn. Clive, who had just settled India's future, was the chief guest at the celebrations.

Nabakrishna, by hosting Clive, set a trend. Other *babu*s too began inviting East India Company officers to grace the pujas at their homes. The social status of a *babu* would be directly proportional to the number of sahibs attending his puja. The sahibs and the memsahibs would be treated to nautches and plied with an array of meat dishes and wine. The entertainment would go on till late in the night, for three nights in a row.

Nautch—even though the word is merely an anglicised corruption of *naach*, which means dance—denotes performances given by young women dancers for the pleasure of a male audience, a practice that originated in the Mughal courts and over time travelled to the drawing rooms and courtyards of the wealthy.

By early nineteenth century, many *babu*s were celebrating 'Doorga Poojah' at their homes just so they could throw 'grand nautches' to entertain the sahibs. Invitations would be sent to every European who mattered and reminders printed as advertisements in newspapers. Durga Puja became an exercise in public relations—a tool to climb the social ladder.

Not everybody was amused. Newspapers run by Christian missionaries reminded the Europeans that they were only encouraging idol-worship by accepting invitations to the nautches, and that if they stayed away, the *babu*s would be disinclined to host grand Durga Puja celebrations and idolatry would automatically be checked. Bengali papers retorted that festivities across the city would not come to an end just because of the absence of the European community at the homes of a few wealthy natives.

Despite the war of words in the newspapers, the *babu*s continued to throw nautches with pride, and the sahibs continued to accept their invitations with pleasure. The practice continued every passing autumn almost until Independence.

It was in 1940 that nautch girls danced for the last time at the Shobhabazar Rajbari—they must have danced at the same spot where I am standing now, watching the artisans groom the divine ladies. Robert Clive, and later Warren Hastings, too must have sat somewhere here, on a golden sofa.

The Rajbari, royal palace, stands under a blanket of silence at this hour. The artisans are working wordlessly:

each is carrying out the task assigned to him. Every now and then a visitor drops by, sometimes a photography enthusiast and sometimes a wide-eyed tourist, and leaves quietly after taking pictures.

The altar, or *thakur dalan*, forms the northern wing of the palace and is the only portion that shows signs of activity. The residential wings, even though freshly whitewashed and painted, no longer appear to be inhabited. The structure, after all, is almost three centuries old, and is most likely to have been hollowed by the passage of time. It stands like a museum whose most precious artifact is a living tradition called the Durga Puja.

I climb down the altar and walk across the grassy courtyard, to find a small portion of it fenced off by iron railings. Here sat Swami Vivekananda, during a public reception accorded to him upon his return from the Parliament of Religions in Chicago.

Until moments before, I was trying to imagine the forever-morose Robert Clive sitting on a golden sofa in 1757, being entertained by nautch girls, and now I am trying to imagine the saffron-robed Vivekananda sitting on a mat on the ground in 1897, being feted by orthodox Bengalis. The two images are not difficult to reconcile, this being Calcutta.

I AM STILL in the courtyard when I find the door of one of the rooms of the palace to be open. Curiosity leads me to it and as I peep in—the images of nautch girls, the wine, and the array of meat dishes still dancing in my head—I find a mound of freshly-fried *samosas*. They are most probably the evening snack for the workers and artisans who are preparing the Rajbari for the puja. I want to ask the men who've just fried the *samosa*s whether they are for sale, but decide to save them the embarrassment of telling me that they aren't.

4

TURNING THE PAGES of the *Telegraph* may be easy, but getting into its offices isn't.

'Look at me,' the receptionist tells me with the grimness of an immigration officer. I comply, and realise that I am being photographed. Soon I am handed a visitor's pass bearing my picture, which I am supposed to hang around my neck before taking the lift to the editorial section. I regret that the receptionist handling me was a man.

I have come to meet Rudrangshu Mukherjee, the editor of its editorial pages and—also because he is a distinguished historian—one of the few public faces of the paper. From him I learn that starting *saptami*—the day after *sashti*—all the newspapers in Calcutta will close down for four days in celebration of Durga Puja, thus reviving a practice that had ended in 1993.

It is clearly not the idea of the managements to celebrate puja by declaring a four-day holiday—this is the time of the year when they are flush with advertisements—but hawkers have suddenly decided that they will not work at a time when the rest of the city is in a festive mood. The proprietors had to give in to the whim, considering that the hawkers are led by powerful unions backed by Mamata Banerjee.

'What can be done in a day takes seven days in Calcutta,' Mukherjee sums up the general attitude towards work in the city. 'This is the sole contribution of irresponsible trade unionism, and now it has become part of the society's DNA. The same Bengali, when he goes to Hyderabad or Bangalore, works. In Calcutta, because of trade unionism, they know they will get their wages irrespective of work.'

Mukherjee is surrounded by piles of books that have come to be reviewed in the *Telegraph*, and they complement his soft-spoken, scholarly persona. I was expecting a man sure of himself, who would chide me for knowing very little about Calcutta, maybe throw a clever remark or two my way, making me regret seeking an appointment with him in the first place. But he has turned out to be unassuming and most helpful: I might not have looked at certain aspects of Calcutta's history had it not been for this meeting with him, which lasts about thirty minutes.

Mukherjee is the typical anglicised, intellectual Calcuttan, who grew up in the ambience of Tagore but went to Oxford, who is a foodie, who loves his single-malt whisky, who has stopped watching Bengali films ever since Satyajit Ray died—and who was a family friend of Ray.

'One of the pillars of my sustenance, western classical music, came from Ray,' he says, 'We discussed more music than films. We exchanged a lot of records. He had fantastic knowledge and an incredible ear for music.'

Mukherjee, who should be in his late fifties, has spent all his life in Calcutta except the thirteen years (1974–87) that he was away, first completing his Master's degree from Jawaharlal Nehru University in Delhi and subsequently earning a doctorate in modern history at the University of Oxford.

'Back then, there was more space to move around,' he

reminisces about the Calcutta of his college days, Presidency College at that. 'I could easily walk from Ballygunge to College Street, there were no crowds. Today I would think four times, maybe age is also a factor now. My favourite hangout used to be the Cosmopolitan Coffee House at Gariahat junction. Those were also the days when you could go for walks to the Dhakuria lake without being solicited for custom.

'(Since I was studying in Presidency College) I also spent time at the Coffee House on College Street. The Naxal movement was at its peak at the time. If you went to college, you were not sure if you would come back home safe. The police could catch you, the Naxalites could catch you, or you could be caught in crossfire. I saw, with my own eyes, one boy being shot dead by the police. He was merely leaning from the balcony of the college.

'Calcutta used to be a gracious city, now it has lost its grace. There was a sense of space, a sense of class, but now all that is completely gone. It's a city where one can't even walk. The only business that seems to be doing well is real estate.'

THE SAME EVENING I visit a friend in South City, a just-completed residential complex in the heart of south Calcutta, rising to a height of almost 400 feet. It comprises four towers, each tower thirty-five floors high, each floor housing twelve flats. As of now, it is the tallest housing complex in the whole of Calcutta: something even taller is coming up on EM Bypass, near Ruby Hospital.

I had always marvelled at its height during my visits to the South City Mall, a plush shopping plaza that adjoins the complex, and wondered how Calcutta looks from the rooftop of its towers. And now I am on the rooftop, watching the sun set over my favourite city. Far on the horizon, my eyes are able to pick up the silhouette of the Vidyasagar Bridge, the dome of Victoria Memorial, the floodlights of Eden Gardens. Between these landmarks and South City is spread out 300 years of history, a jumble of concrete and greenery when viewed from a height of 400 feet.

5

ON SASHTI MORNING I wake up to the beats of the *dhaak* and chanting of mantras, relayed directly from the neighbourhood pandal by loudspeakers tied to bamboo posts erected throughout the block. From time to time, the microphone picks up the voices of women from the block who are assisting the priest in conducting the rituals: 'Where should I place these flowers?' 'Do you need me to light more lamps?' 'Here are the *tulsi* leaves you asked for.'

Durga Puja has begun. I feel I am visiting home—home being the memories of sights, sounds and smells that surrounded you until the age of fifteen; before increasing testosterone levels made you want to get away and chart your own course. Then one day you left, seduced by new sights, sounds and smells, almost embarrassed by the old ones, but two and a half decades later, once testosterone deposits begin to decline, you yearn to return home and become fifteen all over again.

When I was a child, growing up in Kanpur, my mother would drag me to the nearest pandal for *pushpanjali*, the ritual offering of flowers to the goddess. A batch of devotees would stand in front of the idols and, clutching a few flowers in their right palms, repeat the mantras chanted by the priest. As soon as the priest finished with the mantras, they would fling the flowers in the direction of the goddess. The process would be repeated thrice, after which a new batch of devotees took over.

The smell of flowers would soon be dominated by the smell of *bhog*—food for the goddess—being prepared in a secluded corner by volunteers, mostly enterprising Bengali men from the neighbourhood. With *gamchhaa*s tied around their waist, they would be attending to gigantic aluminium pots placed over burning wood, constantly stirring the contents. It can be back-breaking for a pen-pusher to cook for 200 or 300 people, but they would cheerfully take on the responsibility for the joy of puja.

The food would first be served to the goddess and then to the waiting multitude, who would be seated in rows on the ground, eager for their leaf-plates and clay-tumblers to fill up. The *bhog* comprises the simplest of Indian foods: *khichuri*, which is rice and lentils boiled together; *labda*, the crudest form of mixed-vegetable curry; *payesh*, the rice and milk dessert; and tomato chutney. Yet, when eaten in the pandal, it becomes a delicacy. But back then, during my adolescent years, I did not think so. I would find it embarrassing to dutifully follow my parents for *bhog* and *pushpanjali*.

Soon *pushpanjali* begins in the Salt Lake pandal. The priest's intonations, broadcast by the loudspeakers, sound all too familiar. For a moment, at the age of forty-two, I feel fifteen again.

AT FOUR IN THE afternoon I step out of home to look for a taxi. I want to go back to Kumartuli, to see what the artisans are up to now that puja has begun.

But taxis are difficult to find. The few that stop move on once I tell the drivers my destination. No one wants to go to Kumartuli today, that too at this hour, when pandal-hoppers and traffic police would soon be taking over the roads. Suddenly, I too begin to worry about getting back home. I almost abandon the idea when a taxi comes to a halt.

'Kumartuli?' I ask the driver.

'Would you mind paying twenty rupees over and above the fare shown by the meter?' he smiles at me.

'No problem.'

'No problem, right?'

'Not at all.'

'Very good, get in,' he says, as if warming up for a conversation. I instantly know he is a Bengali. His face is soft and chubby, he is wearing a thin moustache, and his hair is parted from the middle: he could well be a man from the Kalighat-style paintings.

'You must be wondering why I am asking for an extra twenty rupees, aren't you?' he asks me, as the taxi rolls through the wide roads of Salt Lake.

'No, I am not.'

'How can you not? It is natural for any passenger to wonder: why is this taxi driver asking for an extra twenty rupees. But let me tell you, it has nothing to do with the rising costs of petrol and diesel.'

'What is the reason, then?'

'You know how difficult it is to drive through Kumartuli this time of the year. Moreover, I was headed for Tollygunge, that's where my stand is. I should have been there by now. Kumartuli is out of the way for me, but I felt bad saying no to you.'

'I don't mind paying that little extra.'

'I know that, of course.'

I light up a cigarette and look out of the window. He too lights up a *bidi*. We are passing through Maniktala. Blaring from loudspeakers tied to electric poles and bamboo posts is a Tagore song, in Kishore Kumar's voice: *Aamar bela je jaaye*. I have always loved this song. I sit back and enjoy the ride.

But even before the song could get over, another song—from a new Hindi film—suddenly starts blasting from the loudspeakers. I quickly realise what has happened: I have moved from the jurisdiction of one pandal into another's. Each pandal in Calcutta boasts of a robust sound system and a network of loudspeakers, and each has a distinct taste in music.

'But why Kumartuli on a day like this?' the taxi driver finally asks the question I had been expecting. 'I am not even sure whether they will allow taxis there today.'

When I tell him the reason the driver, who had only been friendly so far, becomes an ally. He suddenly feels responsible for dropping me at Kumartuli. He takes a short cut, but we emerge on a road where traffic has come to a standstill. The loudspeakers here are playing another Tagore song, sung by Hemanta Mukherjee: *Diner sheshe, ghumer deshe*. I would relish this particular song in the silence of the night, but at this moment, when our path is blocked by a dozen other yellow Ambassadors, Hemanta's golden voice is more of an irritation. Why do they have to play songs so loudly in public? The reason, I would believe, is the same behind having a pandal of your own: to assert your existence.

Even as we wait for the traffic to move, the driver is

thinking aloud how to get me to Kumartuli. 'If they are allowing traffic into Chitpur Road, well and good,' he tells me, 'or else I will drop you at Shobhabazar, from there you can take an autorickshaw.'

There is little else he can do anyway, but he keeps on repeating the strategy to me as if he had hit upon a new idea. '*Aami aapnake* Shobhabazar-*e phele debo* . . .' he is telling me perhaps for the tenth time, as the traffic moves slowly from Hathibagan in the direction of Shobhabazar. '*Phele debo*' literally means 'I will throw you', but what he actually means is 'I will drop you (at Shobhabazar).' Bengali wordsmithery is at play.

Unfortunately for him, he doesn't get to 'throw' me at Shobhabazar. At the traffic intersection near the Shobhabazar-Sutanuti metro station, we find that vehicles are not being allowed into Shobhabazar. The driver looks even more crestfallen when, while getting off the taxi, I hand him two crisp ten-rupee notes apart from the fare shown by the meter, which happens to be exactly hundred rupees. He accepts the extra notes with great reluctance, and asks me, '*Kintu aapni back korben ki bhaabe?*'—But how are you going to get back home?

THE WALK TO Kumartuli is not too long and I enjoy it. To walk through the oldest part of Calcutta, that too at the time of puja, running into a tram here and a hand-pulled rickshaw there, and the sound of celebration everywhere, you can't get any closer to the soul of the city.

Bamboo barricades have already come up along the pavements to contain pandal-hoppers. Like any other neighbourhood, Kumartuli too has its share of pandals and draws large number of visitors from the rest of the city.

But Banamali Sarkar Street, where most of the idol-making workshops are located, resembles a house where a party has just ended and the hosts are slumped on the sofa after a long day. I step into a dimply-lit workshop, looking for signs of life, only to find the shed occupied by a row of unfinished Lakshmi idols. Lakshmi Puja is celebrated five days after Durga Puja ends.

On the far end of the shed, under the faint light of a bulb, an elderly man is seated at a wooden desk. He is busy making calculations on a piece of paper. He looks up when he hears my footsteps and doesn't seem very pleased with my presence. When I tell him the purpose of my visit, he grimly motions me to sit on a bench next to him.

His name is Debabrata Pal. He is sixty, a veteran artisan, and owns the workshop. He is sitting all alone now because the artisans he employs have just left for the day. He too will leave soon, have a bath at home, and will pay a visit to the pandal he is a part of. Tomorrow morning he and his staff will be back again to work on the Lakshmi idols.

'There is no holiday in our profession. We work round the year,' he tells me. 'We start work on the Durga idols sometime in March or April. We make 180 to 200 sets of idols every year.

'Durga Puja is followed by Lakshmi Puja; Lakshmi Puja is followed by Kali Puja; Kali Puja is followed by Jagadhatri Puja; a couple of months after Jagadhatri Puja comes Saraswati Puja, which is celebrated in February. By March or April we are back working on Durga idols.

'My great-grandfather, my grandfather, my father—they were all idol makers. I have known nothing but idol-making, right from the time I was born. *Aamar to babar haath dhore sekha* (I learned the art from my father).

'I have two sons. One is twenty-six and the other eighteen. I had asked them if they would like to join me in the business, but they refused. They say they are educated and don't want to make idols. I will carry on as long as I can, with the help of my staff. I don't know what is going to happen once I am gone. I think this is one problem every artisan in Kumartuli is facing.'

'Do you ever go visiting pandals in other parts of the city?'

'Of course we do.'

'Are you able to recognise the idols made by you?'

'Of course, just one look and I can tell which idol came from which workshop,' he finally allows himself a hint of a smile.

'Do you feel bad when the idols, so painstakingly created by artisans like you over a period of several months, get immersed in the river?'

Debabrata Pal takes off his glasses and wipes them with the edge of his cotton vest. After pondering over the question for a minute or two, he says, 'Yes, I do feel bad, sometimes I feel very bad. But that's the custom, what to do?'

'I have been told about another custom, that the clay you use to make Durga idols must be mixed with soil scooped from the home of a prostitute. Is that true?'

'Even I have heard about this custom,' says Debabrata Pal, 'and it was probably followed in the olden days. But today do you think it is possible to collect soil from anywhere in the city? Is there any soil left?'

6

SAPTAMI, THE SEVENTH day. On this day, the pandal at our block serves *khichuri*, the traditional bhog. The fare on the subsequent days, *ashtami* and *navami*, is somewhat lavish, for which residents should have purchased coupons from the puja committee days in advance. Every house buys sufficient coupons to cover not only the members of the family but also the driver, maid, cook and the watchman—and there are no separate queues for the employers and the employees, for this is a community lunch.

Coupons are cheap—twenty rupees for a vegetarian buffet and forty for a non-vegetarian one—and they are mainly sold to give the caterer an idea of how many people he should prepare food for and to restrict outsiders from walking in and helping themselves to a luxurious meal.

The actual cost of feeding lunch to a few hundred people for three consecutive days, for that matter the entire cost of celebrating puja in a neighbourhood, is usually raised through corporate sponsorships, generous donations by wealthy residents, and door-to-door collection.

Today being *saptami*, when coupons are not required, when just about anybody can walk into the dining area attached to the pandal and have a plateful of piping hot *khichuri*, there is no queue to be seen. People are coming to eat of course—people whose taste buds are itching for that gratifying morsel—but not in numbers large enough to call for a queue.

I decide to draw my own conclusion: even though the *khichuri* may lie at the heart of Durga Puja festivities,

Bengalis, at least the Bengalis living in our block, do not want to queue up for a dish so humble. They can always satisfy their craving for it during less-crowded festivals such as Lakshmi Puja, Kali Puja and Saraswati Puja, or even at home on a rainy evening. But for someone like me, who doesn't live in Calcutta, eating *khichuri* on Durga Puja completes the being-a-Bengali experience.

7

ASHTAMI, THE EIGHTH day, most auspicious of the puja days: the four of us—my mother-in-law, my wife, our cook Unnati, and I—are in a queue that has spilled out to the road.

From our current position in the queue, the source of food is still a good 100 metres away. The distance does not seem to diminish even though we have been standing almost at the same spot, under the not-so-pleasant sun, for nearly half an hour. We know the menu—*luchi, pulao, chholar dal, dhokhar daalna, alu bhaja*—and can now even smell it.

A little ahead in the queue is Badan Singh, the one-eyed watchman who had left my mother-in-law's service some months ago to take up a job in another house, even though she continues to believe that he has retired to Bihar. It is Unnati who spots him. She tells my mother-in-law, 'Look, there's *dadu!*'

'Who?'

'*Dadu.* Your Badan Singh!'

'Bodon Singh? Where? I don't see him,' my mother-in-law brushes her aside.

The queue finally begins to move, and we walk barely

a few steps before coming to a halt again. Bengalis are used to queuing up for food: they know that if there is a queue, the wait must be worth it.

Suddenly I hear a woman shouting. A man is trying to calm her. She shouts at him with greater ferocity. As the angry voices travel closer, I realise what has happened. The woman and her children were at the head of the queue when the food—the *pulao* and the *luchi*—got over. The caterer's boys had told her that she would have to wait for another half an hour before more *luchi*s could be fried and more *pulao* prepared.

'How can you be so irresponsible!' the woman, looking even more beautiful in her agitated state, is fuming, 'Do you think that's fair?'

'These things happen,' the man who appears to be the caterer is now raising his voice, 'All I am asking you is to wait for fifteen-twenty minutes. Can't you be a little patient?'

'Patient? It is already two o' clock, how long can my children stay hungry?'

'Look at the people in the queue, they are all waiting patiently.'

'*My* children are hungry, and it is a shame that the food should get over!'

The secretary of the puja committee, a silver-haired *bhadralok*, arrives at the scene. 'The food should be ready in no time,' he seeks to calm the woman, 'please don't leave.'

'Do you see the time?' the woman trains her anger at the secretary, 'it is already past two o' clock. When will my children get to eat? I can't even take them to a restaurant at this hour. And why should I take them out when I have already bought coupons?'

'I am really sorry for this, please stay back.'

'Stay back? No way. I want my coupons to be refunded right now.'

'But we don't refund coupons. Why don't you please wait? Look at the others, even they are waiting.'

'I want a refund, this moment.'

As the fracas drags on, people in the queue turn eager spectators, forgetting about their own long wait for the food. Finally the secretary asks an office-bearer to take her coupons back and refund the amount. The moment she marches off the pandal along with her children, the caterer's boys bring in hot *pulao* and *luchi*s and the queue begins to move.

DURING DURGA PUJA, the daytime is meant for devotion and nighttime for revelry. There is an overlapping hour, when the day has not entirely ended and the night has not fully begun, when devotion becomes a form of entertainment. This is the hour of the *dhunuchi* dance, when some select devotees get to wave the *dhunuchi*—clay goblets stuffed with burning incense—at the goddess, all the while swaying to the beats of the *dhaak* and vibrations from a bell plate. The *dhaakis*—drum-beaters—sway as well, their own feet moving deftly to the rhythm created by their fingers. Soon the drum-beaters as well as the devotee-dancers work themselves into frenzy, the audience watching them equally transfixed. The goddess watches them all, from behind a screen of fragrant smoke.

Right now, I am one of those being watched by the goddess, and the goddess alone knows after how many years I am watching the *dhunuchi* tribute being paid to her. Without realising it, I've spent close to an hour at the neighbourhood pandal, with my wife standing beside me, watching the *dhaaki*s electrify the autumn evening with the beats of their feather-adorned drums.

It is seven-thirty now, and those who had been watching the show will soon head back home, get dressed in their best clothes and set out for pandal-hopping in different parts of Calcutta. The best part of their evening will be spent in queues leading to the famous pandals and being part of crushing crowds, but that's precisely what they are looking forward to. Who wants to walk on an empty street during Durga Puja? And each pandal has sufficient food stalls to keep the revellers going all night: the kitchen is the most neglected corner of a Bengali home during the festival.

We walk back home, I pour myself a drink and write for a while (the beats of the *dhaak* seem to have cleared my mind), and it is not before eleven in the night that we set out on our own pandal-hopping trip. Pradeep, the watchman, is chauffeuring us.

Our first stop is Park Circus, then Mohammad Ali Park, after which we head straight to south Calcutta—to the Maddox Square pandal, supposedly the most fashionable puja in town. Fashionable because, I am told, it attracts the 'happening' crowd of Calcutta, including actors and actresses.

I have been here once before, some years ago, and at the time had found it no different from other pandals. Maybe because my personal circumstances were different then: I was newly married, yet to fall in love with Calcutta, and found pandal-hopping a painful chore thrust on me by my ever-enthusiastic wife. Maybe things will look different now, because I have begun to love Calcutta and its ways, even though I doubt whether I will spot any actors at one in the night.

The Maddox Square pandal, at this hour, resembles a college carnival. Groups of young men and women—the women, unlike the men, are dressed for a cocktail party—occupy almost every inch of the grassy compound, sitting on the ground in small circles. If you discount the women and the air of festivity, it would perhaps resemble a railway platform where passengers are stranded because of late arrival of trains. A hawker steps forward to offer me a sheet of the *Telegraph*.

'How much?' I ask him.

'One rupee.'

I am about to accept the sheet gladly, believing that this is the newspaper's way of making up for its absence in the mornings, when my wife points out that he is selling sheets from old issues as paper mats. I notice that all the young men and women are seated on pages from the *Telegraph*.

We wade through them to walk into the pandal and join the crowd of pandal-hoppers gathered in front of the goddess. Dozens of arms are raised in the air, taking pictures of the idols with mobile phones. I hand my phone to my wife and ask her to take a picture of me with the goddess in the background: I want to show my friends on Facebook that I had been to Maddox Square. Another woman is taking pictures of a man, who may be her brother. As she aims the camera, she instructs him: '*Taak dhaak*'—Hide your bald patch. The man, embarrassed, quickly adjusts his hair to look less bald.

Walking out of the pandal, I feel as if I am exiting a stadium where a much-awaited football match has just ended in a victory for the local team. The road outside is a river of revellers, determined to drift all night, blowing cheap plastic horns, shouting, laughing. Our next stop is Ekdalia, yet another famous puja, about a mile away. We join the river. Pradeep, who is parked in a lane nearby, will later pick us up from a point.

At Ekdalia, however, there is a long queue outside the pandal even at 1.45 am. After having walked all the way, the plastic horns torturing my eardrums all along, I have no patience left to stand in yet another queue. I suggest to my wife that we head to the nearest main road and ask Pradeep to pick us up from there. As we find our way out of the madness, the place suddenly begins to look familiar to me. It then strikes me that I had come here once before, nearly two years ago, to interview the writer Sunil Gangopadhyay. Two questions spring to my mind: Would he also be required to stand in the queue if he wished to visit the pandal at this hour? And, what if he takes ill on a day like this, because the streets leading to his house are so clogged with people that an ambulance won't be able to enter?

I have no idea that, precisely at this hour, my two questions are being rendered invalid.

NAVAMI, THE NINTH day: a call from my father wakes me up early in the morning.

'Sunil Gangopadhyay has died,' he tells me.

'How do you know?'

'The news is all over the channels.'

'When did he die?'

'They are saying he died late last night, around two o' clock.'

I switch on the TV and find a channel showing an old interview with the writer. He is saying how he is never in Calcutta during Durga Puja and likes to go away to Shantiniketan because of the crowds and the noise created around his house, especially by boys blowing plastic horns all night.

But this puja he was home, having just returned on the day of Mahalaya from Mumbai where he underwent treatment for prostrate cancer, taking his final breaths at a time when I happened to be a few metres away from his house.

A PILLAR HAS fallen. I had expected tremors across Calcutta. But the queue for the food is longer this afternoon, quite expectedly so because the *navami* meal boasts of, besides several vegetarian delicacies, a bowl of spicy mutton curry and a large piece of *rui* fish.

After lunch, everybody lingers in front of the goddess, for tomorrow afternoon—*dashami*, the tenth day—she and her children would be gone, to be consigned to the river as clay idols. Bengalis have only until tonight to soak in the puja spirit. But then they live Durga Puja all year: celebrating it for five days and waiting for it for the remaining 360.

WINTER

WINTER

1

IN THE END, all the revolutionary fire and intellectual arrogance boils down to a tiny white ball—spongy and syrupy.

Calcutta, once upon a time the city of cities, nourishing minds that shaped the social contours of modern India, is today best known across the country for the *rossogolla*. Vivekananda, Tagore, Subhas Bose, Satyajit Ray: all these icons come much later for the lay non-Bengali, who identifies Calcutta most instantly with the celebrated sweet.

Whether the *rossogolla*—cottage cheese rolled into the size of a ping-pong ball and soaked in translucent syrup—is actually a Calcutta sweet remains a matter of dispute. There are historians who claim that it originated in the temple town of Puri, in Orissa, several centuries ago and was brought to Bengal by Oriya cooks. Even if there is truth in the claim—there just might be—it is far too late in the day to make amends. Calcutta's ownership over *rossogolla* is now etched in stone.

On the busy Jatindra Mohan Avenue, one of the arterial roads in old Calcutta, stands a sweet shop with a hard-to-miss orange signboard:

NOBIN CHANDRA DAS
INVENTOR: ROSSOGOLLA

I would pass the shop during my visits to Kumartuli and other places in old Calcutta, and find it funny that someone should call himself the inventor of *rossogolla*. Perhaps an eccentric man, this Nobin Chandra Das, I would think. How can one invent a popular sweet or, for that matter, any dish? These things usually evolve over generations, through trials and errors and also embellishments along the way.

Each time I would pass the shop, I would be tempted to stop by and seek an interview with Mr Das. One afternoon, on my way to the Shobhabazar Rajbari, I did finally stop at the shop, only to find that in order to interview Mr Das I would have to travel nearly a century back in time. He turned out to be the father of the confectioner KC Das, who himself died a long time ago but remains alive as a famous brand.

Fortunately, I had not revealed my ignorance to the staff at the shop. I had taken into consideration that a man claiming to be the inventor of a sweet as ancient as the *rossogolla* may no longer be alive after all, and therefore had not asked directly if I could see Nobin Chandra Das.

I had only asked them whether I could meet the owner of the shop, upon which they had given me the family tree and told me that I could meet the present owners at their *rossogolla* factory in Baghbazar, further up the road.

'The man to meet is Mr Dhiman Das. He looks after the business in Calcutta,' an attendant had said.

'Will I find him in the factory now?'

'Unlikely. He is on the local puja committee. He is very busy with the preparations. You will have to come after puja.'

That afternoon, I had decided that Baghbazar would be my first port of call when I returned to Calcutta again.

2

AT FOUR O' CLOCK on this cold December afternoon—'Take a chill-pill, Cold-cutta,' the *Telegraph* headline had said in the morning—the tiny riverside station of Baghbazar could well belong to a remote town where trains rarely show up.

Not that it would not look any less sleepy another time of the day or year. The riverside of north Calcutta, where one would expect a perennial stream of bathers eager to wash away their sins, is forever engulfed in meditative silence. Its ghats present the same picture of calm: a couple of small tea-stalls, a small temple, dogs sleeping undisturbed, an old idol of Durga or Saraswati abandoned against a tree, the odd couple seated on the steps and gazing at the river, a sprinkling of bathers scrubbing themselves, a couple of country boats bobbing in the river, a steamer gliding past—the noise of its engine barely audible under the canopy of silence.

On the deserted railway platform stands a woman wrapped in a blue shawl, her palms clasped and eyes shut in fervent prayer. She is facing the river—goddess in liquid form—which reflects the orange rays of the setting sun.

Not very far from her are two little girls who are diligently finishing their homework before it gets too dark. The girls are seated on a plastic sheet spread out on the platform, right under the yellow railway signage that identifies the station of Baghbazar in three languages: Hindi, Bengali and English. They are as oblivious of the woman as the woman is of the world: her eyes are so firmly shut in prayer that you wonder what it is that she wants from the river-goddess.

Crows, meanwhile, feast on leftover lunch dumped on the rail track. More crows are perched on the green railing that separates the track from the houses of Baghbazar. Outside one of the houses, a hand-pulled rickshaw comes to a halt and an elderly man, carrying an infant, climbs down. Even as he pulls out money from his pocket to pay the rickshaw-puller, he steps aside to make way for children who are joyously running behind a discarded bicycle tyre spinning down the street. The children, clad in tatters in spite of the cold, are playing the poor child's sport: to keep the tyre rolling by constantly hitting it with a twig.

Baghbazar station may appear to belong to countryside Bengal, but it is part of Calcutta's circular railway. Soon a green-painted train will arrive, stop for a few moments causing minor excitement, and once again calm will prevail.

I have been able to participate in the calm because I've arrived early for my meeting with Dhiman Das, who is Nobin Chandra Das's grandson's grandson and looks after the family business in Calcutta. After having tea at a riverside stall—the temperature this morning was 10.8 degrees, the coldest in a decade—I am now walking to the factory that manufactures KC Das brand of sweets.

The factory, a five-minute stroll from the river, is tucked away in a lane named after Ramakrishna Paramhansa. I can smell the boiling syrup from a distance. The security guard, when I tell him that I have an appointment, courteously shows me into the reception, where I sit under a giant portrait of a man called Sarada Charan Das (1906–92), described in the caption as 'the father of globalisation of Indian sweets.'

Sarada Charan Das, the family tree in my notebook

tells me, was a son of KC Das and grandson of Nobin Chandra Das, the 'inventor' of *rossogolla*. Sarada Charan Das himself had seven children, among them Dhirendra Nath Das, who had opened the shop (the one with the orange signboard) on Jatindra Mohan Avenue and whose son, Dhiman, I have come to see.

'I have been going to that shop right from the day it opened in April 1985. I was thirteen at the time,' Dhiman tells me when I meet him in his cabin, 'I would sit next to my father. That's where I learned the ropes.'

He says, 'My father named the shop after Nobin Chandra Das (and not KC Das) because he wanted at least one shop to be named after him so that people don't forget that he had invented the *rossogolla*.'

'Did he really invent the *rossogolla*?' I ask him.

'Yes, he did. Some people say the *rossogolla* came from Orissa. But we went there, made enquiries and found no evidence. Even if something similar to the *rossogolla* existed at the time, it certainly did not match the quality and texture of what Nobin Chandra Das had created,' says Dhiman.

'Tell me more about him. Tell me how KC Das, the company, came into being.'

Dhiman calls an attendant and orders him to get me some snacks and coffee. He then proceeds to tell me the story.

Nobin Chandra Das was born a posthumous child in 1845 in a family of sugar merchants, which had migrated from Burdwan and made Sutanuti their home for eight generations. By the time he was born the business was on the decline and his mother could not afford his education. In 1864, when Nobin Chandra was nineteen, she advised him to open a sweet shop, even though the family did not like the idea of the young man becoming a *moira*—sweet maker.

Nobin Chandra heeded his mother's advice and opened a shop in Jorasanko on Chitpur Road—a stone's throw from the palatial house where Tagore was growing up at the time. The shop did not do very well on that location and two years later, in 1866, he moved further up the road and opened a new shop in Baghbazar. It was here that he 'invented' the *rossogolla*, in 1868, by making small balls of cottage cheese and boiling them in sugar syrup.

One morning, a horse-carriage carrying the wealthy Marwari merchant Bhagwandas Bagla and his family came to a halt outside his shop. One of Bagla's children was thirsty and they were looking for some water. Nobin Chandra, as hospitality demanded during those days, offered the child a sweet—in this case a *rossogolla*—along with the water. Seeing the child relish the new kind of sweet, the father could not resist helping himself to one, and was so delighted that he bought a large quantity of *rossogollas*.

Nobin Chandra's 'invention' soon became famous by word of mouth. Until then, the *sandesh* was the king of Bengali sweets, but not everybody could afford it. The common man had to make do with sweets made of lentils or gram flour.

Since Nobin Chandra was a simple man who lived in simpler times, he was only too glad to pass on the art of *rossogolla*-making to fellow confectioners. But since no other confectioner could match his skill, the flavour of his *rossogolla* retained its uniqueness.

One friend of Tagore, whenever he visited the poet in Shantiniketan, would always carry along a potful of *rossogollas* purchased from Nobin Chandra's shop. One day, when he stopped at the shop on his way to Shantiniketan, he found that the *rossogollas* were sold out. He bought a potful from another shop, hoping that the poet would not be able to tell the difference. But Tagore only had to taste one to remark, 'These *rossogollas* are not from Nobin Chandra Das's shop, are they?'

Nobin Chandra went on to invent other milk sweets as well. Over time, his sweets became popular with the monks of the newly-started Ramakrishna Mission, which had set up a monastery in Baghbazar. One particular sweet, the *dedo sandesh*, was a favourite of Sarada Ma, Ramakrishna's wife, who spent her final years residing in the offices of *Udbodhan*—the Bengali mouthpiece of the Mission—also located in Baghbazar.

Nobin Chandra died in 1925, aged eighty. His son, Krishna Chandra Das, fifty-four at the time, succeeded him at the shop.

In 1930, Krishna Chandra, who had five sons, opened another shop with the assistance of the youngest, Sarada Charan, in Jorasanko. He called the shop Krishna Chandra Das Confectioner. It was here that he created the *rossomalai* and also introduced canned *rossogollas*. But he died within four years of the shop's opening, leaving the business in the hands of Sarada Charan, then twenty-eight.

Sarada Charan turned out to be a visionary. He began to expand the business. In 1935, he purchased the warehouse of a transport company on Esplanade and turned it into an upscale sweet shop patterned on a Western-style eatery. Liveried waiters served sweets to patrons in porcelain plates. Sweets were no longer packed for customers the traditional way—wrapped in leaf—but in cake boxes. He named the shop after his father. Krishna Chandra Das was shortened to KC Das.

In 1946, Sarada Charan registered 'KC Das' as a private limited company and became its governing director. That year, he also set up a factory in Baghbazar—where I am sitting right now, with his grandson—and began to use steam, instead of open fire, to prepare the sweets. For that purpose he installed the boiler of a steam locomotive in the factory. More KC Das shops opened in the city.

Sarada Charan, who enjoyed a respectable position in society, liked to fund sporting events and help artists. Once when the artist Jamini Roy was hard up for money, Sarada Charan commissioned him to paint images from the Ramayana. The artist depicted the epic in seventeen canvases, which are still on display at the home of the Das family in Baghbazar—built over the shop where Nobin Chandra Das had 'invented' the rossogolla.

A severe blow was delivered to the business in November 1965 when the West Bengal government issued the Milk Trade Control Order, banning commercial production of *sandesh*. The purpose of the government was to ensure sufficient milk supplies for the city's children, expectant mothers, the aged and the infirm. The Calcutta high court struck down the order, saying it discriminated against *sandesh*-makers and favoured other confectioners. Following this, the government issued another order, banning commercial production of not just the *sandesh* but all milk-based sweets—including the *rossogolla*, *pantua* and *ladikeni* (named after Lady Canning, wife of India's first viceroy).

KC Das shut down all its shops, except the one at Esplanade, which had diversified into selling savouries.

The shops shut included the one that had been started by Krishna Chandra Das himself in Jorasanko and the one where Nobin Chandra Das had 'invented' the *rossogolla*. The family, not sure when or whether the government would withdraw the order, rented out Nobin Chandra's shop to UCO Bank. The bank continues to operate out of the building even today.

Even though the order was revoked in 1967, Sarada Charan did not think it wise to invest in reviving the shut shops, that too when he was not sure if sweet-sellers would be slapped with such an order again. He began thinking of taking the business out of Calcutta to somewhere down south, perhaps Hyderabad.

He eventually decided in favour of Bangalore, and in 1972, set up a factory and a shop there. His put his youngest son, Birendra Nath Das, in charge of the business in Bangalore. Birendra Nath, who remained a bachelor and is now in his late seventies, dedicated his life to building the KC Das empire in Bangalore.

Today KC Das has nineteen outlets in Bangalore and only six in Calcutta. Bangalore is sustaining its business in Calcutta, even though one would think it would be the other way round.

'We run at a loss in Calcutta,' Dhiman tells me, 'Bangalore is where we make our profits. It is a good place to do business because cow milk in Karnataka is of very high quality. The workers are efficient and hardworking. We don't face labour problems there like we do here in Calcutta. Here they constantly ask us for hikes and are more eager to earn overtime wages.'

I am now holding a plate that is laden with several varieties of sweets and savouries—including a large flavoured *rossogolla* and something called *Singara Italiano*, or Italian *samosa*, stuffed with corn, capsicum and cheese.

I think of the calories, but at the same time tell myself that it is not very often that one gets to gorge on sweets right inside a sweet-manufacturing factory—KC Das at that. Dhiman makes it easier for me. 'Please eat, don't hesitate,' he urges me. 'They are all fresh, made right here.'

'There is another problem with Calcutta,' he continues. 'Here the consumer is very price-sensitive and not quality-conscious. They always settle for the cheaper stuff. That is why the Calcutta factory focuses mainly on the canned *rossogolla* business.

'This factory produces close to 30,000 *rossogollas* a day. Of them 24,000 go into cans. Each can holds twenty *rossogollas*, so we produce 1,200 cans a day—most of them go to the Howrah and Sealdah stations and to the airport. That's where they sell the most. The remaining is sold loose in our various outlets in Calcutta.

'In Bangalore it is the other way round. There the number of *rossogollas* we make in a day is one and a half times of what we make in Calcutta, and almost all of them are sold loose. It shows that people in Bangalore appreciate the quality of KC Das *rossogollas*. But here in Calcutta, *rossogolla* from any shop will do,' he says.

I make sympathetic noises, but it is easy to see why KC Das is running at a loss in Calcutta—the city with a sweet tooth—but making profits in Bangalore. In Bangalore, which is a thousand miles from Calcutta, KC Das offers authentic Bengali sweets. But in Calcutta, sweet shops are dime a dozen—nearly 16,000 across the city—and each shop commands the loyalty and respect of the neighbhourhood it is located in.

My mother-in-law, for example, always buys her sweets from a shop called Ghosh Brothers in Maniktala. Their *rossogollas* are the best I've ever had: not too spongy, but succulent. They taste local, not global. KC Das, on the other hand, has always aspired to be global right from the time of Sarada Charan Das. Maybe their premises and products are a bit too refined for the taste of Calcutta.

Once I have emptied my plate, Dhiman offers to show me around the factory. He leads me into a shed where a dozen men in khaki shorts, wearing hospital masks and caps and aprons, are seated in two rows facing each other—each man with a large *karhai*, the hemispherical cooking vessel, in front of him. Each *karhai* has countless *rossogollas* floating in it.

In one corner of the shed, a small group of workers is busy putting the freshly-minted *rossogollas* into cans. If I am to mischievously slip a coin—or a strand of hair—into one of those cans, I will never know in which part on the world my crime will eventually be caught. It could be in New York, or Bombay, or Kerala, or somewhere in Madhya Pradesh—such is the reach of KC Das *rossogollas* and the lure of Bengali sweets.

In another corner of the shed, yet another bunch of khaki-clad workers is deftly carving out pieces of *sandesh*. The boiler of a steam locomotive that Sarada Charan Das had got installed in the late 1940s still stands there—like a tall iron Shiva lingam—even though it is no longer in use. The steam used for cooking the sweets is now generated by electricity.

Adjoining the shed is a small laboratory where a microbiologist determines the levels of 'good' bacteria in the sweetened curd, or *mishti doi*, produced in the factory.

The microbiologist—a young attractive Bengali woman—explains her role, and the bacteria's role, in the KC Das scheme of things, though it all goes over my head. But I get the point: that the company has traditionally been investing in scientific research to ensure quality control.

'Did you know that Sarada Charan Das started off as a research assistant under Dr CV Raman, the Nobel laureate, before he joined his father, KC Das, in the sweet business?' Dhiman asks me.

'Really? I didn't know that.'

We walk out of the shed, back into Dhiman's office, where a young man is waiting with a framed canvas. The canvas contains a pen and ink sketch, depicting a musician conducting an orchestra. Dhiman's face lights up at the sight of the canvas.

'Do you know who the artist is?' he asks me, delighted.

'No, who is it?'

'Debojyoti Mishra. Have you heard of him?'

'No, I haven't.'

'You haven't heard of Debojyoti Mishra? He is a well-known music composer. He composed the music for *Autograph*, the Bengali film. Haven't you heard of it?'

'Of course I have. I liked its songs.'

'Very few people know that he is also an artist,' says Dhiman, as he holds up the frame with pride. As he admires the sketch, he tells me, 'We may be into business, but we are not business-minded people.'

3

SOME DAYS LATER I happen to visit the home of the Das family.

The four-storey house in Baghbazar, located right on the historical Chitpur Road, was built in the 1920s. On the ground floor used to be the shop, the only shop the family had at the time, where Nobin Chandra 'invented' the rossogolla several decades ago. The shop now serves as the Baghbazar branch of UCO Bank. On the outer wall of the building is a plaque that marks its importance:

The famous institution of the inventor of *rossogolla*, Mr Nobin Chandra Das, was located here. The institution was shut down by the order of the government banning production of milk-made sweets in 1965. This stone inscription commemorates the centenary of the invention of *rossogolla*: 1868–1968.

And so, Calcutta's claim over the *rossogolla* is etched on stone.

Since the ground floor of the house is occupied by the bank, the central courtyard, a distinctive feature of a traditional Indian home, sits on the first floor. A set of rooms form a rectangle around it: drawing rooms, dining rooms, kitchen, bathrooms. On that rectangle sit two more levels of rectangles: they comprise bedrooms of individual members of the family.

In one such bedroom, Ajay Das is watching a football match on TV. He is nearing eighty and a bachelor, and is the oldest surviving member of the KC Das family. He is a grandson of KC Das. His father, Ambika Charan, was the elder brother of Sarada Charan, the visionary.

Ajay Das is known, even related, to the friend who has brought me to the house this afternoon. Since the friend—a fellow journalist—happens to be the wife of one of my cousins, I can say that even I am related to the family, although very remotely.

Ajay Das smiles at us and motions us to take our seats. He makes polite enquiries even though his eyes are fixed on the game. I look around. His personal belongings—eighty years of existence—seem to be confined within this room. The four-poster bed is strewn with clothes. The table around which we are sitting is laden with bottles containing herbal concoctions. About ten minutes later he switches off the TV.

'Why did you stop watching the match?' I ask him.

'How long can one sit in front of the TV,' he says, 'It is nice to have people over.'

'When was this house built?'

'1926 or 1927. I was born in 1934. I've lived all my life in this house.'

'Were you part of the KC Das business?'

'No. I had my own shop for a while, a sweet shop, but it did not last long. After that I never got into any business.'

Ajay Das, even though he is pushing eighty, does not look more than sixty-five, and when I tell him that, he says, 'I stick to certain rules. I walk every day. I never touch rice after two in the afternoon. I may eat a snack for lunch, but never a heavy meal if it is past two o' clock. And I have curd every day after lunch. A hundred grams of curd—it is a must. Curd is good for health, it makes you glamorous.'

'What about sweets? Do you touch sweets?'

'Of course, I have sweets every day. It is often said that a *moira* (confectioner) never eats sweets, but that is not true. Ours is a family which has sweets even with tea. I have a *rossogolla* and a *sandesh* after breakfast, and another *rossogolla* and *sandesh* after dinner—every day.'

'I am told this house has Jamini Roy's paintings of the Ramayana?'

'That's right. Seventeen canvases in all. He did them in 1941 or 1942, I'm not sure about the exact year. I was a small boy then. Our family has always been connected with the arts. The kind of people who would visit us or stay with us: Ashok Kumar, Kanan Devi, Uday Shankar, Ravi Shankar, I could go on and on.'

'Can I see those paintings?'

'They are in the drawing room downstairs. I will have to get the key.'

We step out of Ajay Das's bedroom when a head pops out from an adjoining bedroom. It's an elderly woman, who looks scandalised. 'You people are leaving so soon, that too without eating anything!' she is almost shouting at my cousin's wife, 'This is not done!'

'They are not leaving,' Ajay Das intervenes, 'I am only taking them downstairs to show them a few things.'

We climb down to the courtyard where I suddenly notice a prominent circular patch on the floor. I had missed it while coming into the house. Seeing me looking at the patch, Ajay Das says, 'That used to be the outlet for the chimney in Nobin Chandra's shop.'

He opens the drawing room and ushers us in. It a large rectangular room lined by sofas. But the most prominent piece of furniture is a dining table, which would have seated many a celebrity and served dishes that Bengalis always dream of.

'There, those are all Jamini Roy,' Ajay Das points to the walls. I look at the paintings—I would have missed them had he not pointed them out, they hang so high on the walls—and count the number of canvases: there are indeed seventeen of them, depicting various scenes from the Ramayana. Then there is another work by the artist, made from straw mat, showing child Ganesha resting his head on the lap of Durga.

Assuming the market value of each work is Rs 10 lakh—though that's a very modest figure for a Jamini Roy of the 1940's vintage—the drawing room holds a treasure of nearly two crore, or twenty million, rupees. No wonder it remains locked.

Ajay Das puts the lock back and shows us into yet another drawing room that is adjacent and more tastefully done up, complete with a piano. I suddenly recognise a familiar frame on the wall: the pen and ink sketch by Debojyoti Mishra, the music composer.

Soon the refreshments arrive: two plates, each containing three different kinds of sweets and a *samosa*, and tea in flasks. 'Eat without worry,' Ajay Das tells me. 'We use just the right amount of sugar in our sweets, unlike other confectioners who use far more sugar than is required.' He goes on, 'When I was your age, I would eat dozens of sweets in a day. I am a little careful now because of my age, but I have had no health problems.'

My cousin's wife, who has just started going to yoga classes, reluctantly picks up a sweet and pushes her plate away. 'Why are you doing that?' Ajay Das gently admonishes her.

'It is with great difficulty that I wake up early in the morning to go for the classes. I don't want that effort to go in vain,' she replies and then, turning towards me, says, 'Ajay *dadu* is a great palmist, do you know that?'

'What rubbish, I am not a great palmist,' Ajay Das gives out a laugh of modesty, 'I am just an amateur palmist.'

'Do you mind reading my palm?' I ask him.

He looks outside the open door. The sun has not set

yet. The last rays of the sun are still streaming in, beautifully illuminating a vacant chair placed between the door and the piano. 'One is not supposed to read palms once the sun has set. You are just in time. Let me get my magnifying glass,' he says and leaves the room.

Taking advantage of his absence, I quickly eat the *samosa* and the sweets from the plate meant for my cousin's wife. 'How shameless,' she giggles, 'he will think I ate them up after making all the fuss about losing weight.'

'How does it matter,' I tell her. She punches my arm.

When Ajay Das reappears with the magnifying glass, he sits on the vacant chair between the door and the piano. I can see the last rays of the run shine a spotlight on the oldest surviving member of an old Calcutta family, who is sitting by a door that leads to a balcony overlooking the Chitpur Road, which had existed long before the city of Calcutta did. Somehow, it doesn't strike me that I should take a picture of the old man sitting on that chair. I am more nervous that he has got the magnifying glass: will he get to know something about me that I may never know myself—my future?

He beckons me to come to the sofa next to him and asks me to extend my right palm. He feels the bulges on the palm with his thumb and then proceeds to read the lines with the help of the magnifying glass. He suddenly grows pensive and asks me, 'Is there anything particular you want to know?'

'Nothing as such, but tell me something about my career.'

He feels my palm again and tells me, 'You are highly ambitious. You don't settle for smaller goals.'

'But will I be able to realise my ambition?'

He runs the magnifying glass over my palm and says, 'You are on the right track, but you will reach the peak of your success only at the age of fifty. Not before that.'

'Nothing is going to happen before fifty?'

'Unlikely,' he says, 'How old are you now? The lines suggest you must be forty-one or forty-two?'

'That's right, forty-two.'

'So you have eight more years to go. Don't worry, time flies. Before long, you will be famous.'

'Eight years? You mean nothing is going to happen in the next eight years?'

'I never said that. I only said that you will reach the peak of your success at fifty.'

'What about the book that I am working on right now, the one about Calcutta, will that be successful at least?'

'I should think so,' he says, 'Unless your books are successful now how are you going to reach the peak of success at fifty? But if you want me to be precise with my predictions, I need to take a look at your horoscope. Do you have one?'

'I think I do. But I need to find where it is.'

'Come back when you find it. Come back even if you don't find it,' he grips my hand, 'Come whenever you feel like.'

I promise him I will and step out into the dusk of Calcutta.

4

WRITING A BOOK on Calcutta was not even remotely on my mind when, one afternoon in August 2009, I stood inside St Mary's Church in Chennai, looking at the granite font in which Job Charnock's three daughters were baptised 320 years before.

That afternoon, when my first book, the one on railway junctions, was still with the printer, I had formally begun the legwork for my second, the one on Chennai, which I called *Tamarind City*. Fort St George, where the 1680-built church stands, had been my first port of call because the city of Chennai, or Madras, had originated from the fort.

What was Charnock, who is synonymous with Calcutta, doing in Madras? The question hadn't struck me at the time because he was not relevant to the history of Madras. Nevertheless, I had noted down the inscription on the plaque explaining the importance of the font:

> Baptisms have taken place at this font since 1680. It is made of black Pallavaram granite known to geologists as Charnockite from the fact that Job Charnock's (founder of Calcutta) monument at Calcutta is built of it. On the 19th August 1689, Job Charnock's three daughters were baptised here. Job Charnock had carried away by force a Hindu widow who was about to be immolated on the pyre of her husband. Charnock rescued her and she lived with him for the rest of her life ...

Three years later, on a crisp December afternoon, I am standing in front of Charnock's mausoleum in Calcutta, with a clearer idea of history.

Charnock, along with other servants of the East India Company posted in Bengal, had cooled his heels in Madras for seventeen months in 1689–90 when conflict with the Mughals had forced the Company to wind up business in Bengal. Elihu Yale, who was Madras's president at the time, was hardly pleased to see 'the Bengal gentlemen' idling away in Fort St George and must have been relieved when Aurangzeb restored the Company's trading rights in Bengal and Charnock and his men took the first boat out of Madras, landing in Sutanuti on 24 August 1690.

Charnock died two and a half years later, aged sixty-three. A mausoleum, said to be commissioned by his son-in-law Charles Eyre, was later built over his grave. The burial ground was closed in 1767 when it ran out of space, and fifteen years later, Warren Hastings, then the governor-general of India, purchased the land from Nabakrishna Deb, the local landlord, to build St John's Church on the site of the graveyard.

During the construction of the church, nearly all the graves were dug up and their remains taken away. Left untouched were the tombs of Charnock and Vice-Admiral Charles Watson, who had accompanied Robert Clive from Madras in the expedition to recapture Calcutta but had died, at the age of forty-four, within weeks of Clive's victory at Plassey. And thus they came to be located in St John's Churchyard.

Not many in Calcutta seem to know that Charnock lies buried in the city, or that his mausoleum stands in the backyard of St John's Church. For that matter, not many seem to know where St John's Church is, even though it stands at an important intersection in Dalhousie Square, once the seat of administration and business for the British and now for Bengal.

At least I have some difficulty locating the church, or

maybe I have been asking the wrong people for directions. But it is ironical that while Charnock has become a brand name in Calcutta—there is a Charnock Hospital and plazas called Charnock City—his mausoleum, where the man actually lies buried, is visited mostly by well-fed cats, as I discover when I am finally able to locate St John's Church.

Christmas is just a couple of days away and the trees in the front yard of the church are all wrapped in chains of tiny electric bulbs that will come alive once the sun goes down. Since a large number of cars are parked in its compound, I step inside the church making as little noise as possible, half expecting a mass to be in progress.

But I find the entire church to myself—not a soul around (I later discover that the compound is being used as a parking lot, perhaps for a fee, by visitors to Dalhousie Square). So overpowering is the silence inside that I can hear my own breath, and if I am to feel a tap on my shoulder, it could well be the hand of Warren Hastings.

Hastings was present when its foundation stone was laid in 1784, but by the time the construction was completed three years later, he had resigned and left Calcutta. The consecration was attended by Lord Cornwallis.

On a wall hangs a depiction of The Last Supper, painted by the German artist Johann Zoffany shortly after the church was opened. 'When the picture was originally hung'—to quote from the Kolkata Municipal Corporation signboard that stands outside the church—'Calcutta society was scandalised by Zoffany's indiscretion in introducing the features of important local persons in his picture. It is said that the Greek priest Father Parthenio sat for the figure of Jesus. The auctioneer, Tulloch, who had been given to believe that he was sitting for St John, took recourse to law to avenge the insult of finding himself depicted as Judas. The Police Magistrate, William Coates Blaquiere, is supposed to have been the actual model for St John in the picture.'

But the signboard—such signboards, titled 'Beautiful Bengal', have been erected by the municipal corporation outside every protected monument across Calcutta—only drops a hint about the presence of Charnock's grave in the churchyard: 'This was the old burial ground, closed since 1767, where rose the mausoleum of Job Charnock.' Visitors will have to guess whether the mausoleum belongs to the past or the present—if at all they pause to read the signboard.

The tombs of Charnock and Watson lie in a separate enclosure in one neglected corner of the churchyard. Charnock's mausoleum, a white octagonal structure, looks more Mughal than British but in no way matches the grandeur of a Mughal monument. It is infested by lazy, overweight cats who stare at you evilly and is grossly dwarfed by a modern high-rise office building, numerous air-conditioning panels jutting from its wall, just across the boundary wall of the church.

But the mausoleum must have cut an imposing figure in the early eighteenth century, when Calcutta was just a collection of villages, and contributed to the belief among the locals that the man who lay buried under it ought to be the founder of the settlement.

In another corner of the churchyard stands the replica of Holwell's monument, built by Lord Curzon in memory of the 123 Europeans who had supposedly suffocated to death in the Black Hole—the original being built on the site of the Black Hole by Holwell himself.

John Zephaniah Holwell had survived being locked up in the Black Hole and had lived to tell the tale—much of which was considered exaggerated by latter-day historians. Holwell had built the monument at his own expense but it was demolished in 1821 when the government found that it had become a base for local barbers. Lord Curzon, after he became the viceroy and governor-general of India in 1899, built a replica of the monument on the very spot in 1902. But in 1940, when the movement for India's independence was at its peak, Curzon's monument was shifted to St John's Church, where it stands today, surrounded by shrubs and overlooked by modern buildings that are way taller but aesthetically incongruent.

The backyard of St John's Church, come to think of it, serves as the ultimate museum of colonial rule in Calcutta. The three monuments—the tombs of Charnock and Watson, and Curzon's obelisk—explain, more clearly than anything else, how the city came into being. And yet I had a difficult time finding the church.

5

DALHOUSIE SQUARE—RENAMED BBD Bagh after Independence—is Calcutta's own Westminster. It was built that way, to serve as another London, from where the British would rule India forever.

The old name sticks, like many things British. Calcuttans call it Dalhousie—the 'Square' is usually dispensed with. In grandeur and elegance, Dalhousie Square surpasses anything that is British in this country, except that its neglect has been equally Indian. Conservation efforts have picked up ever since heritage became a fashionable word, but the decay is still heartbreakingly visible in several of the imposing buildings: façades worn out, intricate carvings hidden under decades of grime, branches growing out cracks in the walls.

At the same time one feels happy for the structures that have been salvaged. Town Hall, one of the most magnificent buildings in Dalhousie Square, is among those. The story of its rescue is told by the municipal corporation signboard outside its gates:

> The construction of this building was completed in 1814. It is a fine structure built in the Doric style of architecture with steps leading to a grand portico in front. The carriage entrance is at the back under a lofty covered portico. The building is two storeyed and originally used for public meetings, receptions, balls, and concerts that generally took place on the upper floor, which is boarded with teak with the thirty feet high ceiling. After Independence, the Town Hall fell into disuse. A unique step was taken to create a fund for restoration. Through an auction of paintings and outside support, a trust fund was created. On April 14, 1998, the restored Town Hall was handed over to Kolkata Corporation. On August 15, 1998, the Town Hall was opened to the public with an exhibition of paintings.

The story may have a happy ending, but it is illustrative of the neglect Calcutta has been subjected to after the British left. The realisation that Town Hall must be saved had dawned only in 1998, half a century after Independence; even then, the money for restoration had to come from an auction of paintings and 'outside support'. The government, clearly, had other pressing concerns.

In Dalhousie Square is located the red-brick Writers' Buildings, the seat of West Bengal government. It was built in the late eighteenth century, on the site of a demolished church, to house writers, or clerks, of the East India Company. Several additions were made to the structure over the next two centuries.

In 1930, three young Bengali revolutionaries—Benoy, Badal and Dinesh—shot dead Col NS Simpson, the inspector-general of prisons, at his office on the first floor of Writers' Buildings. They had apparently killed the wrong officer. The man they were looking for was Charles Tegart, the much-hated police commissioner of Calcutta who had escaped similar assassination attempts.

Cornered by the police after the shooting, Badal swallowed potassium cyanide, while Benoy and Dinesh shot themselves. Benoy died a few days later in hospital. Dinesh survived and was hanged.

And so, after Independence, Dalhousie Square came to be named after the three Bengali revolutionaries: Benoy, Badal, Dinesh, or BBD. Writers' Buildings, however, retains its name. On the wall of Simpson's office, now occupied by an IAS officer, is a plaque that commemorates their act.

I visit Writers' Buildings—Calcuttans call it Writers'—the day before Christmas. I show up sharp at noon. Swapan, the friend I have come to see, had told me over the phone in the morning: '*Lunch-er aagey aagey chole aaye kintu*'—Try and make it before lunch.

'But why not after lunch?' I had asked him.

'I am not sure how long I will stay in office after lunch,' he had replied, 'Why? Why can't you come before lunch?'

'I've just woken up. But I will come.'

'Come to the rear gate, the one that is opposite stock exchange, and call me. I will get you in.'

But at noon, Swapan is not in Writers'. He had to suddenly go to the court for a hearing. Since he works with the Land and Land Reforms department, he is often required to show up in the court for some land-dispute case or the other. 'Stay there,' he tells me when I call him, 'I should be back in twenty minutes.'

And so I walk up and down the lane between Writers' and the stock exchange. It smells of food, just like many other busy lanes of Calcutta.

'*Alu porota hobey*!' calls out one vendor—We have *alu parathas* here!

'*Kochuri hobey*!' shouts another.

'Chow mein! Chow mein!'

'Biryani *hobey*!'

People are eating with relish. The moment they put down their plates on the pavement, the crows take over. They peck at the remnants of the delicacies until they are shooed away and the plates dunked into a bucketful of water for washing.

A little away from the crows, along the same pavement, two men in their underwear are enjoying the force of the water gushing out of a hosepipe and are scrubbing themselves vigorously. This must be their pre-lunch bath.

A little away from the bathing men—but far enough from the splash of the water—is sitting a bald elderly man peeling boiled eggs.

Further down the lane, a vendor has spread out, on a wooden table, the hottest produce of the season: *nolen gur*, or date-palm jaggery. The arrival of *nolen gur* is the befitting finale in the sweet-toothed Bengali's calendar year—English calendar, that is. During winter, even the celebrated sweets, such as the *sandesh* and *rossogolla*, acquire a brown tinge because they are flavoured with the jaggery instead of sugar.

I walk on. The lane ends with a tall regal building that must have been constructed over a century ago but seems to have remained locked for half that period. Calcutta is replete with such ghostly structures: built with great ambition once upon a time, but now uninhabited for reasons that remain mysterious to the bystander.

I would like to see what's inside the building but there is no way I can. I can only see what is outside of it: hawkers have dug nails on its walls to hang their tarpaulins to protect their wares from the sun and rain.

In the shade of one such tarpaulin, a barber is busy lathering the chin of a customer. The tarpaulin's shadow on the pavement marks his territory in Calcutta.

As I retrace my steps, I begin to feel hungry. I had been told once that one can eat with 'eyes shut'—denoting blind faith—at any of the roadside stalls in Dalhousie Square. But I am not sure what Swapan, my friend, has in mind for lunch—maybe he will take me to the canteen at Writers'—so I give up the idea of eating on the street.

Soon Swapan arrives and as I follow him into Writers', I notice a small signboard reminding visitors that they are entering a no-smoking area and warning them against spitting 'here and there' (a literal translation of the Bengali phrase for 'indiscriminately'). But the first thing we do, as soon we reach his office on the second floor, is light up cigarettes.

'*Cha khaabi toh?*' Swapan asks me—You will have tea, won't you?

But even before I can reply he has sent the attendant to get two cups of tea. The attendant returns with two miniature plastic cups containing lemon tea: *lebu cha*, as Bengalis call it.

Swapan shares the room, which is not very large but appears spacious because of the high ceiling, with three fellow officers from the Land and Land Reforms department. But right now no one is around other than my friend and the attendant, who is sitting on the chair of one of the officers and listening intently to our conversation.

The room, illuminated and warmed by the sunlight streaming in, has a mirror and two calendars (both bearing pictures of the goddess Kali) hanging from the walls. The tables are all laden with files. They seem to contain records of land-related cases that the government of West Bengal is fighting.

The file sitting right in front of me is marked with a felt pen: *Sudhamoy Ghosal vs State*. I try to picture Mr Sudhamoy Ghosal. The image that immediately comes to my mind is that of a plump distinguished-looking Bengali man, clad in a dhoti and kurta and reclining on an easy chair. In real life he might be anything but like that. There must be thousands like him, whose identities stand immortalised on the covers of dusty files that sit on the shelves and tables at Writers'.

Land and Land Reforms is not only the oldest and the largest government department in West Bengal but also the most significant, especially ever since the communists came to rule the state in 1977 and began implementing the existent land-reform policies with an iron hand—a pro-peasant move that supposedly kept them in power for thirty-five years.

Even today, no single individual in West Bengal can own more than 24.22 acres of land. Anything in excess is taken away by the government and distributed among the landless—the idea being that the poor, instead of being at the mercy of landlords, can grow their own crops and earn an honourable living.

'What should we have for lunch?' Swapan asks me.

'I leave that to you.'

'Sandwich?' he suggests. And then, same as before, reaches for his wallet and gives the attendant some money to get sandwiches from one of the eateries across the road, even before I can say yes or no. 'Wait a minute,' he tells the attendant and hands him more money, 'get some *nolen-gur sandesh* as well.'

Soon we are all biting into sandwiches—Swapan, me and the attendant. 'These are the safest thing to have,' Swapan tells me, 'I could have ordered something else but I cannot guarantee that your stomach won't be upset tomorrow.'

'*Biryani ta kharap hoye na*,' the attendant interjects— The biryani isn't so bad.

'*Dur!* You call that biryani!' Swapan reprimands him. 'For all you know they might be putting crow meat. Sandwich is safe.'

'But,' I tell Swapan, 'I have heard that you can eat anywhere in the Dalhousie area with your eyes shut?'

'*Dur!* All nonsense!'

The sandwiches appear to be fresh and I like them, but I was secretly hoping to eat at the canteen. I like eating at office canteens: the food is almost like homemade, and the fact that fifty or hundred others are simultaneously eating the same food under the same roof brings about a collective gratification and enhances the pleasure of eating.

We are still at the sandwiches when three men burst into the room. I presume they are Swapan's colleagues who share office space with him. They slump on their seats with loud sighs of relief, as if back from an arduous assignment, and light up cigarettes. The attendant has moved to the chair meant for him.

'How did it go?' Swapan asks them.

'It went off rather well actually,' replies one of them, blowing cigarette smoke in the direction of the roof. 'She heard us out and seemed positive. Let's see what happens eventually.'

I soon gather that the three men were part of a delegation that had just met Mamata Banerjee, the chief minister. They had sought an appointment months ago to present her with their long-pending demands—better pay-scales and faster promotions—but had finally got an audience only this morning. The meeting itself, therefore, was a small victory for them.

'What are we waiting for,' Swapan tells them, 'Let's order sweets right away.'

'We already have some sweets here,' the peon interjects again. The *nolen-gur sandesh* is passed around.

Swapan introduces me to his colleagues as a journalist.

'Oh journalist!' says one of them, 'then you must write about the new circular.'

'What circular?' I ask the man.

'It says all Writers' staff must report for work latest by 10.15 am and not leave before 5.15 pm.'

'What are the working hours?'

'10 am to 6 pm—that is the official timing, but who

can stick to that? Employees who live in far-flung places, can they make it by ten, that too in such severe winter? And can the same people, unless they leave office early enough, say by three-thirty or four, reach home before the cold gets bone-chilling?'

'So what are you going to do?' I ask.

'We are going to stage a protest if they insist on us following the circular. Though I don't think they will; such circulars come and go.'

'But when do people usually come in to work and when do they leave?'

'There are many who come in just to sign the attendance register. They come in by noon and are out by four. But don't write that.' The room breaks into laughter.

Just then a newspaper hawker walks in. He is an elderly man, wearing a smile and carrying a knitted wire bag that is bulging with fresh copies of newspapers and magazines. A bunch of magazines are also tucked under his arm.

He slaps two magazines, including a copy of *Desh*, on Swapan's desk. 'Here, these have hit the stands just today,' says the hawker.

'That reminds me, I am yet to settle last month's bill. Can I pay you tomorrow?' asks Swapan.

'Who is asking you to pay right now? I am not going away anywhere. I have known this place for sixty years, long before you people were even born,' the hawker says, not just to Swapan but to the entire room.

'You have been selling newspapers in this building for sixty years?' I ask him, astonished.

'Selling papers? I used to work here, in the health department. I started selling papers only after retirement, just to keep myself active. How times flies, I am already seventy-two.'

'When did you join service?' I ask.

'A long time ago, how can one remember? Wait let me think, yes, I joined in 1956. At the time Dr Bidhan Chandra Roy was the chief minister.'

'And what is your name?'

'Madan Mohan Ghosh.'

'So you joined the health department?'

'Yes, I started in the health department, retired in the health department. Those days were different when I joined. People had more work and less of ailments. Now they have less work and more of ailments.'

'What did you join the health department as?'

'I joined as a Group D staff. *Mithye kotha bolbo kano? Mithye kotha boley to kono laabh nei* (Why should I lie? One does not gain anything by lying).'

No one had even remotely suggested that he could be lying. It's just the case of verbosity that afflicts many Bengalis who tend to be theatrical with their speech. What he simply means is that he is not embarrassed telling people that he had joined service in Group D, the lowest rung in officialdom that comprises employees who are known variously as peons, attendants or messengers.

It is a different matter that in Writers', a messenger is never called a messenger and an attendant never an attendant. They are all respectfully referred to as 'Group D staff'.

Such courtesy extends to the rest of Calcutta, perhaps even Bengal, where servants and domestic helps are never ever referred to as *chaakor* or *jhee*—two words I would hear often when I was growing up in Kanpur. In Calcutta, domestic help are always known as *kaajer lok*—people who work.

Whether such courtesy was born out of the long communist tradition, or was already enshrined in the Bengali *bhadralok* culture—I would not know, though common sense suggests that the former is more likely.

'I joined service wearing half-pants,' continues Madan Mohan Ghosh, 'those days it was compulsory for Group D staff to wear half-pants. Why just Group D, we even had a minister back then who wore half-pants.'

'A minister?'

'Yes, a minister, Nikunja Maity. Haven't you heard his name? *Shey ki*? He always wore half-pants and full socks to work, even though Bengalis did not dress like that. At the time a pair of half-pants cost twelve annas, and the ones with drawstrings came for even less, just six annas. Full-length pants came for six and a half rupees, and a Hawaii shirt came for three and a half rupees. Those days the rupee had value, unlike today.'

Madan Mohan Ghosh goes on and on about the olden days. If there is one thing that remains unchanged from the times that he is reminiscing about, it is Writers' itself.

The offices—tall slatted doors, aged furniture, heaps of musty files, empty cups of tea everywhere, cigarette and *bidi* smoke in the air—could well belong to the late twentieth century. At least in the room we are sitting in, even the desktop computer, which could have served as a reminder that we are in the twenty-first century, is missing.

If I am to discount Swapan's laptop—which is most likely his personal—and our smart phones, this room will appear to be frozen in time from the days of Jyoti Basu or even Bidhan Chandra Roy. And now we have a man who actually belongs to those days and is remembering them fondly.

'Dr Bidhan Chandra Roy was a great man,' Madan Mohan Ghosh continues, 'I got to watch him from close because I knew his personal assistant Bhola quite well. I would often sneak into his office under the pretext of meeting Bhola. There, I would often find a very skinny man sitting with Dr Roy. Do you know who that man was?'

'Who?' I ask.

'Jyoti Basu.'

'Really?'

'Yes—why should I lie? Jyoti Basu was nobody then. Who could've imagined he would be the chief minister someday? But Dr BC Roy was the greatest of them all. He was not only a great leader, but also a great doctor. Once, a couple came to see him along with their ailing son, in the hope that he would suggest a cure. The son was obese, and the moment Dr Roy saw him, he told the parents, "This boy won't live beyond three months." Hearing this, the boy lost all interest in eating, and as he lost weight his ailments too began to disappear. The family came back to meet Dr Roy after three months and this time the boy was perfectly healthy. That was how he treated patients—you know what I mean?'

Perhaps due to this remote association with Dr Roy, during which he must have heard countless health tips being handed out, Madan Mohan Ghosh still looks a decade younger than his age. He lives across the river and walks all the way to Writers', crossing the Howrah Bridge.

'I need to watch my weight. The moment you lose control over your weight, you start getting all the diseases. I have no sugar, no pressure because I walk a lot and don't overeat. Nowadays everybody has become conscious about what they eat. Earlier, guests would feast on *rossogollas* during weddings, but these days you see them squeezing out the syrup. Times have changed,' he says.

'Tell me about your family,' I ask him.

'We are just the two of us—my wife and I. We have four daughters, but they are all married. We also raised one of the granddaughters, but even she is married now and has a son. Only the eldest son-in-law does not keep too well, otherwise life is not too bad. I get a monthly pension of Rs 9,500—enough for the two of us. By the way, can you guess what my salary was when I joined service?'

'How much?'

'Forty-four rupees!' he exclaims, and then proceeds to dig one more nugget from the past—and then another. He even tells us a ghost story: how one of the rooms in the health department was haunted and no one dared go into it once night fell. According to him, an officer of the deputy secretary rank had even fainted once at the sight of a ghost in that room.

'But all this used to happen long ago, when Writers' was not so populated,' he says. He is possibly referring to the pre-communist days when work culture in Calcutta was different from what it is today. The ghosts might still be around, who knows, just that no one gets to see them anymore because no one stays back till the night descends.

As I listen to his stories, narrated with childlike innocence, I wonder why he had chosen to sell newspapers inside Writers' after retirement. He certainly didn't need the money. Perhaps he wanted to remain connected to the corridors of Writers', where he had spent nearly all his life, and did not want to become completely irrelevant to the giant machinery in which he was once a small cog.

Earlier he would carry files, now he carries newspapers. The corridors, which recognise Madan Mohan Ghosh by the sound of his footsteps, cannot tell the difference.

AS I GET up to leave—I've spent over three hours at Writers'—I ask Swapan if he could show me the plaque that commemorates the assassination of Col Simpson by Benoy, Badal and Dinesh.

He takes me down to the first floor, on the VIP corridor, where the plaque is mounted on the outer wall of what was Simpson's office, now occupied by principal secretary, Land and Land Reforms. It was unveiled by Jyoti Basu in 1980, to mark fifty years of the sensational event.

I wonder if the bureaucrats who are allotted Simpson's office harbour any special emotions. Are they proud to be on the site of one of the most daring acts carried out by Indian revolutionaries, or feel uneasy because it involved bloodshed? Has any of them ever seen Simpson's ghost?

'Let's have one more round of tea before you leave,' Swapan tells me.

'Not lemon tea again, I want regular tea, with milk and sugar.'

'I will get you regular tea. Come with me,' he says.

We walk through a maze of corridors, enter a large hall, and emerge into an enclosed area where there are more empty desks. Here, in one corner, behind a wooden partition, a tea-seller carries out his business.

Swapan orders two cups of tea and we seat ourselves at one of the vacant desks whose rightful occupant—considering it is past four o' clock now—should be on his way home.

I ask Swapan what are the departments—apart from Land and Land Reforms—that function out of Writers'. He does a silent calculation on his fingers and gives me a rough list: Chief Minister's Office, Home, Law, Information, Prisons, Public Works.

The list of departments that have moved out of Writers' over the years (many have been relocated in Salt Lake) is equally long: Education, Power, Industries, Irrigation, Fisheries, and Health (where Madan Mohan Ghosh, the newspaper hawker, had worked all his life).

The tea-seller places two small ceramic cups on the desk. As he pours the tea from an aluminium kettle, we light up cigarettes. But he doesn't leave even after he has filled the cups.

'*Aagey kheye dekhoon,*' the tea-seller insists, 'Taste it first.'

I take a sip. The tea is really good—neither too strong and nor too milky to mask the flavour of the leaves—and I tell him so.

'I have never compromised on the quality of tea leaves,' he tells me proudly, 'I have been using the same brand of leaves ever since I set up shop in Writers'. Back then they cost Rs 32 a kg, now Rs 250 a kg.'

'So when did you start selling tea in Writers'?' I ask him.

Basanta Pramanik, the tea-seller, begins telling me his story.

In the 1970s, when he was still a teenager, Basanta worked in a liquor shop in Lake Town. He hailed from 24 Parganas, a district neighbouring Calcutta. At the liquor shop, he made about a thousand rupees a month and got a new set of clothes twice a year. (He remained a teetotaller himself: as is likely the case with nearly all people working in liquor shops.)

One senior officer in the Land Reforms department, who bought liquor from that shop every evening on his way back home, took a liking to Basanta. 'Why are you wasting your life in a liquor shop?' the officer would ask him often, 'why don't you do something more respectable?'

Basanta, only eighteen or nineteen at the time, had no idea what else to do. The officer told him one day, 'I can arrange a place for you in Writers'. Would you like to set up a tea stall there?' Basanta replied that he did not know how to make tea. The officer told him that making tea was the simplest of things—all he needed to do was boil water and put some milk, sugar and tea leaves in it.

And so, with an investment of sixty rupees, Basanta started a tea stall in Writers' in 1978. He set up a table on one of the corridors. Apart from tea, he sold four to five varieties of biscuits, puffed rice, *chanachur* and *laddoo*. His tea cost only ten paisa. He began to sell. But the Public Works Department, which maintains Writers', wasn't amused by his presence. He was an illegal entrant, after all. Basanta was soon shown the door.

He returned, in 1984, after the officer who had got him into Writers' pleaded his case with the minister concerned. The minister wanted a petition, signed by at least twenty-five employees, which was organised in no time. Basanta now had a permit to carry out business in Writers'. He was soon sending tea to the offices of ministers as well.

The purple patch stretched for nearly three decades until in March 2011, on the eve of the state elections, his permit did not get renewed. He had hoped the renewal would come through after the elections, but the government changed and Writers' suddenly had new rulers. Basanta, once again, became an illegal entrant.

And so he occupies this secluded corner now, making himself as inconspicuous as possible and surviving on the kindness of the staff he has been serving all these years. He knows he could be thrown out any day.

Basanta, fifty-seven now, is more worried about the future of his two sons. The elder son, who has studied in Ramakrishna Mission, is looking for a job; while the younger one, who has been assisting him in the tea-selling business, faces a future that is as uncertain as his father's.

'I have raised them to the best of my ability,' says Basanta, 'Now I hope they get decent jobs, only then I can sleep in peace. Other than that, life has not been too bad. I got a lot of affection from the staff at Writers'. Nobody has ever insulted me because I am just a tea-seller.'

6

CHRISTMAS DAY IS called *boro din*—the big day—in Calcutta. On this day, all Calcuttans like to have fruit cake. The adventurous ones venture to Park Street in the evening, and those who have the money and luck find a table to dine in one of its restaurants.

My wife and I leave home early, when the sun is still setting over the Eastern Metropolitan Bypass, so that we can find a place to park near Park Street, which has been under a canopy of decorative lights for several days now. We find a place to park on Theatre Road and walk down Camac Street, which joins Park Street.

The sidewalks of Park Street are bursting with people. We walk a few inches at a time, literally rubbing shoulders with total strangers. It is part of the festivity: to be the crowd. People from across the city have come here just to be part of the crowd that chokes the sidewalks of Park Street on Christmas Day.

'Oh my God!' gasps a woman, middle-aged and very beautiful, who is walking right in front of us. 'You know what I did just now?'

Two men accompanying her—undoubtedly her husband and her young son—look at her in horror. 'Why, what happened,' the husband, highly alarmed, asks her.

'I just grabbed the hand of a total stranger thinking he was Mintu. What must he be thinking of me?' the woman's cheeks are red.

The son—Mintu—bursts out laughing. 'But I have been walking right behind you. How could you mistake him to be me?' he asks.

The husband, unlike the son, does not find the episode very amusing. The family forms a chain—this time they get the hands right—and resumes its walk.

My wife wants to have tea at Flurys—that was part of her plan when we had set out from home—but finding a table is out of the question. A notice outside its door requests prospective patrons to leave their names with the security guard and await their turn. We keep walking—rather the crowd from behind carries us forward.

We eventually reach the end of the sidewalk and want to cross over to the other side of Park Street, but face an obstacle in the form of a nervous-looking police officer who refuses to remove the rope that is serving as a barricade.

All along, as I could see from a distance, the rope was being removed periodically to let the crowd walk across in batches. But once the batch we belong to begins pressing against the rope, the police officer, who seems to have taken position at the spot only moments before, starts shouting, in English, 'Disperse! Disperse!'

The officer, one of those chubby delicate-looking Bengali men, appears to be a new recruit even though he appears too old to have joined the police force only recently.

'Disperse! Disperse!' he waves, wanting the crowd to just melt away.

Two men try to breach the barricade but he waves them back, 'Nobody! Nobody!' And then again, 'Disperse! Disperse!'

The police officer does not realise that he is pitted against the Calcutta crowd—a crowd that is now wondering why it is being detained behind a rope when the sea of humanity preceding it had been allowed to cross over in batches. Soon the crowd is gripped by a sense of injustice, and it bursts through the cordon, ignoring the chubby officer.

The defeated officer, wanting to show that he is still in command, orders the crowd, in English, 'Go fast! Go fast!'

Much later, when the crowds have thinned out, I spot the same officer in a corner of Park Street, standing next to a vendor who is selling sprouted lentils. The officer, looking morose, is eating the lentils from a small leaf-bowl, using a leaf-spoon to put the contents into his mouth.

The lentils, I can see, are garnished with chopped tomato and green chilli and, I am sure, mixed with condiments that can set the taste buds on fire. But the chubby officer is chewing on them emotionlessly: his mind is clearly elsewhere. Perhaps he is wondering whether he makes an efficient cop: what better place to test your policing skills than on Park Street on Christmas evening.

I feel sorry for him. At the same time, the sight of him putting the sprouted lentils into his mouth, that too with the help of a leaf-spoon, kindles my desire for street food. Walking back on Camac Street, we stop outside Vardaan Market, where you will always find a lively congregation of snack vendors. Someone is selling *pani-puri*. Someone else is selling *alu-kabli*. Men in white dhoti-kurta and Gandhi caps are selling *chanachur*. Mr Chauhan from Jaunpur is selling Victoria brand of *vadas*—hot lentil *vadas* served with spicy garlic chutney.

I settle for *alu-kabli*. For me it's always been the forbidden snack. One morning, more than thirty years ago, while visiting my uncle in the railway settlement of Liluah, not very far from Calcutta, I happened to accompany his two sons, who were almost my age, to the nearby market. The boys had been strictly instructed by their mother to stay clear of all roadside food, particularly the 'unhygienic' *alu-kabli*, but they only had to spot the pushcart of an *alu-kabli* seller to start counting the coins in their pockets. I watched as they ate: I had refused to be a partner in the crime, the obedient child that I was. That was the closest I had ever come to having this famous spicy snack of Bengal.

And now, almost a lifetime later, I place my order with a flourish and watch the hawker's deft fingers at work. He first peels a large boiled potato—the *alu*—and cuts it into small cubes. He drops the cubes into a steel bowl along with a small portion of boiled chickpeas, or Kabuli *channa*. He then sets about chopping a tomato, half an onion and a green chilli into tiny pieces, which are also put into the bowl. He then shakes the bowl so that the ingredients blend nicely. On the mixture he sprinkles salt, chilli powder and cumin powder and squeezes the juice of half a lemon. He shakes the bowl again and empties its contents onto a leaf-plate. The *alu-kabli* is ready, but not before he has sprinkled thin slices of ginger and spread, with the help of a leaf-spoon, some tangy tamarind chutney over it.

The beauty of street food lies in watching it being prepared. The same *alu-kabli*, were it to be sold readymade, would evoke no special feeling: it would have been just a soggy salad. It is the live demonstration of the hawker's skill that works your salivary glands.

All along, while the hawker was putting the *alu-kabli* together, a young Marwari woman standing next to me had been making familiar noises. It is the noise you instinctively make when lips are pursed against a mouth that is watering. As soon as the hawker begins sprinkling the thin slices of ginger over the *alu-kabli*, she pleads with me, '*Bhaisaahab, pehle mera number hai*'—Brother, it's my turn first.

She grabs the plate and moves to a corner and the hawker begins the intricate process all over again, starting with the peeling of a potato. The long wait has only heightened my craving. Finally, when I get to put a spoonful into my mouth, I think of that innocent morning thirty years ago: which *alu-kabli* tasted better: the one that my cousins had, in defiance of their mother's orders, or the one that I am having now?

7

TWENTY-SIXTH DECEMBER, my birthday. My wife is taking me out for lunch to Park Street. I want to have Chelo Kebab at Peter Cat.

Just as we leave home, she realises that the car is low on fuel and drives to the nearest petrol station, which happens to be right next to a big hospital in Salt Lake. We are awaiting our turn when I notice a small crowd standing in a semi-circle around a white woman, who is slumped on the pavement and is wailing uncontrollably. She is beating her chest and repeatedly hollering a word that I am unable to catch.

I step out of the car and join the semi-circle. The woman, who must be in her thirties, is howling, 'Kancha! Kancha!' I wonder what she is trying to say.

'What's wrong?' I ask the man standing next to me. He has an ID card from the hospital next door hanging around his neck.

'Her lover died this morning in the hospital,' he tells me. 'He was a Nepali, who worked as a watchman. And this woman is a doctor from Germany. They were living in. Five days ago he began vomiting blood and she got him admitted here.'

Now I understand what she is hollering. Kancha, in Nepali, means little boy, and often serves as a generic nickname for young Nepali men. So she has been calling out to her dead lover.

'I was at the reception counter the day she got him admitted,' the man from the hospital continues telling me. 'I have been talking to her. She works for an NGO, from what I gathered, and came to Calcutta some years ago.

The man happened to be the watchman at the place she was living or working. She fell in love with him, so much so that she even took him along to Germany during one of her trips back home. They had been living together for some time now, even though he had a wife and children back in Nepal.'

'Kancha! Kancha!' the woman howls again, stamping on the road with her bare feet.

'Look how she is crying,' the man from the hospital says, 'can you believe that a German doctor is crying like this? What love can do to people!'

A saree-clad woman emerges from a Maruti van that is parked close by and walks up to the distraught German doctor and offers her some water. She then consoles her and persuades her to get up and get into the van.

The German doctor, looking dazed, walks a few steps towards the van but suddenly breaks free from the comforting arms of the saree-clad woman and throws herself back on the pavement. 'Kancha! Kancha!' she is howling again.

'This drama has been going on since morning,' the man from the hospital tells me, 'they have been persuading her to get into the van but she is simply refusing to leave this place.'

'Who is that woman in a saree?'

'She is the Nepali man's wife, as far as I know.'

I soon leave the semi-circle and get back to my wife in the car. I tell her all that I've just seen and heard. 'I am a little surprised,' I tell her, 'because Westerners usually show restraint in times of grief, don't they?'

'Maybe she subconsciously adopted the Indian way of displaying emotions, having worked here for so long,' my wife tells me, 'or maybe she loved him a bit too much.'

We drive down to Park Street in silence. Peter Cat is packed and the waiting list is long. We move to other restaurants but they are packed as well. Finally we find a table, with some difficulty, at Bar-B-Q, which also has the Chelo Kebab on its menu. I eat it with relish.

After lunch we stroll down to the Maidan and take a walk across its breadth. It is littered with the previous night's waste: paper wrappers, plastic packets, plastic glasses. Crows, bold enough not to be intimidated by human footsteps, hop from one leftover to another. Dogs, coiled up against the chill, are taking their afternoon nap. Dozens of football games are on, dozens of picnics in progress, dozens of card games underway. Lovers, unmindful of the presence of the multitude, are cuddling up to keep themselves warm. We walk—it's a long and a pleasant walk, on a perfect winter afternoon—but something is bothering me, I don't know what.

Soon the outline of the Victoria Memorial shows up on the horizon. I decide to take pictures of the silhouette of Calcutta's most famous building, and as I train my phone camera, I find the sun, by now an orange ball, also fitting into a corner of the frame. I wish I could stop time for a while so that the silhouette and the sun stay where they are. All my life Calcutta had not meant a thing to me, but I now feel glad spending my birthday in its lap.

Once we reach the Victoria Memorial, we have *phuchkaas* and take a taxi back to Park Street, where we claim our car from the parking lot. As I get into the car, I suddenly realise what's been bothering me all afternoon. It's the voice that's been playing in my head: 'Kancha! Kancha!'

8

TWO BOTTLES OF Scotch whisky, Glenlivet at that, have been sitting at home for several months now. They had been handed over to my wife for safekeeping by a friend of hers who happened to be transiting through Calcutta. The friend hadn't showed up after that, but there was every possibility of him knocking at the door any day, and so I had been staying away from the bottles.

But tonight, the night of my birthday, I am determined to open one of them. More than anything else, I want to get the cries of the German woman out of my head. Since it is no fun drinking such expensive whisky all by myself, I think of people I could call over, but I hardly know anyone in Calcutta who would come all the way to Salt Lake at such short notice.

Finally I ring the bell of the tenant living on the ground floor. I know him as Dr Sharma—a young dermatologist, a native of Uttar Pradesh, who had spent much of his childhood in Calcutta and had studied medicine in Chennai. He had married his classmate at the medical college and together they practised for a few years in Pune, where his in-laws live, before he left his wife and a child behind to set up his own skin clinic in Calcutta.

Dr Sharma has moved in only recently to the house and I have met him a few times, and found him the agreeable sort, someone you could have a drink with. When he opens the door, I notice a two-litre bottle of whisky placed on top of the fridge.

'If you have not made a drink for yourself yet, come and have a drink with me.'

He seems pleased with my invitation. 'What's the occasion?' he asks me.

'No occasion. I just needed some company.'

Soon Dr Sharma and I are sitting in the balcony, nursing the single malt that does not belong to me. Kebabs, ordered from Shiraz, are at hand.

He talks about his childhood in north Calcutta, where his ancestors still have large properties, and about his college days in Chennai. He says he had liked Chennai because the people—including his professors—were humble and sincere. And that he has chosen Calcutta to set up his clinic because, he believes, Calcuttans have more disposable income to spend money on skin enhancement.

'I've exhausted my entire savings setting up this clinic. Not only that, I've had to take loans—thirty thousand from one friend, fifty thousand from another friend, one lakh from yet another friend. Forget about the bank loan, which itself is a huge amount. Now I am pinning my hopes on Calcutta,' he says.

As I pour the second drink, he lights up a cigarette. 'You know, it is a do or die situation for me,' he leans back on the chair and exhales the smoke.

'I can understand,' I say in sympathy.

'You want to know why I really came to Calcutta, leaving behind everything—wife, kid, an established practice, a secure future?'

'Why?'

'I came here because I wanted to be on my own. I could not take it any more, living in the shadow of my in-laws. They are also doctors, by the way, and they have a flourishing clinic in Pune. But why should I live off their success?'

'I can understand.'

'True, I miss my wife and child. But if I had stayed on in Pune, I would have always lived in their shadow. A man must have his own identity, shouldn't he?'

'I can understand.'

'Suppose if your mother-in-law tells you to come and live here permanently, will you do that? Will you drop everything in Chennai and move to Calcutta?'

'I will if it suits my needs. To begin with, I will be saving on rent. But I see what you mean.'

We have moved on to our third drink when he asks me, 'Tell me, boss, how can you live in Chennai? What do you do for entertainment in a dull place like that?'

'I have friends coming over all the time. We drink, we listen to music, that's about it.'

'But what do you do for entertainment?'

'I go out for movies, but only occasionally. I like having friends over. We drink and listen to music, sometimes till three or four in the morning.'

'But what do you do for entertainment?'

'By entertainment you mean?'

'Calcutta is a good place for entertainment. There is so much one can do here. Even dance bars have opened here now.'

'Dance bars in Calcutta?'

'You didn't know about it? After the dance bars were shut in Mumbai, the business quietly moved to Calcutta.'

'And where are the dance bars?'

'Why, there is one right here in Salt Lake, in City Centre.'

'City Centre? But I go there almost every day.'

'Not exactly inside City Centre, but in a building right outside it. You will recognise the building if you see it.'

'You go there often?'

'Not very often, maybe once or twice a week. If you had not called me over tonight, I would have gone there after a couple of drinks.'

'Will you take me there someday?'

'Why not tonight? What's the time now'—he looks at his watch—'only nine-thirty. Are you game?'

'Why not?'

I swiftly get dressed and tell my wife that I might be late. We are about to step out of the door when my mother-in-law intercepts us. 'Where are you off to on the night of your birthday?'

'To collect matter for my book, *ma*,' I tell her.

'May God bless you,' she tells me, 'I am going to bed now.'

'Today is your birthday?' Dr Sharma shakes my hand vigorously, 'you never told me. So the treat is going to be on you!'

City Centre is barely a five-minute drive from home: I know the route and the mall like the back of my hand. But once I get into the dermatologist's car—it's an SUV—I suddenly feel I am in some foreign land, headed for a secret destination in pursuit of forbidden pleasure.

I instantly recognise the multi-storeyed building in which the dance bar is located. I have walked past it countless times without paying any attention to it, but now I am seeing it in a new light. The watchman salutes Dr Sharma as soon as we enter the lobby to take the lift.

'I didn't see you last night?' the watchman asks him sheepishly.

'I had to go for a Christmas party. How are you? All well?'

'All well, sir,' the watchman, flattered, salutes him again.

We get out of the lift on the second floor and enter a large hall where sofas are arranged around low tables. Against one of the walls is the stage where seven chairs are placed in a row. These chairs are meant for the young women who are known as 'bar girls'—who shake their hips in a bar in order to cheer patrons.

Four of the chairs are occupied at present: the women, the lights shining on them, look bored and are browsing through their mobile phones. The remaining three chairs are empty: their occupants are now dancing to recorded music on the dance floor. All the girls appear to be in their twenties and are decently clothed in Indian attires.

We sink into sofas around one of the front tables and a waiter comes over and effusively greets Dr Sharma.

'Sir, where were you last night? I didn't see you.'

'I had to go for a Christmas party. All well?'

'All well, sir, all well,' the waiter grins. He places menu cards before us and withdraws.

The hall is nearly empty. Only three tables, including ours, are occupied. Dr Sharma glances through the menu and throws it back on the table. He suddenly gets up. 'Come let's go to the third floor. It's no fun here.'

We climb the stairs and enter another hall with a similar setting, only that this hall is dimly lit, decorated with red balloons and nearly packed. Also the music here is louder and there are more women on stage than in the hall downstairs. Four saree-clad women are dancing to a popular Hindi song, while six others are seated on their designated chairs, talking among themselves or fiddling with their phones. The patrons have their eyes fixed on the dancing women, not wanting to miss a single movement, even though the women are fully clothed.

In the song the women are dancing to, the female is beseeching the male: '*Bharo, maang meri bharo*'—Come, fill the parting-line of my hair with vermillion. In Hindu tradition, a man applying vermillion on the *maang*—parting-line of a woman's hair—means he is taking her as his wife. I was expecting a raunchy dance number—not something so conventional.

'Welcome my friend, welcome,' a young man rushes to greet Dr Sharma as soon as we seat ourselves at an empty table.

Dr Sharma introduces the young man to me, 'Meet Sohail, a good friend of mine.'

Sohail shows no interest in me and goes on to slap Dr Sharma's shoulder. 'Where were you last night, brother?'

'I was at a Christmas party, brother. I had better things to do there.'

'I am glad you came tonight. I was getting thoroughly bored.'

'Why bored?'

'Look at that Marwari man!' Sohail points to the stage. 'He has been standing there for the past one hour, insisting on the same song to be played again and again. Anyone else in his place would have produced a kid by now, but this fellow has been applying the vermillion forever!' He laughs at his own joke.

I look at the stage. A large man in a batik shirt, who looks used to the comforts of life, is standing on the edge of the dance floor and showering the women with hundred-rupee notes as they dance to '*Bharo, maang meri bharo.*' An attendant, trying to remain as inconspicuous as possible, is collecting the currency notes from the floor with the help of a plastic scoop.

I order drinks for the two of us. This is my first time in a dance bar. But the women are not even dancing; they are barely swaying to the music, with minimal effort, to give the impression of activity on the stage. They are obviously aware that the men who come here are not connoisseurs of dance. The sight of so many young women, in flesh and blood, shaking their hips to music in a watering hole, is titillation enough for the men. The glimpse of the midriff, if the woman is wearing a saree, is a bonus.

'Really, I am telling you,' says Sohail, 'any other man would have produced a kid by now, but this man has been applying the vermillion ever since I came here.' He has fallen in love with his own joke.

The song finally changes. Dr Sharma and Sohail settle into a conversation while I nurse my drink alone. Even though the music is loud, I am able to catch parts of their conversation and can tell that they have not known each other for too long. Their friendship was forged in this dance bar and now—from what I can gather—Dr Sharma is trying to get Sohail to invest in his business. I also gather that one of the 'bar girls' dancing on the stage is already a client at Dr Sharma's skin clinic. It is clear that he finds this place useful for networking.

Dr Sharma asks me to order another round of drinks and excuses himself from the table, saying he would be back in a moment. While I look for a waiter, I can see Dr Sharma walking up to the stage and, instead of flinging currency notes into the air with flourish, handing out money to each of the dancing girls. He looks embarrassed as he does so and wants to make a quick job of it. The women accept the money without making eye contact with him.

The waiter brings us the drinks and tells us that if we want to drink more, we should order right away because the bar is about to close. Dr Sharma waves him away and returns to his conversation with Sohail. I spend the rest of the evening sipping my drink and sending Thank You messages to friends who have wished me on my birthday.

When the waiter brings the bill, Dr Sharma looks away. I pay with my credit card and add a small tip amount to the receipt before signing it.

'Some tip, sir?' the waiter asks.

'Here, I just added some tip to the bill,' I tell him.

'That will go to the owner, sir. Tips added with credit card payments never come to us. Please give me some cash, sir.'

'No way, I've already paid a tip.'

The lights come on, an indication that patrons must wind up. I can see the large man in his batik shirt walk up to the stage. He can barely stand now. He waves angrily at the bouncers. Suddenly, the women resume dancing as the loudspeakers come alive with the song, '*Bharo, maang meri bharo.*'

Sohail slaps his forehead. 'I swear,' he says, 'any other man would have produced a kid by now, but he is still stuck on the process of applying the vermillion!'

The man is now swaying in delight and he pulls out a bundle of notes and flings them in the air, his hands going as high as his drunkenness can allow him. They are all five-hundred rupee notes. The attendant armed with the plastic scoop swings into action.

'And people say Calcutta does not have money!' remarks Dr Sharma as he leads us out of the dance bar.

9

SONAGACHHI, CALCUTTA'S FAMOUS red-light district, is also said to be Asia's largest. I do not know if there is any truth to that, but this piece of information, which I have come across from time to time, had led me to form my own mental image of the place.

Sonagachhi, in my head, had always been a large shabby township—milling with prostitutes, pimps and policemen—whose presence could be smelt from a distance. Asia, after all, is the world's largest continent, and the largest red-light district in the largest continent could not be just a narrow street.

But Sonagachhi turned out to be just that—a long narrow street, the spinal cord of commercial sex in Calcutta, with the maze of alleys branching off it serving as the vertebrae.

I had strayed into Sonagachhi unknowingly on a beautiful Saturday afternoon, just two days after my birthday. I was waiting outside the Shobhabazar-Sutanuti metro station for a cousin—one of the brothers who, as kids, had defied their mother's orders and had had *alu-kabli*. I was going to meet him after twenty-five years, and he was going to take me to meet a Bengali writer on College Street. Since he was still on his way when I reached, I had decided to take a short walk along Jatindra Mohan Avenue, where the station is located.

I had crossed the road and turned left. If I had turned right, I would have reached the shop with the orange signboard that proclaims Nobin Chandra Das as the inventor of *rossogolla*. Since I had already seen that part of old Calcutta, I turned left. The idea was to not go very far from the station because the cousin was expected any moment.

I would have walked barely a hundred metres when I had found myself at the mouth of a bustling street festooned with colourful paper triangles. Some sort of a festival seemed to be on.

Curiosity had led me into the street, and I only had to walk a few paces to realise that I was in a red-light area. Women of various ages, attires and ethnicities had lined the street, eagerly looking for customers. I could see a young man, a rucksack hanging from his shoulders, being pulled in different directions by women who had surrounded him. They were refusing to let him go.

I had panicked at the sight—and plight—of the young man and retraced my steps quickly. At the taxi-stand on the mouth of the street, I had asked a driver who was leaning against his taxi and reading *Ganashakti*, the CPM mouthpiece, 'What's the name of this place?'

The taxi-driver, a kind-looking elderly man, had looked up from the newspaper and said, 'Sonagachhi. Right from this end of the street till the other end, it is all Sonagachhi. And you are?'

I introduced myself, upon which he had put the newspaper aside and smiled. 'The street has a name, Durga Charan Mitra Street, but people know it as Sonagachhi. Do you know why it is called Sonagachhi?'

'No, I don't.'

'That's because at the other end of the street is the *mazaar*'—tomb—'of an Islamic preacher called Sanaullah

Ghazi, who was known by that locals as Sona Pir Baba. It is because of him that this place came to be known as Sonagachhi. Since you are a writer, you must know all this.'

'And when did Sanaullah Ghazi live here?'

'I really don't know, but it must have been sometime during the British rule, if not before. You will have to do your own research if you want to find that out. I don't know much about history.'

'But why is the place all festooned?'

'That's because the pimps are celebrating Narayana puja today. They organise Narayana puja'—propitiation of Lord Vishnu—'this time of the year. They consider Narayana to be their god.'

Just then my phone had rung. My cousin was on the line. 'Where are you?' he had demanded to know.

'Sonagachhi,' I had replied instinctively.

'What?' my cousin had cried in surprise, 'I hope you have not changed your plans.'

'I will be with you in a minute.'

I had then quickly taken down the phone number of the taxi driver—who gave his name as Shankar Das—and told him that I would be meeting him soon.

'Come before nine any morning, you will find me at this stand,' he had said.

And so I had set foot in Sonagachhi, after having heard many stories about it all these years. My favourite story is the one told to me by a fellow Bengali journalist who lived in Calcutta for many years before moving to Delhi, where we happened to work together. This is something that had happened to him:

One night, during his encounter with a prostitute at Sonagachhi, an argument broke out between the two, even while they were in the act, over money. The woman was not letting him touch her breasts, saying it was not part of the deal and that if he wanted to do so, he should pay two hundred rupees more. My friend argued that touching of the breasts should be considered part of the deal. Suddenly there were loud knocks on the door. Police had raided the brothel. My friend, aggressive until a moment before, was now touching her feet. '*Behenji, please bachaa lijiye,*' he pleaded with her—Sister, please save me.

She hid him under the cot—or did she let him out through a secret door? I am unable to recall that detail: the story had been told to me many years ago.

10

AT TASTY RESTAURANT on College Street, I meet Prithviraj Sen, who takes only a day—at the most two days—to write a book. He says that he has written 1,091 books so far, and that he needs to write just one more to enter the Guinness Book of World Records.

'Who is the current record-holder?' I ask him.

'He is supposed to be a famous British writer, Robert-something. My record-breaking book is going to be released at the book fair, which is just a month away. You must come,' says the man who claims to be the world's most prolific author—someone I hadn't heard of until my cousin brought me here.

Prithviraj Sen is fifty-eight, but looks far younger. He is soft-faced, clean-shaven, bespectacled and curly-haired — you can tell from a mile that he is a Bengali. His attire, however, is very Mughal: *sherwani* and *churidar*. I order Mughlai paratha for all of us, since a notice at the restaurant warns patrons against whiling away their time over soft drinks alone.

Prithviraj Sen tells me, 'I live nearby, with my parents, my wife and a son. My father was a senior officer in the income tax department. No one in my family was ever connected to literature. I began to write when I was very young. I first wrote at the age of twelve, for a Bengali magazine, and went on to write nearly 700 pieces for various magazines.

'I was twenty-one when my first book got published. It was a novel, released in 1976, during the first-ever book fair held in Calcutta. The book became an instant bestseller but it also attracted a lot of criticism.

'The novel was called *Kamonar Casanova* (The Desirable Casanova). The principal character is a Calcutta girl, who gets married into a Bengali family settled in America. She not only experiences culture shock in America, but also gets sexually assaulted by her father-in-law. She returns to Calcutta traumatised, falls in love with another man but eventually commits suicide.

'It's a true story, based on the life of my ex-girlfriend. I only had to change her name in the book. The book had created a sensation and people had criticised me for writing it. I was just out of college at the time.

'I studied at the Presidency College. I studied biochemistry. I was in the 1973–76 batch. I have been writing ever since I left college. I have to write one book daily, no matter what.

'I write by talking into a recorder. There is no other way for someone as prolific as me. I wake up at five in the morning and dictate the story on tape until about noon. I visualise the characters and the details in my mind before I begin to talk.

'Once I start dictating, the story just flows. I do not pause to think. You cannot tell from any of my books that it has been done almost in one go.

'Around noon, I break off for *adda* and lunch. Then I go to my office, which is in a flat nearby, and once again dictate the story till four in the afternoon. Each of my novels is about 5,000 words long—that's the lower limit. I speak about 500–1,000 words an hour. In about ten hours I finish a book.

'I have a five-member staff to listen to the story and transcribe it. They pass it on to the copy editors, who then pass it on to the proof-reader. I have a system in place, you see. Everything is set. Mine is a stereotypical, professional life. I cannot do away with it. I am yet to finish ten books before the book fair.

'I have never had problems finding publishers for my stories, right from the first book onwards. The number of publishers who have accepted my works so far easily adds up to over a hundred. A number of them are not rich and can hardly afford to pay me, but they still publish me because of my reputation. I don't write for money.

'But I make enough money from my books. Every month, after paying my staff—and I have a big team—I am left with Rs 30,000 to Rs 40,000, all of which I earn as royalty. I have no complaints, I am happy.

'Writing is not an easy task. You know how difficult life can be for a Bengali writer. In the early 1980s, soon after

I got married, I had stopped writing. I did not write for twelve years. To earn a living, I had become the chairman of a small bank. My wife, however, was very unhappy that I was not writing. She would tell me that she had married a writer and not the chairman of a bank.

'Her words would haunt me, and so I started writing again—after twelve long years—on the *poila baisakh* (Bengali New Year's Day, celebrated mid-April) of 1995. I quit the bank that very day. That's because Samaresh Basu, the great Bengali writer whom I consider to be my mentor, had once told me, "If you want to be a writer, do not take up any other job. And if you are in a job, do not take up writing."

'And so I have been a writer ever since. I have done no other job. I hope you are coming for the book fair? I would like you to be there when I break the world record,' Prithviraj Sen tells me earnestly.

I tell him that I would like to come. I have never been to the book fair in Calcutta—an event almost every Bengali in the city seems to be sentimental about.

A boy clears our plates and I order coffee. I ask Prithviraj Sen if the reader's preferences have changed over the years.

'When I began writing, my books were a rage,' he tells me, 'adult literature was much sought-after back then. My books used to be bestsellers at the book fair. But today readers want information, not stories.'

'You mean to say your books are adult literature?'

'Not all, but many of them are. But people still read my books, and I have more women readers than men. What is your book about?

'It is about Calcutta.'

'Are you writing in Bengali or English?'

'English.'

'Good, very good,' he says. 'Guinness *ta hoey gele aami-o English-e aaschhi*'—Once I have made it to the Guinness book I will also switch to writing in English.

11

I DON'T KNOW if Sonagachhi sleeps at all, but it is already up and about at eight o' clock on a chilly December morning. I am standing right at the spot where Durga Charan Mitra Street branches off Jatindra Mohan Avenue—right between Shankar Das's taxi stand and a small brick structure that serves as a nursery for the children of the prostitutes. But Shankar Das, the taxi driver, is not to be seen at the stand even though he knew I was coming.

I have not come to Sonagachhi alone. I have brought my wife along so that I am not mistaken for a prospective client by the women or the pimps. Just as we wonder what to do next, since Shankar Das is not to be seen, we hurriedly step aside to make way for a hand-pulled rickshaw that ploughs into the street. Seated on the rickshaw is the largest woman I have ever seen. She must be in her fifties: her eyes are big and terrorising, and she wears the authoritative air of an ill-tempered queen. She is clad in a black night dress, which is wet, and has an aluminium *ghoti*, a small pot used for storing or pouring water, gripped between her thighs. She must be the madam of one of the brothels, returning home after bathing in the Ganga. Many, many winters ago, she must have entered the same street for the first time as a young, nervous and needy woman—never to leave again.

'You have come to see Shankar *da*, haven't you?' a taxi driver, suddenly appearing from nowhere, asks me.

'That's right.'

'He will be here any moment. He wants you to wait in the school,' he says, opening the door of the shack that serves as a nursery for the children of prostitutes. 'It's not a good idea for you people to wait in the open.'

He seats us on a wooden bench and leaves. I look around the room. The blackboard, which bears the previous day's date, has the sun and an umbrella drawn on it with a chalk. Obviously, the nursery is functional. Against the wall opposite the blackboard, battered aluminium trunks are piled up. Rolled-up red flags rest in a corner. Patriotic Bengali songs are blaring from a park across the road: I recognise many of them. Bengal has easily produced far more patriotic songs than many other regions of India put together, and they remain in circulation, played at homes and during political functions, even though the British left sixty-five years ago.

Shankar Das arrives. He apologises for keeping us waiting. The Bengali taxi driver is a rare breed to begin with, and Shankar Das, who is wearing a monkey cap, a pair of spectacles and a sombre expression, looks more like a knowledgeable school teacher this morning. He certainly talks like one.

He is fifty-seven now. He grew up across the road in Dorjipara, in one of the numerous houses around the park from where patriotic songs are blaring now. Right now the loudspeakers are playing the famous Tagore song which wasn't exactly meant to be a patriotic song but was a source of strength for many patriots: *Jodi tor daak shune keyo na aashe tobe ekla cholo re*—If no one pays heed to your call, walk alone.

'I came to the taxi line because I could not find a government job. For a while I drove for the Writers' Buildings. I would drive around the personal assistants of ministers—this was in the mid-1980s—but even then I could not find a government job. So I began driving a taxi full time.

'Once I started driving a taxi, I realised life is not easy for taxi drivers and I joined the Bengal Taxi Association. Later I became a member of CITU'—Centre of Indian Trade Unions, run by the CPM—'and eventually brought this taxi stand under the CITU umbrella. I also take care of this nursery, which is run by an NGO. There are several nurseries and schools in this area, meant for the children of the women who live here.'

'What about your children?' I ask him, 'What do they do? Who all do you have at home?'

'I have my wife, two sons and a daughter-in-law. The elder son is into animation and the younger has recently joined Axis Bank in Jadhavpur.'

'You obviously did not want them to join the taxi line.'

'They had asked me, but I refused. I wanted them to study. This line is tough. Every single day I see people behave badly, hear them talk filth. I do not like it at all. How could I have exposed my sons to such filth? Decent people do not take the taxi from this stand. I myself don't stay here beyond 8 pm on most days: I like to leave home safe and reach home safe.'

'Who exactly owns the brothels of Sonagachhi?' I ask him.

Shankar Das adjusts his spectacles and says, 'In north Calcutta, the prostitution business originally began in Baghbazar and Bowbazar. While it continues to thrive in

Bowbazar, although on a smaller scale, the business in Baghbazar moved to Sonagachhi a long time ago, even when the British were around.

'Most of the houses are owned by women we call Agrawaali. They are women who hail from Agra and belong to a community that is known to have been in the prostitution business for centuries.

'The brothels were originally houses belonging to Bengalis. These women moved in as tenants, made money and eventually bought over the houses. Today there are hardly any Bengali houses in the neighbourhood.

'Most of the prostitutes these days come from Bangladesh. There are many from Nepal as well, even though they say they are from Darjeeling, Sikkim and other places in the northeast. They mostly change their names.

'Some girls come on their own, while some are promised work and tricked into coming here. Once they come here, they cannot go back. They are poor and in need of work and money, so they have no choice but to stay. How well a girl is treated depends a lot on the *maalkin*—the owner of the brothel. Every brothel is run by a *maalkin*, who is a retired prostitute herself.

'There are two kinds of brothels here: the ones that are run with the help of pimps, called *dalal bari*; and the ones that are rented by girls who live in other parts of Calcutta and come here for sex work during the day time. They have to pay Rs 125 per day as rent.

'In a *dalal bari*, it is the pimp who finds the client, helps him choose a girl, fixes the rate and takes all responsibility. Girls living in such brothels cannot leave, they are like prisoners, but they are usually protected against sadistic behaviour by clients. Clients can ask them to sing and dance but cannot subject them to any kind of sexual torture. The girls too are punished if they are caught stealing from the clients. The pimp gets twenty-five per cent as his commission.

'In the brothels that are rented on a daily basis, the girl has to share fifty per cent of her earnings with the *malkin*. This is called the *aadhiya* system. There are no pimps involved here, but at the same time no one can be held responsible if anything untoward happens. A client can lose his valuables, a girl can be subjected to sexual torture, but there will be no one to complain to.

'Sex can be cruel here. Once there was a girl travelling in my taxi, who showed me cigarette marks on her body. She said, "How will I go home now?" I was shocked when I saw the burns and asked her why she had not complained to the *maalkin*. She replied that the *maalkin* herself had insisted on her spending time with the man.

'Clients often have the strangest of fetishes. One man who comes here occasionally likes the girl to only spit on him—and he licks the spittle. He does not have sex. Another man comes here just to apply vermillion on the girl's head. No sex, he just comes here to "marry" a new girl each time. One night there was a raid and this man was among those rounded up by the police. It turned out that he had "married" for the $1,001^{st}$ time that night.

'I know these things because I have been here for more than thirty years. I know many of the girls, I know the cops, I am also familiar with some of the clients because I drop them home. Sometimes a client might get emotionally involved with a girl and even end up marrying her.

'I know of a girl from Maniktala who fell in love with a salesman and married him. They had two sons, but soon the husband lost his job. Unable to bear the expenses, he sent her to Sonagachhi to work under the *aadhiya* system. The neighbours were told that she had found a clerical job in Sealdah. A Marwari man who would often visit the brothel fell in love with her. He bought her a two-acre plot in the outskirts and built a house for her. She now lives there and he visits her every weekend.

'But I know of another girl, who got married to a client only to be sold by him to a brothel in Bombay. She was locked up in a room for days. She refused to eat. The watchman there took pity on her and helped her escape to the railway station. She got into a train to Howrah and hid in the toilet to avoid getting caught by the ticket checker. But she was caught in Burdwan, just an hour before she was to reach Howrah. She was detained for several hours at the Burdwan station before being released by a kind-hearted officer, who put her back on a train to Howrah. Upon reaching Howrah she realised that she was penniless and had nowhere to go. She once again ended up in Sonagachhi.

'There is no end to the sad stories. I can go on and on. I feel sad even narrating them to you. Of late, the Agrawaalis have started a new business. They pool in money and buy posh flats, where they put teenaged girls—virgins. Their rates vary from Rs 1 lakh to Rs 5 lakh per night.'

'Rs 5 lakh for a night?' I ask in disbelief.

'You have no idea how much people can shell out. There are many people who believe that certain diseases can be cured by having sex with a virgin. For a rich man eager to rid himself of a particular disease, five lakh rupees is loose change.'

In the park across the road, patriotic songs have stopped playing and speeches have taken over. I ask Shankar Das if he would like to accompany us to the *mazaar* of Sanaullah Ghazi, supposed to be located on the opposite end of the street. He refuses, politely but firmly.

'We are under strict instructions from the party not to walk down the street or be seen near any of the brothels. We are supposed to stay in the taxi stand. But do not worry, it is safe for you to go up to the *mazaar*,' he says.

I thank Shankar Das and take my first determined step into what has always been believed to be Asia's largest red-light district, with my wife walking by my side. The morning sun has divided the breadth of the street into two equal halves: shaded and sunny. Dogs are asleep on the sunny side. We walk on the shaded side, since we are keeping to the left.

My nervousness begins to melt away when I find signs of normal life in a locality that most Calcuttans have only heard about: fish stalls, *paan* and cigarette stalls, sweet shops, shops selling mobile phones and recharge coupons, hand-pulled rickshaws, girls in uniform rushing to school. If I look hard, I just might find a second-hand bookshop. But right now I am looking straight ahead in order to avoid eye contact with the women lining the street.

They are of different shapes and sizes and ethnicities, clad in skirts, jeans and sarees, standing apart from one another as if strangers at a bus stop. Some appear as young as the school-going girls, who are mostly likely to have been born in Sonagachhi. The younger prostitutes are shy: they sport a suppressed smile and look embarrassed. The older ones gape at passersby and are eager to strike a bargain. What unites them is their eagerness to look presentable, which makes them wear gaudy makeup—you can tell from a mile that they are waiting to sell sex.

I am not sure whether these women, soliciting business themselves, work under the *aadhiya* system or belong to *dalal baris*. There is no way I can find out. According to Shankar Das, the taxi driver, the best girls in the trade don't even get to see the sunlight: they are presented only to rich clients.

If you were to ignore the prostitutes, Sonagachhi would be just another busy neighbourhood in old Calcutta. But the prostitutes are hard to ignore. Their dominating presence is what sets Sonagachhi apart from the rest of Calcutta.

AT THE GRANITE-WALLED tomb of the preacher who gave Sonagachhi its name, I am met by a signboard which forbids visitors from coming to the tomb after eating beef.

A *muzawar*—caretaker—appears from inside and eyes us suspiciously at first. When I explain him the purpose of my visit, he breathes easy.

'Sanaullah Ghazi came from Iraq to preach Islam about 700 years ago. He was also known as Sona Pir Baba,' he tells me. 'This place used to be a graveyard during his time.

'Over the centuries, a settlement came up here, and until 1947 there were a number of Muslim houses in Sonagachhi. But during the riots of 1947 and 1964, most of the Muslims living here left.

'Even today, thirty to forty people come to the *mazaar* everyday from far and near. They are people who are troubled, who want a job, who want a child, who want disputes to be resolved.

'But unfortunately, decent people are unable to come here because of the reputation of this place. We have nothing against (the prostitutes), but we would like the government to relocate them to another place. They also need to earn a living, after all.'

12

AS DUSK FALLS, the neon signs of the jewellery shops in Bowbazar come alive. But the lights have no effect on the face of Mahadeo Yadav, who is perched on the footrest of his rickshaw that is parked by the road, staring ahead blankly. He is sitting on his haunches, hugging his knees to keep himself warm in the biting cold, so withered and lifeless as if he had been dead for days without anyone noticing.

Who would, after all, notice a rickshaw-puller parked by the road to check whether he is breathing or not. Yet when the same rickshaw-puller goes about his work, playing the human horse, he becomes the most-noticed man in Calcutta. He makes a great subject for photographers, writers and filmmakers. He is the icon of poor Calcutta. Many a renowned actor has pulled the rickshaw in films set in the city.

Calcutta is said to have about 6,000 rickshaw-pullers running on its roads, confined mostly to the old neighbourhoods. They have some things in common, apart from their poverty. Nearly all of them hail from Bihar. All of them wear the *lungi* to work, perhaps for better mobility. And almost all of them are elderly: I am yet to see a young man hand-pulling a rickshaw. It can be a heart-rending sight to watch a man almost as old as your father panting his way through the roads and streets of old Calcutta, clad in just a vest and a *lungi* and often barefooted.

Mahadeo Yadav, the rickshaw-puller, is in fact my father's age. He is seventy, and has been pulling a rickshaw—it's been the same rickshaw—in and around Bowbazar for fifty years. For him fifty years, half a century, is not a landmark but merely the time that has lapsed ever since he came to Calcutta from Gaya in Bihar to earn a living.

He lives all alone in Calcutta, in a lodge inside a nearby lane, paying a monthly rent of fifty rupees. He is out with his rickshaw between three in the afternoon and ten in the night, sometimes earning sixty or seventy rupees a day and sometimes nothing. Every month, without fail, he sends Rs 300 to his wife back home, and once every year, visits her. The wife lives with the extended family in the village. They have a daughter, who is married and lives in another village.

'I will pull rickshaw as long as I can,' he tells me, 'this is my only source of livelihood.'

'But you are already seventy. Are you able to manage?'

'These days I tire easily. Sometimes my feet hurt, sometimes my back hurts. But do I have a choice?'

He answers all my questions without looking at me even once, but continuing to stare ahead blankly, his arms folded around his knees. I take a good look at his rickshaw. If you discount the rexine upholstery, it could well belong to a museum, so antiquated it looks.

The two—the rickshaw and the rickshaw-puller—make quite a pair.

13

'IF SOMEONE KILLS your father,' Tarun Dutta tells me, 'and you want to avenge his death, just take the killer to the races. He will destroy himself sooner than later. Races destroy people.'

Mr Dutta, who is the father of a dear friend of my wife, is a member of the Royal Calcutta Turf Club, and we have come to his house in old Calcutta to collect passes for the New Year's Day races at the club.

'I have always taken the races casually,' says Mr Dutta. 'Had I taken it as a means to gamble, I would have been a pauper today. Many of my friends have been ruined, completely destroyed, just because they made a habit out of betting on horses.

'You make money one day, but lose for the next three days, before you win again. By then you are an addict. And then you start losing again and wait for the next win, betting even more heavily. By then you are on the path to becoming a pauper.'

Mr Dutta lights up a cigarette and pulls out a tip sheet—a crudely-printed booklet meant to guide bettors—and briefs me about the different forms of betting. Only two names register in my mind, quinella and tanala, because they sound exotic.

As he hands us our passes—badges that are meant to be worn on the wrist—his wife arrives from the kitchen to say that lunch is ready. She has prepared mutton biryani because she knew my wife and I were coming.

Over lunch they talk about their recent holiday in Australia, where Mrs Dutta, by her own admission, wore a bikini for the first time in her life. I imagine her on an

Australian beach. She wouldn't have looked too out of place. Even though she is, by her own admission again, sixty-three, it is evident that she looks after herself.

For that matter even Mr Dutta doesn't look his age. He is seventy-five—that makes him five years older to my father—but he doesn't come across as an elderly man, even though he is diabetic and comes to Chennai once a year to see his doctor. He remains a heavy smoker and, as far as I know, he continues to drink heavily every night. Since his children are settled into high-paying jobs, he spends his money—he manufactures cartons for big companies—travelling around the world with his wife and visiting casinos.

'Come, I will show you my office,' he tells us after lunch, 'I've just done it up.' The carton-manufacturing plant is on the ground floor, he lives on the first floor, and his office, where he is taking us now, is on the second floor.

We climb up the stairs and are shown into a hall which is bare except a freshly-polished wooden desk on which sits an outdated computer monitor with a bulging screen. One look at the computer and you can tell that it was last switched on some ten years ago.

'Poor Mr Dutta,' I tell myself, 'he doesn't even know how to operate a computer, but still he has kept one, that too an antiquated model, on his desk to give the hall a semblance of an office.'

Suddenly I notice a pair of Bose speakers, placed diagonally across the hall. 'Wow, Bose speakers!' I exclaim, 'but where's the music player?'

'Come I will show you,' he leads us into an adjoining room, where I find a cot and a couple of plastic chairs. In a corner is a desk, on which sits a 27-inch flat-screen computer monitor.

'Is this your son's room?' I ask Mr Dutta.

'My son lives in Bombay, don't you know that? This is my office, my room. This is where I relax in the evenings. This computer is also mine.' He switches it on.

The sound that a computer monitor makes when it comes to life is amplified by the Bose speakers—two in the hall and two where we are sitting now. It is the most familiar sound of the twenty-first century and yet I had never heard it this loud. Mr Dutta, with the flourish of a magician, unravels his latest passion: collecting videos and songs from the internet.

The folders on his computer are very well-organised. There is one that contains only Hollywood classics, another that has only Hollywood action films, yet another that has only Bengali classics. Then there are folders containing only songs, classified under 'English', 'Hindi' and 'Bengali'. Even the porn sitting on his computer has been categorised under 'X', 'XX' and 'XXX'.

To show off his impressive collection—more than that, his ability to build such an enviable collection single-handedly—he clicks on a couple of files from every folder except the ones containing porn. I can see that he is tempted to click open even the porn videos, but feels restrained by the presence of my wife, his daughter's best friend.

He then shows us pictures from his recent trip to Australia. I wait to see Mrs Dutta in a bikini, but she is fully clothed in all the pictures that we see of her. She presently walks in with tea.

'Did you tell them that you are also on Facebook?' she asks her husband.

'Not yet,' responds Mr Dutta, losing no time in clicking open his Facebook profile page. 'Both my children are not on Facebook, but both my grandchildren are. I chat with them in the evenings.'

I decide to like Mr Dutta. At seventy-five, he has already lived out most of his life, living it his way. Even if he were to live five more years in the same fashion, which is mostly likely to be the case considering he seems to be in good health, he would have conclusively proven that the lust for life wins over disease and old age.

The lesson I learn from him this afternoon is that life is not just about living but looking forward to live, to unapologetically keep on doing things that give you pleasure no matter how old you are — even if that means smoking, drinking, gambling and watching porn at the age of seventy-five.

I HAPPEN TO spend New Year's Eve at Princeton Club on Prince Anwar Ali Shah Road in south Calcutta, in the company of my wife and her former colleague who is a member of the club.

It is not one of those snooty Calcutta clubs where aristocratic Bengalis still ape their erstwhile British masters, but one of the new middle-class-friendly clubs that are a little less fussy about the dos and don'ts.

The hostess who is guiding revellers through the evening decides to have an on-the-spot contest in between performances by a singer wearing a short dress. She invites five men to the stage and challenges them into downing as many pints of beer as possible in under a minute.

The winner turns out to be a lean, dark, curly-haired man clad in a white jacket. He was already drunk when he went up the stage. He bears a faint resemblance to Mr Dutta, the father of my wife's best friend. He is barely able to stand and has to be helped off the stage once the hostess hands him his gift, contained in a box wrapped in shiny paper. I only hope the gift is not another bottle of beer or wine.

Soon the DJ takes over and we all drink and dance until the stroke of midnight, when we hug and wish one another a Happy New Year. By the time we leave the club, after a hearty dinner, it is one-thirty. Most of the revellers have already gone home. The lawn, bristling with young men and women until an hour ago, is now empty.

But wait, I see one man in the lawn, sitting all alone, conspicuous in the darkness because of his white jacket. He is sitting upright on a chair—his chin on his chest—firmly clutching the gift that is still wrapped in shiny paper.

13

THE FIRST DAY of 2013. I put on the best clothes I have in my temporary wardrobe in Calcutta, and get into a new jacket, a birthday gift from my mother-in-law. My wife had been insisting that I dress well this morning because, according to her, the fashionable come to the New Year's Day races at the Royal Calcutta Turf Club.

As we drive across the Maidan, past the Victoria Memorial, past Fort William, I feel like an important man, clad in an expensive jacket and the badge of the club tied to my wrist. But a prick of regret as we pass Fort William: it's been almost two years that I've been coming to Calcutta to write this book and yet I have never been inside the fort, whose construction in 1758 effectively marked the beginning of British rule in the subcontinent.

Fort William now belongs to the Indian Army, serving as the headquarters of the Eastern Command. I have been speaking to my officer friends from time to time, asking them if they could help me get in. But none of them seem to have sufficient clout to remote-manage my visit from their current locations. It looks like the fort is going to remain out of bounds for me. The gates of the Royal Calcutta Turf Club, however, are wide open for us.

I am as illiterate about horse-racing as a bus driver would be about flying a plane. I have come here to watch not the horses but the people, and I find three categories of them: 1. The 'British' Bengali, the stiff upper-lipped Chatterjees and Roys and Senguptas who would like to believe that India is still being ruled by Lord Dalhousie, 2. The 'Indian' Bengali, the humble variety of Chatterjees and Roys who like to be British on occasions such as this and who speak the language of the British with a Bengali accent, and 3. The others, including rich Marwaris, Sindhis and Punjabis, who are comfortable in their own skins and who rarely pretend to be anybody else.

From what I gather—though I am not sure if I am entirely right—it's only the 'British' Bengalis and the suave Punjabis who have brought their women along—most of the women dizzyingly beautiful and dressed for Paris. For the 'Indian' Bengalis, a day such as this is perfect for a solo outing: their traditional wives would serve them tea once they return home.

Then there is another category of people whom I haven't counted because you find them everywhere: the commoners, who have come here not for an outing or to make a fashion statement but in the hope of making quick money. They are all serious worshippers of Lady Luck: what if she decides to smile on them this morning?

As we watch the races from the members' gallery, I realise it is no fun being there unless you are rooting for particular horses, which means you have to bet. Suddenly I recall two words I had taken down in my notebook: quinella and tanala.

Quinella is a betting in which you predict the first two finishers, irrespective of who comes first and who second. In tanala, you need to predict the first three finishers in correct order, and even if your choices for the second and third places interchange positions, you still make some consolation money.

I decide to play quinella for Rs 200 — after nervously asking several genteel citizens how to go about it — and get back Rs 320. Emboldened by the stroke of luck, I play tanala for Rs 400 in the next race, but get back only Rs 160. I lose the double of what I had earned. I now know what Mr Dutta, the father of my wife's friend, meant when he said that people destroy themselves at the races.

We walk down to the lawn where food stalls — this being Calcutta — are doing brisk business. There is also a makeshift bar, where I buy a can of beer and then walk up and down the lawn, watching people eat. I come across a sight I am not going to forget in a long time:

A 'British' Bengali — a tall, handsome middle-aged gentleman, clad in a suit — is quietly standing in a corner, tucking into hot chicken *tikka*s. An 'Indian' Bengali — also a middle-aged man clad in a suit, but bald and dark — happens to pass by. When he notices the contents of the 'British' Bengali's plate, he suddenly stops and, pointing to the plate, demands to know in heavily-accented English, 'Oowhere phrom you got this?'

The 'British' Bengali, taken aback by the intrusion, ignores the question and moves away.

14

JANUARY 3. INDIA AND PAKISTAN are playing a day-night match at the Eden Gardens. I merely watch the floodlights illuminating the sky over the Maidan, as I neither have the inclination to watch the game nor the contacts to get me tickets or free passes at the last-minute.

I would much rather spend the evening on Park Street, especially in the Oxford Bookstore, considering I am going to leave in a couple of days and am not sure if I am going to come back anytime soon. And so I spend an hour at the bookshop with my wife, looking for nothing in particular and yet looking at everything, even Bengali books, whose titles I read with some difficulty.

Eventually I buy five copies of a slim volume of *Gitanjali*, containing facsimiles of Tagore's selected poems, handwritten in Bengali as well as English by the poet himself. I intend gifting them to friends in Chennai. As soon as we reach the exit after paying for the books, a voice calls out from behind.

'Excuse me, aren't you the guy who wrote the book about railway junctions?'

'That's right.'

'Do they have a copy here?'

'I don't think so, though I can see a copy of my second book right there.'

'The one you wrote about Chennai?'

'That's right, how do you know?'

'I am Colonel Shankar,' he extends his hand. 'We are friends on Facebook in case you didn't know. I come from Chennai.'

He buys the only copy of *Tamarind City*, my Chennai book, which has been sitting on the shelves of the Oxford Bookstore for several months now. I feel happy as well as sad: happy, because someone has finally bought the copy, sad because I am not sure if it would be replenished anytime soon. He pulls out a felt pen to get it signed by me.

'Are you posted in Calcutta?' I ask the colonel.

'I was a few years ago. At present I am posted in Pachmarhi. I came all the way just to watch the match, because Dhoni happens to be a good friend of mine.'

'Oh, really? Who won?'

'We lost, unfortunately.'

'Would you know anyone posted in Fort William? That's one place I am yet to see in Calcutta.'

'Why, I am staying there tonight. Why don't you guys have breakfast with me tomorrow morning? Eight o' clock?'

Who ever thought that *Chai, Chai*, the book about railway junctions, published at a time when this book was not even on the horizon, would someday earn me friends and help open doors in Calcutta.

THE NEXT MORNING I wake up earlier than usual so that we are able to reach Fort William on time. If an Army officer says eight o' clock, it has to be eight o' clock. We make it by 8.10 and find Colonel Shankar waiting for us outside the checkpost at the main gate. He gets into our car and we enter Clive's Country, which is cut off entirely from the noise and the pollution and the politically-charged air of Calcutta.

Fort William, which is spread over 177 acres, is indeed a separate country within Calcutta. Its lingua franca is not Bengali but Hindi, which happens to be the language of every serving Indian soldier, irrespective of which corner of the country he hails from. Unlike Fort St George in Chennai, where you are constantly reminded that you are in a Tamil city because the seat of the Tamil Nadu government happens to be inside the fort, Fort William is strictly Army property. It even has its own traffic lights. The lights must be obeyed without fail, which is not at all difficult for its inhabitants because discipline is their second nature.

The colonel guides us to the officers' mess, and we soon enter a gate guarded by two white lions. From a plaque I learn that until 1977, the two lions adorned the nearby Princep Ghat, but when a portion of the ghat was taken away to build the Vidyasagar Bridge, the two majestic figures, already decaying and much vandalised, were rescued by the Army and placed inside Fort William.

At the mess, where, like most other officers' messes, a smell from the British days hangs in the air, orderlies serve us hot *alu parathas*, toast and omelette. Over breakfast we get to know Colonel Shankar better. After a recent stint in Bhutan, he is now teaching the Bhutanese language to Indian soldiers at Pachmarhi. He is also a serious autograph hunter and likes to have pictures taken with celebrities. Friendliness seems to come naturally to him: he even speaks to the orderlies in a manner as if they were his buddies. He is the kind of officer about whom everybody will have something nice to say. But then, autograph hunters have to be friendly.

After breakfast he shows us around the mess, which is decorated with memorabilia related to India's victory in the 1971 war against Pakistan that led to the creation of Bangladesh. Even though Clive's Fort William was built 250 years ago to protect the military and commercial interests of the East India Company, its most glorious military moment came twenty-five years after India's independence from the British, when it sent soldiers to help Bengalis across the border win their freedom from Pakistan. Needless to say, the main mess hall is dominated by a three-dimensional mural replicating a photograph that Indians of my generation have grown up with: the head of Pakistan's Eastern Command, Lt Gen. AAK Niazi, signing the instrument of surrender in the presence of his Indian opposite, Lt Gen. Jagjit Singh Aurora, and a host of other senior Indian officers.

Soon we are driving past Dalhousie Barrack, said to be the largest military accommodation block in the world. The four-storey building houses 1,000 soldiers along with their rations, weapons and equipment. On the large ground that separates us from the barrack, a football match is about to begin in one portion while soldiers are going through drills in another.

We drive into the Kitchener House, built in 1771 to house British Army officers but which in 1784 became the official residence of the commander-in-chief of the British Indian Army. Lord Wellesley, when he was the governor-general of India, stayed here from 1799 to 1803. When the capital of British India shifted to New Delhi in 1912, Kitchener House became the officers' mess of the Bengal Presidency, and continues to serve as the officers' mess of the Bengal Area of the Indian Army.

This morning, however, the silence of a hermitage prevails over the perfectly-preserved palatial house from where the destiny of India would be decided once upon a time. In any case, our entry is allowed only up to the verandah where, among the exhibits on display, is a 'time gun' manufactured in 1756, which would be fired at one o' clock every afternoon to indicate the time to the ships on the Hooghly. In a corner sits a hand-pulled rickshaw, the only native element I have noticed so far in Fort William.

On our way out, we stop at St Peter's Church, built in 1784, which now serves as the library of the Eastern Command. What used to be the altar—complete with the depiction of scenes from the Bible on stained glass—is undergoing renovation. The young workers giving this corner a facelift are hopefully aware that the building is almost two-and-a-half centuries old and that the wall they are working on needs to be dealt with care.

The rest of the church is occupied by bookshelves, which are overlooked by the portraits of Raja Ram Mohun Roy and Subhas Chandra Bose—two more native elements in the Army-controlled fort. When was the church converted into a library and, more importantly, why was it converted into a library? The two questions were to strike me only later, much later.

Right outside the church is placed a small cannon, identified as the 'oldest gun of Fort William'. But the gun was never fired on an enemy. As I run my palm on its pockmarked surface, trying to get a feel of history, I read the information about the fort provided on a plaque that covers an outer wall of the church:

'From the ramparts and fortifications hundreds of guns could be fired, but never was a single shot fired on a besieging force. The fort could be defended against any enemy but none came to test its impregnability. Fort William has a reputation of being the only fort in India which was never besieged.'

Robert Clive had got the East India Company to spend two million pounds in building the fort. He chose to build it on Gobindapur, one of the three riverside villages that constituted the original township of Calcutta. The construction began in October 1757, four months after he won the Battle of Plassey, and finally ended in 1781, seven years after his death. The end result was that Gobindapur vanished from the face of Calcutta and the jungles around it became the Maidan.

So far, I had walked on the riverbank at Sutanuti and also walked the streets of Kalikata. This morning, I have, at last, set foot on what used to be Gobindapur. My Calcutta experience is complete. I have gathered enough material for the book. I am not going to return in a long, long time.

15

I WAKE UP feeling sad. A city is a goldmine as long as you are still writing about it. Everything around you is a nugget of gold. But once you have turned in the manuscript, you return to the same city only to stare at an empty pit, stripped of all the gold. Calcutta would be one such pit when I come back again, whenever that may be.

The flight to Chennai is at eight-thirty in the evening. But right now it is only eight-thirty in the morning, which means I have the whole day in Calcutta. I want to go back to the village of Sutanuti and spend some time on the riverbank. I would like to end this journey at the spot where Calcutta began.

So once again I am walking down Chitpur Road, or Rabindra Sarani, trying to absorb the atmosphere as much as I can so that it stays in my head long after I have returned to Chennai.

One moment a hand-pulled rickshaw makes way for an oncoming taxi, and the next moment the same taxi makes way for an oncoming tram. Call it near-collision or coexistence.

On the sidewalks, meanwhile, life goes on the way it must have for over three centuries: shopkeepers killing time, pedestrians hard pressed for time, labourers carrying loads on their head, locals idling away.

Even though I have had breakfast, I stop at a modest snack stall, a grimy cubbyhole, unable to resist joining the small crowd that is gathered outside it. The stall is manned by two grim-looking Bihari men who seem to be taking their jobs very seriously: one of them is dealing with the customers and the other, sitting in the deep end, is frying the snacks to keep up with the demand. I have *radha ballabi* (stuffed *puris* served with potato curry) followed by *kachoris* laced with *heeng* (asafoetida). I pay the bill—ten rupees—and move on.

I know I am in Kumartuli because I see a row of idols of Goddess Saraswati, still straw and bamboo, placed by the road. Saraswati Puja is about a month away. In one of the workshops, a young artisan clad in Bermuda shorts and perched on a stool, is giving finishing touches to the outstretched arm of Subhas Bose, whose birth anniversary is barely two weeks away.

A few metres ahead, two young artisans, also clad in Bermuda shorts, are working on a larger-than-life statue of Rabindranath Tagore. As far as I know, neither the poet's birth anniversary nor his death anniversary falls anytime soon, but then, when has Calcutta needed an occasion to celebrate Tagore?

I know I am walking parallel to the river and all I need is to turn left into one of the lanes to reach the ghat. But to be doubly sure, I ask a man how far the ghat is.

'Not even a two-minute walk. Just get into that lane,' he tells me.

'Thank you.'

'Have you come here to watch the shooting?'

'What shooting?'

'There is a film-shooting going on in that very lane. Rupa Ganguly and other stars have come. Go, go, take a look,' he urges me.

I get into the lane and find reflectors set up outside an aged mansion. From unit hands loitering in the compound I learn that the set is on the first floor. I climb up the stairs. No one stops me. The camera has been fixed in the drawing-cum-dining room of what appears to be the house of a once-wealthy Bengali family. On the walls hang several framed black-and-white pictures showing the landlords—or perhaps their ancestors—in their younger days. There is a portrait of Tagore as well, apart from a calendar that carries a picture of Goddess Kali. The film unit has a free run of the house, including the bedroom, where the bed and the bedside furniture look as old as the house itself.

It is one of those houses where the nineteenth century has come to terms with living in the twenty-first century, and I wonder why a family in its right mind should blindly hand over its house to a film unit. I even see a spot boy scratching the wall of the drawing-cum-dining room in some places with a knife to further give it a dilapidated look.

Many members of the crew, including the director and the cinematographer, warmly shake my hand when I introduce myself. They tell me that the film they are working on is called *Kaancher Dewaal*, or Wall of Glass.

So far, back in Chennai, I have seen action sequences or songs being shot for movies. But never have I seen intense scenes, which call for real acting skills of the actors, being captured by the camera. Today I am finally going to see actors emote—up close.

As I chat with the cinematographer, who gives his name as Manoj Mishra, I learn that the entire look of the house—the furniture, the portraits on the walls, the clay pickle jars—is part of the set. The black-and-white portraits on the walls, apart from the other artefacts and embellishments adorning the various rooms, have been sourced by the art director.

So the family that owns the palatial but decaying house is not so foolish after all. If I belonged to that family and had a say in its matters, I would have either chosen to live in this house or turned it into a heritage guest house. The Hooghly is barely a minute's walk away, and the ghat not very far from the spot where Job Charnock had landed three centuries ago—how much more heritage can you get?

I am still talking to the cinematographer when the actors arrive for the shot. I instantly recognise Rupa

Ganguly: I was still a teenager when she played Draupadi in the TV serial *Mahabharata* and the boys in my class found her immensely sexy. She is clad in a purple saree and is smoking a cigarette. She looks far less curvaceous than she does on screen and in photographs. She is accompanied by a tall, slender man, who is wearing a white shirt and pyjamas and is also smoking a cigarette.

'Who's the man with Rupa Ganguly?' I ask the cinematographer.

'That's Adil Hussain. Haven't you seen *English Vinglish*?'

'No.'

'Have you seen *Life of Pi*?'

'No.'

'He was there in both the films.'

Rupa Ganguly stubs out her cigarette and sits down at the dining table to discuss the shot with the director, who had introduced himself to me as Anindo Sarkar. At the same time, Adil Hussain removes his shirt and is now clad only in a white vest and pyjamas, ready for the shot.

I move to a corner so that I am not a hindrance to anyone. The director is still explaining the scene to Rupa Ganguly when a unit hand taps my shoulder.

'I am afraid you will have to leave now. Please don't mind,' the man tells me very politely.

I look in the direction of the director and the cinematographer, hoping they would intervene. But I already don't exist for them. Until a few moments ago, I was a welcome guest, and now I am an intruder. I leave quietly and walk towards the river.

AN ABANDONED IDOL of Goddess Durga, who is seated on a tiger instead of a lion, stands on the ghat facing the river. As if the devotees who had brought her here for immersion changed their minds at the last minute and left her on the banks.

I sit near the idol, on the steps of the ghat, and gaze at the river. Under the noon sun, it is almost the colour of the sky: grey. The monotony is broken by a steamer that glides past, the noise of its engine subdued into a hum by the powerful silence hanging over the ghat.

I count nineteen bathers in all: the men are in their underwear or wearing *gamchhas*, the women in sarees or in petticoats. Barely a couple of kilometres downstream, at the Princep Ghat, in the erstwhile village of Gobindapur, fashionable young men and women must be boarding country boats for a ride on the river. You won't find bathers in *gamchhas* and petticoats there.

Calcutta is indeed a city of paradoxes—more paradoxical than any other in the country. Trade unionists who fearlessly challenge the might of the masters often surrender meekly to the changing weather, reaching for the monkey cap at the slightest hint of chill. The hands that vote for the hammer-and-sickle symbol often sport silver rings embedded with gemstones supposed to have miraculous properties. The minds that epitomise culture, when angered, can forget all about culture and plunge the entire city into chaos. The people who conduct Durga Puja in their neighbourhoods with gaiety are also capable of calling for crippling strikes.

Calcutta, to me, is a sturdy, grime-coated grandfather's clock, whose pendulum was set into motion over 300 years ago and which continues to swing with the same precision between extremities: despair and joy; anger and celebration; chaos and culture; the permissive and the conservative; defiance and deference. As long as the pendulum continues to swing between these extremities, Calcutta will live on.

Why can't I come back one more time—to have yet another drink with Sajal at Floatel, to visit the book fair, to buy some more books from Oxford Bookstore—before I submit the manuscript? So far the idea has been to divide the book into four seasons: Spring, Summer, Autumn and Winter. What stops me from adding one more chapter: Spring Again?

SPRING AGAIN

SPRING AGAIN

1

AND SO, TWO years have passed since I started coming to Calcutta with the purpose of writing this book.

My visits have been of varying durations, most lasting a week and the longest a month, during which I left my footprints in many places, gave out more business cards than I collected, filled up many small notebooks. Whenever memory gets hazy, I only have to look up the notebooks, and suddenly everything comes back.

But memories remain fresh, almost crystal clear, of that pleasant March morning of 2011, when I arrived at the Howrah Station, for the first time not as a son-in-law but as someone who now had the licence—publisher's contract—to roam the city on his own.

That entire day remains etched in my mind: the taxi ride from Howrah Station; the fragrant spring breeze sweeping through the room as I lay on the bed reading the *Telegraph*; browsing through new arrivals at the Oxford Bookstore; the brief chat with the pimp of Park Street; sitting across the Bengali beauty at the restaurant of the hotel afloat on the Hooghly.

I must say, at the risk of sounding clichéd, that there is something magical about the spring in Calcutta. Walks are pleasant, songs sound better, food smells better, drink tastes better—and the women look more beautiful. Or is it all in my mind?

It's spring again. Only that I am two years older now. But some people never seem to grow up.

'*Beware! Didi in the mood to whip,*' the main headline of the *Telegraph* screams when I pick up the paper on reaching home from the airport. Mamata Banerjee, it turns out, had visited the book fair the day before, and because her car had delayed showing up as she prepared to leave the crowded venue, she had shouted at her security officer, '*Chabkano uchit aapnader!*'—You people should be whipped!

This evening I also need to be at the book fair. I am one of the five 'dignitaries' who are launching a set of four slim books. The authors of these four books are: my cousin, my cousin's father (my father's elder brother), my cousin's friend, and the husband of the cousin's friend.

My cousin's father—my uncle—is a talented wordsmith, his biggest claim to fame being the famous Manna Dey song *Ei kule aami*, whose lyrics he wrote. He never had to buy a fridge or colour television or motorcycle for his home: he would win them in slogan-writing contests. And now this was his proud moment: his book being released, in front of an audience of some two hundred people, by five 'prominent personalities', one of them being his nephew.

Each of the 'prominent personalities' are handed the four books packed in colourful wrappers. Each time we tear open a wrapper, a book is released. The audience claps.

One of the 'personalities' sharing the stage with me is Prithviraj Sen, who is aiming to enter the Guinness Book of World Records as the world's most prolific writer. We smile at each other. The next event is his, when his

1,092nd book—the one that supposedly breaks the existing record set by Mr Robert-Something and makes him eligible for the Guinness Book—will be released. So while the rest of the 'dignitaries' get off the stage, Prithviraj Sen remains seated on the ornate chair.

I decide to give his event a miss. Having fulfilled my family obligations, I now need to take a look at the stalls and buy some books for myself. But I return for the post-event press conference organised by Prithviraj Sen's well-wishers to announce to the world his just-accomplished feat. The hall where the press conference is being held is packed.

'He will be immortal someday,' a speaker is thundering into the microphone, 'it's just a matter of time. I pray that he finishes 1,500 books soon. The world has not acknowledged him so far, but you can't deny that he has published 1,092 books. It shows that there are people who are willing to publish him. He needs acceptance, how else will he write!'

The speaker then turns to Prithviraj Sen and exhorts him, 'The media will come to you one day, you just keep writing. The day the media discovers your genius, I'll have to hide you somewhere or else they won't leave you alone!'

Prithviraj Sen retains a smug smile throughout the speeches made in his honour. When it's his turn to speak, there are cheers from a section of the audience. 'For the past twenty-five years,' he tells the gathering, 'I have been busy chasing this record, because of which I could only think of quantity and not quality. Now I will have to think of quality.'

2

'DO YOU REMEMBER there was a huge controversy when the song "*Chhukar mere man ko*" came out?' Atri asks me.

'I do,' I replied, 'even though I was only nine or ten years old then.' The opening bars of the song, composed by Rajesh Roshan for the Amitabh Bachchan film *Yaarana*, were supposed to be a copy of the famous Tagore song "*Tomar holo shuru*", inviting objections from the Visva-Bharati.

'And do you know how the controversy got diffused?'

'No, I don't.'

'It got diffused when RD Burman said in an interview that the Tagore song itself was based on a Scottish folk tune. You see, Tagore used to travel far and wide, and he too would be inspired by folk songs from other countries.'

'And have you heard that Bengali song, sung by RD Burman himself, "*Bolo ki achhe go, tomari aankhitey*"?

'Yes, of course.'

'RD Burman had changed the scale of this song to create a very famous Hindi song—a very popular Kishore Kumar song. Guess which one?'

'No idea.'

Atri lowers his voice and starts singing, '*Phir wohi raat hai, phir wohi raat hai khwaab ki . . .*'

'Oh, the song from *Ghar*! It is one of my favourites.'

It's eight in the morning and Atri Bhattacharya and I are having breakfast at Tollygunge Club, sitting by the golf course which runs like a green carpet as far as the eyes can see. '164 acres,' says Atri, chewing on a sausage, when he sees me admiring the velvety expanse.

Atri, a 1989-batch IAS officer, is the secretary of the

water resources investigation department of the government of West Bengal. From this morning, he is also going to hold the additional charge of information and cultural affairs department—the *Telegraph* had the news this morning.

It is, however, only a coincidence that West Bengal's cultural affairs secretary is discussing music with me. We both happen to be fans of Kishore Kumar and RD Burman and he, additionally, of Satyajit Ray as well. It helps that we are nearly the same age—he is only four years older—because it means we have grown up with the same songs.

We had mostly discussed music on our way to the Tollygunge Club. Since he too lives in Salt Lake, he had picked me up, in a white ambassador fitted with a red beacon light. I had tried getting him to talk about the functioning of Mamata Banerjee's government, but like any conscientious bureaucrat, he changed the subject each time I brought up Mamata Banerjee. And so we had stuck to the safe gods, Kishore Kumar and RD Burman.

Atri Bhattacharya is a true blue Calcuttan. The son of a civil servant, he studied in Don Bosco and St Xavier's and followed his father's footsteps into taking the civil services exams. When he joined the IAS, he opted for the home cadre—he was the only Bengali in the batch—so that he could live in Calcutta, at the most a few hours away from it, even though West Bengal was a decrepit state at the time and Rajiv Gandhi had just called Calcutta a dying city.

I have known him for sometime now, and even though he, like Tagore, travels far and wide, sometimes on work and sometimes on holiday, he sounds happiest when he is back home—in Calcutta. That's when he cracks the best jokes and is at his sarcastic best, sarcasm being a literary skill in Bengal.

Calcutta is his anchor. So much so that in 2001, when he went on study leave to do a PhD on political economics (whatever that means) at Stony Brook University, he couldn't last beyond two months in America. On the other hand my own IAS-officer cousin, who too had gone on study leave to America, had never returned.

Atri tells me: 'I had a lot of issues with the place, with the intellectual content. Within three weeks I realised, *byapar ta jomchhena* (things are not working out to my liking).

'As an Indian, you are used to a milieu where the people who teach you know more than you. But by the time I went to study there, I had been working with the government for twelve years. I had a lot of experience, a lot of practical knowledge.

'People there, they are nice guys, reasonably bright guys, but about my subject, which was participatory development, they didn't know a thing. One of the teachers was an ex-Marine, who was developing a computational model for elections. His area of knowledge was only the American presidential elections. Whereas back in India, I had conducted all kinds of elections—parliamentary elections, assembly elections, panchayat elections, you name it. I thought, *Ey amaye ki shekhabe?*—What is *he* going to teach me?

'Not only that, I also found people choosing arcane subjects for research. For example, a Greek girl in my class, a very sweet girl, had spent seven years researching sex scandals in American presidency. How is such research going to be relevant to the society? It's like saying, I have done the research, now let somebody else find use for it.

'Moreover, all the calculus and statistics was getting on my nerves. You don't like doing certain things after you have left school. And so I was in two minds, whether to stay on or go back.

'My wife was in New Jersey at the time, she was living with her sister and brother-in-law. I had no class on Fridays, so on Thursday nights I would go down from Long Island to New Jersey.

'One evening, at a party in New Jersey, I happened to mention to an elderly Bengali man that I was in two minds about staying on in America. He told me, "Everybody will tell you to stay on, they will tell you that there is nothing left in Bengal to go back to. But deep inside, they all want to go back to their motherland. I have been living here for forty years. I want to go back too, but it's too late. The longer you stay here, the more difficult it becomes to return. If you want to return, return now."

'What he said made immense sense, but I still hadn't made up my mind. Then one Thursday night, when everybody was sleeping, I happened to watch an interview of Satyajit Ray. Somebody had given me the tape. When the interviewer asked Ray why he hadn't ever worked in Bombay, leave alone Hollywood, he replied'—he imitates the baritone of Ray—"I was born in Calcutta. I grew up here. My entire creative ethos has evolved from here. I do not think my creativity will survive transplantation to any other city."

'I immediately woke up my wife and told her, "We are going back. Boss says there is no city like Calcutta. We are buying the tickets tomorrow." We were back within a month.'

The coffee arrives. There are now more golfers, many of them women, waiting to tee off. Two men among them are wearing red trousers. If you are a member of the Tollygunge Club, often shortened as Tolly Club, you are a somebody in Calcutta. The only people who don't care if you are a somebody are the waiters of elite clubs such as these: for them everybody is a somebody, and therefore a somebody is a nobody.

'But tell me,' I ask Atri, 'what is it about Calcutta that you like?'

'People are very important here. I am not talking about people who are in power or in influential positions, they are important everywhere, in fact less so in Calcutta. I am talking about people as humans. Let me give you an example:

'About two years ago I got a call from a very good friend of mine, a classmate at college, who is the head of one of the top corporate houses in Calcutta. He told me that a classmate of ours, who had become a drug addict, had been found unconscious on a footpath near Deshapriya Park. So a few classmates got together and got this man off the street, put him in a hospital, got him to stay in a house, got him treatment, got him counselling.

'Now this man, the man who had called me, is a highly influential person. He could have just picked the phone and seen to it that the drug-addict classmate is attended to. But he not only involved himself but also other classmates because the man found on the street was one of ours.

'The drug-addict classmate eventually ran away, but that's a different story. The point is this man, the head of the corporate house, spent nearly a year trying to rehabilitate his classmate. This human bond is typical of Calcutta.

'I used to know a media consultant called Shilu Chatterjee. He was a big man in Calcutta and would be travelling all over the world, but on Sundays, come what may, he would go back to his old neighbourhood for *adda* with the people he grew up with. That old bond is important.

'Take Mithun Chakraborty, for example. He is basically a Calcutta boy. After he had become a big star in Bombay, he was once being interviewed on Doordarshan. The interviewer, who knew Mithun very well, began one of his questions like this, "Mithun, you used to live in Jorabagan (a neighbourhood in old Calcutta) . . . " Mithun instantly corrected him, "Please don't say I *used to* live there, I *still* live there. That is my home." This attitude sums up the spirit of Calcutta. One never forgets the old bonds.'

'There is another reason why I came back. My parents are now old. Who will look after them? If something happens to them, it would have taken me thirty-six hours to get back. My father is now over seventy, he keeps saying he has five to ten years more. When your father is contemplating death, the least you can do is be with him.'

3

ON VALENTINE'S DAY, I meet Protima at Flurys. She happens to be the best friend of a friend of mine.

My friend, who I have known from school and who now lives in Singapore, had been telling me of late, 'The next time you are in Calcutta, you *must* meet Protima*di*. She is the most gorgeous woman I've ever known. She is not just a friend, but almost like an elder sister to me.'

And a few days before I left for Calcutta, she had again

reminded me over the phone, almost gushing with pride, 'Do meet Protima*di*. Did I tell you that she is also an accomplished yoga teacher and a face reader? The most gorgeous woman I've ever known. You will like her.'

However, the woman whose hand I shake on Park Street on Valentine's Day turns out to be lean, elderly and sunburned. Only when she sits across the table at Flurys do I notice that she is not just lean but actually fit, and even though she may not qualify as gorgeous, she must have turned heads once upon a time.

'So you teach yoga?' I ask her.

'I just finished a class. How about you, are you also into yoga?'

'Sort of, in the sense that there are phases when I practise religiously, and then there are phases when I barely lift a finger.'

'That's not good. You must practise every single day, just like I do. I can give up everything else but not my practice.'

'It shows.'

'Does it?'

'Yes, you look supremely fit.'

'Oh, I am nothing compared to what I used to be once upon a time. You should have seen me then. Now I look my age.'

'I don't know how old you are.'

'How old do you think I am?'

Years of experience—and commonsense—told me that she would easily be above fifty. But it would be ungentlemanly to disclose to a lady what I thought her actual age was. So I tell her, 'You must be about my age, early forties?'

'Wrong,' she beams, 'I am fifty-four.'
'I am surprised. You don't look it.'
'You are being kind, but thanks anyway.'
'I am sure men still hit on you.'
'Men are men, even when they are old.' She then talks about some of her admirers who, unmindful of their own age and hers, still try to seek her attention, the most persistent of them being a retired teacher, who often drops in at home unannounced.

Soon we are chatting like old friends. Her age, looks and fitness levels become irrelevant. Nearly two hours pass before we step out of Flurys.

Outside Flurys, I light up a cigarette and we stand in a corner of the pavement to say our goodbyes. Suddenly, someone calls out her name: 'Protima! What are you doing on Park Street?' The voice belongs to a stocky grey-haired man who is now standing between us.

'What are you doing here?' he repeats his question.
Protima ignores his question and makes the introductions. 'This gentleman is a journalist from Chennai who is writing a book on Calcutta. And this is Mr Banerjee, he has just retired as a teacher from'—she names a school—'and is also a well-known bodybuilder.'

'But what are you doing here?' he persists with the question.

'I happened to be passing by when I ran into him,' she lies.

'But how do you know him?'
'He is a friend of a very dear friend of mine.'
'And you had to run into him of all people?'
'Forget about that, you tell me how have you been? It's been a while since I last saw you.'

'I have been busy with the contest. Did I not tell you about it? Wait, I will show you some pictures.' The retired teacher takes out his mobile phone and clicks open the photo folder. 'Here, take a look,' he holds the phone in front of our eyes. We see a man, old enough to be a grandfather, clad in a bodybuilder's brief and showing off his rippling muscles. I still don't know if the sight of a sculpted, semi-naked male body has the same effect on women as the image of a semi-naked female body has on men, but Protima shows no emotion except a polite smile as she looks at the pictures.

'But tell me, how do you know him?' the bodybuilder asks as he puts the phone back in his pocket.

'I just told you, he is a friend of a friend.'

He regards me with amusement, and then pats my stomach. 'You need to reduce this. Look at mine, feel it,' he makes me touch his belly, 'Isn't it rock-hard?' He makes Protima touch his stomach too.

I look at my belly. It is true that there are phases when I don't exercise at all, but for the past few months I have been regular at the gym and even though I may not have acquired a six-pack, I certainly don't feel embarrassed about my waistline. I suspect the bodybuilder wants to put me down.

'I had come home the other day,' he tells Protima, 'but you had gone out.'

'Yes, my son told me you had come.'

'These days it is so difficult to find you at home. You seem to be roaming all the time. But tell me, how did you meet this gentleman?'

'I just told you, he is a friend of a friend.'

'I got that, but how did you meet him today? You just ran into him.'

'Yes, I just ran into him.'

'Interesting. But it's not a good idea for you to be standing on the road with a man. Today is Valentine's Day.' He walks away, hesitatingly.

Once the bodybuilder is out of sight, I too say goodbye to Protima and hail a taxi. At a traffic intersection, a eunuch puts her hand inside the window to ask for money. I look away, pretending I have not seen her. She waves her hands at me, as if flinging invisible objects on my face, and curses, *'Baaj parhe'*—May you be struck by lightning.

THE SAME EVENING I return to Park Street to mark Valentine's Day with my wife. We have a drink at Roxy, one of the nightclubs at Park Hotel. She expects the dance floor to fill up so that we can dance, but Roxy remains deserted for most of the evening. Nightlife in Calcutta doesn't seem to be the same anymore.

Walking out of the hotel, I stop at a cigarette shop. A beggar woman comes over, jingling coins in a steel tumbler. The noise is irritating. The shopkeeper shouts at her, *'Bhak!'*—Get lost.

The beggar walks away, but not before delivering a curse, *'Aag lagey teri dukaan ko'*—May your shop catch fire.

4

ON SARASWATI PUJA, I get a taste of life in an aristocratic home—and the *khichuri* cooked in its kitchen. The *khichuri* and the hospitality are warm, but the aristocracy—just like the palatial house—has been weathered by the passage of time.

Saraswati Puja, which marks the beginning of spring, has a youthful flavour, which is natural, considering that the devotees who flock to the goddess of learning are mostly students. On this day, young women drape themselves in yellow sarees, letting it be known to those who matter that they are no longer little girls but are stepping into the spring of their lives. It could be seen as Bengal's Valentine's Day, and very often the two are just a few days apart.

The scale of its celebration is not as large as that of Durga Puja, which is about crowds, and not as small as Lakshmi Puja, which is mostly a household affair. Idols of Saraswati are installed in roadside pandals or in homes and stay there for two days or three before being immersed. Like any other Hindu festival in Calcutta, Saraswati Puja too is more of a social occasion than religious. *Khichuri* is served, gossip is exchanged, music is played—often loudly—in the pandals, teenage romances bud in neighbourhoods.

'Would you like to come to our home for Saraswati Puja,' a young man, who lived in Chennai until recently and would occasionally communicate with me online, had messaged me a couple of days before the festival. He was back in Calcutta now and had come to know that I was in town as well.

I had asked him if I could bring my wife along, and he had said that she was most welcome. The address he had given me was of a house on Debendra Ghose Road in Bhowanipore.

Getting to Bhowanipore, or for that matter Debendra Ghose Road, was not a problem—the taxi driver knew the place well—but finding the house was. On the precise address he had given, stood a faded palatial house that looked abandoned. I only had the name of my would-be host and his phone number. His name did not ring a bell to the shopkeepers in the neighbourhood, and his phone went unanswered.

Eventually, and quite nervously, we entered the tall iron gates of the weather-beaten palatial house to look for signs of habitation inside the building. We hesitantly climbed up the wooden stairs, past a wood-panelled landing where we found a mirror and hooks to hang coats and umbrellas, and were greeted by the smell of incense and of *khichuri*. Soon we could hear the priest chanting the mantras.

Our host, when he spotted me, rushed out to greet us and showed us into the hall where people sat in a semi-circle around the goddess as the priest waved an oil lamp. The hall had been cleared of furniture so that it could become a shrine for a couple of days.

Presently the priest places the lamp in the centre of the room so that the worshippers can warm their palms on the fire and rub the warmth on their foreheads—a way of imbibing the goddess' blessings. I am already hungry for the *khichuri*.

Our young host, Arijit, introduces us to his family members—his mother, his sister, grandaunts and a granduncle. The granduncle, who is eighty-three, takes a liking for us and makes us sit next to him at the dining table.

'You have come home for the first time, but let this not be the last time. I want the two of you to drop by as often as you can,' the granduncle tells us as we all bite into sweets and pieces of fruits—the offering made to the goddess—from our respective leaf-plates.

From him we learn that Debendra Ghose, after whom the road has been named, was his grandfather and, therefore, the great-great grandfather of Arijit, our host. Debendra Ghose was a prosperous lawyer during the late nineteenth century: his classmates at the law college had been Sir Rashbehari Ghosh (one of the founders of Jadavpur University) and Ganga Prasad Mookerjee (the father of Sir Asutosh Mookerjee and the grandfather of Syama Prasad Mookerjee).

This house was built nearly a century ago by Debendra Ghose's son Dhirendra Nath Ghose, also a well-known lawyer during his time. Debendra Ghose had spent his life in another palatial house, built in the 1840s, located a few yards away on the same road, but in place of that house now stands a multi-storied apartment building.

The granduncle tells us about his own career. He had worked in the aviation industry, at a time when flying was a luxury, and then as an art dealer. He still deals in art, but more as a hobby—something that not only keeps him going but also brings him reasonable amounts of money. His son lives in Bangalore and his daughter lives in Zambia: they are unlikely to return to settle in Calcutta anytime soon. Today he is the eldest male member in this house, presiding over a household that comprises barely half a dozen members, mostly elderly widows, though once upon a time he must have been the youngest, watching from behind the curtains the who's who of Calcutta gathering for an *adda* in the same hall where the goddess is sitting now.

'Where are you off to?' the granduncle asks me as I get up from the table, 'You have just come in.'

'I am going to take a look at the house.'

'That's good. I thought you were leaving. You have come home for the first time, but let this not be the last time.'

'Certainly not,' I promise him. I ask my wife—who too has worked in the aviation industry—to keep the conversation going.

As Arijit takes me from one room to another, I feel as if he is showing me around a museum. There are framed black-and-white pictures everywhere: there is Churchill, there is Syama Prasad Mookerjee, there is Ma Anandamayi, and there are many others, including distinguished members of the family and other distinguished citizens of Bengal. The pictures, evidently, remain where they have always been. The furniture in the rooms—and the manner in which they remain arranged—also belong to the period depicted in the frames, which is the first half of the twentieth century.

I suddenly envy Arijit. At a time when people, used to the constraints of living in an apartment, often shell out a fortune to holiday in heritage homes such as this, he is actually living in one, though he isn't sure for how long. After having lived for nearly a decade in Chennai, where he finished his college and started studying for chartered accountancy, he is now toying with the idea of continuing his studies in Mumbai, where his father happens to work. His sister, who has come home for Saraswati Puja, lives in Norway and will soon relocate to New Zealand. She is twenty-four, two years younger than Arijit, and is vivacious and wearing a yellow saree.

The three of us—Arijit, his sister and I—are now standing by the window of a room that had always been reserved for visiting spiritual gurus and holy men. The large room, with a four-poster bed and an exclusive bathroom, smells fresh enough to be ready for occupation. The window overlooks a small temple in a corner of the compound: it is the family temple, which appears to be fashioned after a Japanese Buddhist shrine.

In an adjoining room where Arijit's ancestors in bow ties are glaring down from photo frames, *khichuri* is being served. The guests—distant family members and neighbours who have been invited—are queuing up with their plates to receive the *khichuri*, *labda*, *beguni*, *papad* and *payesh*. I am under strict instructions from the granduncle not to eat with the gathering, but to eat only with him. And so I return to the dining table, where a domestic help plies us piping hot *khichuri*, saving us the embarrassment of asking for more.

'Do you like the food?' the granduncle asks.

'Very much,' I reply.

'And you?' he asks my wife.

'Excellent,' she replies.

'That's good,' the granduncle says. 'You have come home for the first time, but let this not be the last time. I want you to come again. Consider this as your own home.'

5

EVERY SUNDAY MORNING, my mother-in-law is visited by a soft-spoken elderly lady, who comes home to deliver a copy of *Ganashakti*, the CPM mouthpiece.

My mother-in-law does not support any particular political party and reads only *Bartaman*, known to be a neutral paper. Yet she indulges the woman every Sunday, not only making small talk (something she is unaccustomed to doing) and offering her tea but also paying for the copy of *Ganashakti*. Once the woman leaves, she glances through the headlines of the paper, spending not even five minutes on it, and puts it away. If I happen to be around, she always remarks to me without fail, '*Mohila ti bhalo*' — the woman is a nice sort.

For my mother-in-law, the woman is part of her Sunday ritual. For the woman, who lives nearby, bringing us a copy of *Ganashakti* every Sunday morning is a political ritual. She is, after all, married to Marxism, apart from being married to a man who is also married to Marxism.

The husband and wife, both retired government employees, had been active CPM workers during their younger days. But now, apart from age, responsibilities too have caught up them. They have a daughter, who is married and lives with her husband and child a few streets away. On weekdays, the daughter, a software engineer with a multination firm, leaves the child in the care of her parents when she goes to work. It's only on Sundays that the elderly couple is free from the responsibility of babysitting their grandchild, and the woman sets out to distribute copies of *Ganashakti* to the few homes she has gained access to over the years. She kills two birds with a stone: socialising with women her age in the neighbourhood and at the same time promoting communist thought.

Politics in India remains, by and large, a male domain. It is still rare to find married women — barring the ones who belong to erstwhile royalty or to political families — also wedded to a political party or ideology. India's most famous women politicians, discounting the ones who hail from political families, are all gutsy spinsters.

Only in Bengal, and to some extent in Kerala, do you often find even ordinary married women—the office goers as well as homemakers—being married to an ideology as well. And very often the ideology in question happens to be communism, because it insists on gender equality.

I find such women excessively attractive. They may be very feminine—charming and soft-spoken, blushing when you pay them a compliment—but steely when it comes to defending their political beliefs. They will seldom get into an argument with you, leave alone a confrontation, but will very gently make you see their point.

Indrani Roy is one such woman. She is thirty, married, a reporter with a Bengali paper—and a leftist. She shakes my hand shyly and leads me into Presidency College, her alma mater. It was her idea that we meet in the college.

Students' union elections are round the corner, and the college walls are plastered with posters—the slogans are all in Bengali and it's going to take me a long time to read them. We walk past the slogans, past a yet-to-be-immersed idol of Saraswati standing in the portico, and go behind the college building to where the canteen is. Since the college is closed today, the canteen also is closed, even though Indrani had expected it to be open.

We settle on the steps of the canteen. There is not a soul in sight in the college except a good-natured dog who interrupts our conversation periodically, sometimes by licking my feet and sometimes by sniffing Indrani.

'So you want to know about me,' Indrani fixes her gaze on the ground. 'Where do I begin? I grew up in Bagbazar, where our family had come to live ever since it migrated from East Bengal in 1964. It was an upper-class neighbourhood then, only good families lived there.

'It was a rented house. Before I was born, we had twenty-six people, from the same family, living in that three-storey, ten-room house. Such houses are no longer found in Calcutta, they are all disappearing.

'By the time I was born, there were only eight members left. Many had left to work and had their own places to stay. Those who had stayed behind were my parents, my *jethu* (uncle) and his wife, their son, my grandmother, and my father's aunt.

'The Baghbazar of that time was very different from the Baghbazar of today. Life was not as fast. One of my earliest memories from those days is strolling with my *dada* (uncle's son) to the jetty close by. The Ganga was very close to our house.

'I went to Nivedita School. The school was set up by Sister Nivedita, a disciple of Swami Vivekananda. I also remember the play sessions at the school and the evening play sessions in front of our house. We had a lot of sports, but my mother believed that too much playing would adversely affect academics.

'But *dada* always got to play, and he played with the so-called *basti* (slum) boys. I had this immense desire to play, so much so that whenever I saw an empty space I would start to run. Once I almost met with an accident because of this.

'By the time I got to the fifth standard, my *jethu* and his family left, they went to Belgachhia. *Jethu* was a government servant, and he had got a government accommodation there. We were left behind in that house. I missed them a lot.

'My introduction to communism was through my *jethu*. He was a hardcore communist, unlike the communists of today. He still is one. I also read a lot of Swami Vivekananda, since I went to school started by his disciple. There are two things Vivekananda talked about: 1. Men are in pain and are being exploited, there is sadness all over and 2. The solution lies in devoting yourself to the divine. I ignored the second point.

'We were never a very religious family. My grandmother was the disciple of some guru and she had pictures of him in the puja room, but she never encouraged rituals. My mother too did not practise rituals, not that she was a non-believer. However, my father—who worked as an accountant in a hospital—was a believer.

'I would go to Durga Puja not so much for religious reasons as for fun. We went for the swings and for shooting balloons. And standing at the bookstalls, *dada* and I would finish reading various Chinese and Russian storybooks over these four days.

'After tenth standard, since my results were good, my parents asked me to join science for Plus Two, because if I took science, it was still possible to switch to arts but not the other way round. So I did science from Scottish College, although what I really wanted to be at the time was Feluda (a fictional detective character created by Satyajit Ray).

'In 1997 I joined Presidency College to study Bengali. I will always remember it as the best phase of my life. Presidency College, to me, meant Jibanananda Das. Presidency College, to me, meant Binoy Mazumdar. Have you heard of them? They were great poets. Presidency College, to me, meant the Naxal movement—the romanticism attached to it. Life has no meaning if one didn't study in Presidency College, that's the way I saw it.

'Since the beginning I was part of the Presidency College Student's Association, or PCSA. It doesn't exist anymore, it dissolved soon after I left college, sometime in 2005, I think. The organisation had become weak. The students were getting rapidly globalised, whereas PCSA was orthodox Marxist. There were no organisers left to convince the students of its motto.

'When I joined college, there was a huge movement going on. Our boys' hostel, called the Eden Hindu Hostel, did not allow Muslim students to stay there. The Hindu king who had donated the hostel building had wanted only Hindu students to stay there. But even after the government took over the hostel, the rule did not change. Muslim students who travelled from far and wide to Calcutta to study would not be allowed to stay in this hostel.

'PCSA started opposing this long ago, in the early nineties, when a young man named Shamim Ahmed joined Presidency College to study philosophy. He was from a village near Mushidabad. He had applied for the hostel but was denied admission because he was a Muslim. But nothing came out of the PCSA movement. Today Shamim Ahmed is an intellectual of sorts, he teaches Vedanta at the Ramakrishna Mission Vidyamandir.

'In 1998, when I was in the second year, another Muslim student, Shamim Asgar Ali, joined the college to study political science. He was from a village near Burdwan. He too was denied a seat in the hostel. PCSA resumed its campaign and this time it was a full-fledged movement—pasting posters, collecting signatures of teachers and intellectuals, holding street meetings. It went on for three years. What we need to remember is that we had a communist government at the time.

'After three years of protests, the government finally bowed down and changed the rule. Now, throughout these three years, the role of the SFI (Students' Federation of India, the student wing of the CPM) was very interesting. They opposed us. Although they don't believe in casteism and religion-based politics, they opposed us because the CPM was in power, and the hostel is a government hostel.

'The CPM should have immediately met our demand, but they took three years. The reason why the CPM lost to Mamata Banerjee is that it had stopped being a communist party long ago. Today, the Congress and the CPM have no difference left other than the colours of their flags.

'After the economic liberalisation of 1991, whatever the Congress had done throughout the country, the CPM had done in West Bengal. How were they any different? Communists are supposed to provide an alternative to Congress' policies, not join them.

'Before every election, the CPM would appeal to people to vote for them if they were against globalisation, privatisation and liberalisation, but as soon as they came to power they started to privatise institutions and factories one after another.

'Take Singur, for example. If the government had wanted to set up a factory there, people would have been fine, hasn't the government set up factories throughout the country earlier? But people had a problem with their land being given to the Tata group nearly free of cost to build a car factory.

'That is why Mamata Banerjee scored by siding with the people. We knew that if Mamata came to power, it will be really bad for Bengal, but the communists had to go.

'I am a hardcore leftist, I have five ideological fathers: Lenin, Marx, Engels, Stalin and Mao. But I would not join any of the existing communist parties. What we need today is a brand new communist party—a revolutionary left front. If that does not happen, there is going to be a serious problem in this country.

'But I am not sure if I will ever join active politics. Because I got involved in the students' union and also in politics—I had joined a small group called Centre for Communist Revolution—while in college, my academics did get affected.

'Had I done well in academics, I would have surely been a lecturer today. My first preference was academics, but since that did not work, I became a journalist.

'But I did work as a teacher for three years before I became a journalist. I taught Bengali in a government school. But the administration was feudal. They were communal and discriminated against Muslims.

'With me the school had another issue. After the first two months, I had refused to wear a saree to school, because there is no formal dress code in West Bengal. I said that I would wear *salwar-kurta*. The secretary threatened to physically harm me if I did not comply. I filed a complaint and did not go to the school for seven months.

'When the school management did not find support with the government, they called me back. I taught for another couple of years and then one day I thought: why am I working with such uneducated people? So I quit. Now journalism is my passion.'

'How do you apply leftist ideology in your daily life?' I ask Indrani, 'Is there anything you do or don't do?'

'*Churi kori na* (I don't thieve),' she laughs. 'And when I got married, I had a simple, registered marriage, not a grand wedding.'

'But anything symbolic, such as not drinking Coke?'

'Nothing like that, I don't drink Coke because I don't like aerated drinks.'

'What about wearing foreign brands?'

'See, communists are not RSS (Rashtriya Swayamsevak Sangh, the Hindu nationalist organisation). We are not against imported goods and all. If that was the case, what are we doing with Marx? He too is German.

'What concerns us is that most people in our society toil for a living and yet they don't get a proper meal or education. The fruits of their labour are enjoyed by only a privileged few.'

'But aren't communists responsible for causing strikes that often lead to closures of factories? It is the workers who suffer.'

'That's not true. Workers are always made out to be the villains by the capitalists and capitalist-owned media. Why should communists cause a situation that will make workers go hungry?'

'But isn't it a well-known fact that in government offices in Calcutta, people hardly work because they know they have the backing of powerful unions?'

'You are confusing the two things. Can the women who carry vegetables on their head every morning afford to shirk work? If they shirk work, neither will they get to eat nor will we. The laziness you are talking about—the laziness that one gets to see in government offices—is a middle-class trait. The poor cannot even think about being lazy.'

I SAY GOODBYE to Indrani at the gate of Presidency College and stroll down College Street. I see a man urinating on the imposing red-brick boundary wall of the Calcutta Medical College. The pavement running along the wall appears to have long become a public urinal: wet patches mark its entire length.

From the same pavement sprout brand-new tri-headed streetlights, a part of Mamata Banerjee's plan to make Calcutta resemble London. But London does not have people wetting the walls of historical buildings on Trafalgar Square. But then London has public toilets.

Had the money spent on acquiring the fancy streetlights been utilised for building public toilets, it would have gone a long way in boosting the image of Calcutta abroad. It must not be a pleasant sight for Westerners, coming to Calcutta for the first time with romantic notions of the city, to be watching the backs of men peeing in public, that too on the walls of public property, even historical buildings. To plant fancy streetlights on a pavement that has become a public urinal is like trying to mask the stench of stale urine with deodorant.

It serves the Calcutta Medical College right that people should urinate on its walls. One of its two gates—the one that leads into the rear side of the stately building—resembles the entrance to a dump yard. The pathway leading to the compound is flanked by piled up garbage. I retrace my steps and enter the hospital from the other gate. Here I am struck by the size of the building: a wide stairway leads up to the main facility on the first floor, from where Corinthian pillars rise majestically, supporting a gable roof that has 'Medical College Hospital' engraved on the entablature. Sitting on the steps are people, looking morose and lost in thoughts. They are obviously poor and relatives of patients admitted in the hospital.

Calcutta Medical College, whose origins date back to 28 January 1835, when the government passed an order for its setting up, is often billed as Asia's oldest medical college. While that may be technically true, training in modern medicine began in Madras way back in 1664 with the founding of the Madras General Hospital. And on 2 February 1835—just five days after the government passed the order to set up Calcutta Medical College—a medical hall run privately by the superintendent of the hospital formally became Madras Medical School, which in 1850 became Madras Medical College.

In any case it is Madras, or Chennai—and not Calcutta—that is considered the Mecca of medical treatment in India. Bengalis form a large chunk of patients who are treated in the hospitals of Chennai. A few months ago, a man I had met in a government office, when he came to know that I live in Chennai, had said, 'My wife was having trouble with her knees for many years. These Calcutta doctors, who call themselves gold medallists and all, know nothing about medicine. Finally I took her to Chennai and she is now fine. Can I have your number?'

I could not but agree with the man. I may like to die in Calcutta, but I would not like to fall ill in Calcutta. I have heard too many horror stories about negligence.

Near me is a small group of women squatting on the ground. They are suddenly wailing. I walk out to College Street, back in the direction of Coffee House. The College Street area is dotted with idols of the goddess of learning, standing under tiny decorated pandals. There is one in the compound of the Sanskrit College as well. Iswar Chandra

Vidyasagar, the highly revered educationist, reformer and philanthropist, had studied in this college and later become its principal.

The college is closed today and there is not a soul around, except a sweeper, who reeks of alcohol and who is clearing the compound of dried leaves. The goddess stands flanked by two loudspeakers, and the song blaring from them, full-volume, is a song that came out soon after I had left college: *'Amma dekh, dekh, tera munda bigdaa jaaye'*—Mother, look, your son is getting spoiled.

6

GANDU, THE FILM, could have been made only in Calcutta—and only by a Calcuttan.

The word *gandu* literally means a person who likes to get sodomised, but it is loosely—and freely—used in the sub-continent as an expletive, to describe a loser.

Gandu is a Bengali film, about an aspiring rapper who is in the habit of stealing money from the wallet of his mother's rich lover, crawling into her room whenever they are having sex, to finance his own trip into the world of drugs and debauched fantasies.

Made in 2010, it was first shown at Yale University and subsequently screened at film festivals across the world. It even picked up the best director and best film awards at the South Asian International Film Festival in New York.

Indians, however, have watched it only on the internet because clearance from the censors is next to impossible, considering the film has a longish sex scene, perhaps the most explicit ever performed by Indian actors.

Qaushiq Mukherjee, the producer-director, would rather

retain the sex scene than have it legally shown in India. The film is easily available, and it has made him famous anyway. With *Gandu*, he added a new dimension to Bengali cinema which, as of 2010, could be classified into three genres—the highbrow (classics by Satyajit Ray that are still watched with great pride by Bengalis in their homes), the middle-class variety (sensitive stories about human relationships that are watched in multiplexes), and the mass-viewership films (mostly made in Andhra Pradesh with Telugu-style song and fight sequences, watched by the masses in standalone theatres of Calcutta).

Gandu doesn't belong to any of these genres. It was shot on a modest budget with a handheld camera with the support of barely ten people in all, including the cast and crew. It defies all conventional norms of filmmaking and storytelling. What's more, it has explicit pornographic content. And yet, it was warmly embraced by audiences at Berlin and Slamdance festivals, marking Qaushiq's emergence on Calcutta's horizon as an unconventional filmmaker.

Qaushiq, now forty, has always had an appetite for the unconventional. Once he became a filmmaker he changed his name to its current spelling because he wanted to stand apart from the million other Bengalis named Kaushik. After his first two films he made it further conspicuous by shortening it to just Q. Just like his girlfriend Rituparna, who features in the explicit sex scene in *Gandu*, became Rii.

The couple often find place in the features pages of the *Telegraph*. The captions accompanying their pictures invariably, rather inevitably, contain the word *Gandu*, which is a bad word as it is, even worse in the society of *bhadraloks*. I do not know whether the *bhadralok* feels amused or outraged, what I do know is that Q is not the one to care.

Q's office is in Lake Gardens, and when I call him to request a meeting, he asks me to get down at Lords Bakery intersection. 'Once you reach the intersection, call me. I will give you directions,' he says. The name rings a bell: Lords Bakery was the landmark we would give to taxi drivers on our visits to my aunt's house during my boyhood.

I get down at the intersection and call Q. He tells me how to reach his office. Suddenly the place begins to look familiar. Was my aunt living in the same lane that leads to Q's office, or was it the next lane? I pause for a while to recall other landmarks that might come to my mind, but twenty-five years is a long time to remember anything of a place that had only been a ritual and never a part of you.

And what if I locate her house: it's going to be as good as the house of a stranger. Her two sons have been abroad for decades. Her husband, my *pishomoshai*, died in 1983. My aunt, struck by loneliness-induced depression, died about fifteen years later: she had consumed toilet-cleaning acid and could not be revived. As far as I know, a very distant relative, who had come from the village to help her with domestic chores, now lives in that house with his family.

And so I give up the idea of looking for old memories and start walking in the direction given by Q. That's when I notice Q coming from the opposite direction, riding a sports bicycle. He feared that I had lost my way and has come looking for me. Together we head to his office. He pedals slowly to maintain my walking pace. In his office, which is dominated by *Gandu* artwork, we settle on a mattress.

He tells me, 'I was born and raised in Calcutta. I was working since the time I was fifteen, which is something that wasn't very normal at that point. My school friend and I started a brand called Overdose, designing T-shirts and whatever came to our minds. Bangla T-shirts came first.

'We were great fans of Suman (singer Kabir Suman, formerly Suman Chattopadhyay), whose songs changed my life a lot. So we did some stuff for him, which would now be called branding exercise. We would use lines from his songs on T-shirts, we also created a poster of him—at that time we only had posters of Western idols.

'Through this exercise we also learnt about designing and production and execution, from a very early age. I was fascinated by this whole world of printing and the use of design. Writing was something that came probably easier to me, which is why I was mostly writing. All this, I think, set in an early aesthetic, which was highly influenced by this city.

'But also Kolkata was extremely dry. I was into music big time and post-Suman there was this whole Bangla rock music which had started. I was very much a part of it but I really got scared looking at the set up back then, which was very bad. It was like the guitarists had no guitars. This is how bad it was. I was like this is not going to go anywhere, so I fled. I left the city when I was twenty-one and moved into advertising.'

'What kind of a family did you come from?'

'I come from an archetypal middle-class family. I was the only child. One side of the family, you know, will always be more traditional, Congress-loving and on the other side you will find these stray fuckers, you know, going completely around the bend. My dad was sort of fallout of the early Naxal movement and in spirit he remained in that space. But in life he moved into the mainstream, which kind of troubled him a lot and I grew up in this sort of strife situation which I am sure a lot of Bengali kids have grown up in.'

'What did your father do?'

'He was a cost accountant. He was very young when he started writing for these underground magazines that were popping up. And this we are talking about late 1950s, very pure idyllic scene but entirely in the underground. The Congress was in power and my dad was the nephew of the food minister. He was one of the boys from the village who are sent to the city to live with the uncle.

'So basically he was brought up in a very feudal sort of atmosphere and which was not a nice experience at all, which also probably pushed him into this space. At one point they got found out and the organisation sort of asked them to leave and gave them a way to escape. So my dad went on a ship to London and stayed there for the next twelve years through the 1960s and came back in 1971. He became a senior manager in a large organisation. He was—as they have shown in many films—a white-collared guy who sympathised with the blue-collared and therefore couldn't go anywhere and remained stuck in between. All this shit happened to us.

'I grew up with Russian literature. American literature was not allowed into the house. The first fairy tale I read was by Oscar Wilde. So it was very demented. And no Hindi films or Hollywood films either.

'My mom and her sisters and cousins used to go for these matinee shows and sometimes they took me too so that I wouldn't tell my dad about it. He was the only one in the family who was like this. Everyone else was like a normal Bengali. He could play along with that scene also, which I find very, very difficult to do now.

'I went to South Point School and then to Asutosh College, which I attended very sparingly. Academics never interested me, I was always into extra-curricular. I was into tennis until I discovered smoking, and by that time I was into music and then Suman happened. No more health. It was Bob Dylan does not go to a gym sort of thing.

'I was part of the musical underground of Calcutta, it was a very interesting group. Complete losers, all those guys. We would meet at a spot which is not there anymore, in Gariahat. There was no bridge and at that place was a boulevard. There was a small kiosk called Rhythm and Blues. It was the only music shop in Calcutta where you would get proper music. There was one guy who used to sit there through the day, from ten onwards, popping once a batch of nitro and then some other drug. He was tripping for sometime and then drooping. He alternated until the shop closed and the scene shifted to the double-decker buses parked in Gol Park. Please also note that the Gariahat police station was right there.

'So everyone was doing different kind of drugs. Now, I was always a very cautious person and I love my conscious state, which I have realised much later. So my drug-taking was very cautious and extremely careful. These guys were friends, so I would do nitro and smoke up. And you'd get these cough syrups, which all got banned after they found out what we were doing. And then of course the inevitable brown sugar happened to everyone, except me.

'All these guys were musicians. They all had bands but no hope basically. They knew it was never going to work, no one was going to listen to their music. But it was great fun—that time and that whole crowd. They were extremely rich in terms of information.'

'Then you left the city at twenty-one.'

'Yeah, so after college, I worked for eight or ten months, I had got into advertising. My first job was a bit weird because I was working in my uncle's ad agency, which was highly unlike the setup I had thought for myself, because I had grown up with the idea that there is no family in life. My dad was very clear, ever since I was old enough to understand, that there's no legacy, there is nothing he'd give me, I have to do everything on my own.

'At the ad agency, because I was a trainee, I did everything. I picked up really quickly because I had been doing these kinds of things since I was fifteen. My uncle thought I was manager material and after about ten months sent me to Delhi to manage the Delhi office. I was, in my uncle's mind, going to be the inheritor of the legacy and all, but that was never my plan.

'I lived in Delhi for two and a half years. Then I fled to Bombay. By this time I was twenty-three and I had a portfolio also. And from Bombay, I got into raves in Goa. There was this guy in my office who sort of held my hand and led me through this whole digital revolution that was happening at that time, he introduced me to Goa.

'So I became a raver. From my early teens, I was looking for a revolution to be a part of, and a revolution was happening right here and no one had an idea about it.

'We would take the bus to Goa on Fridays—we would leave after lunch—and from then on, even in the bus, we would be tripping. The music and the drugs sort of went hand in hand, which was the same as in the early sixties.

'It's amazing when you get to a rave. If you have the right energy, if everybody involved has the right energy, it's like Nirvana, full on. I was into psychedelics, I didn't drink, I still don't drink, I did not do heroin. I don't do class A and class B, only class C drugs.

'After three years in Bombay, I was completely fed up of advertising and life there. Then I got this job in Colombo. The CEO of an agency there had come to Bombay and was looking for creative directors. So I had gone to meet him and one look at each other and we knew we were both druggies, so it was immediate bonding.

'By this time I was making commercials. My first commercial had won an Abby—the Abby awards are the Oscars of Indian advertising. So every year Abby sends out a theme and from that theme, they choose five scripts and you can make a film on one of them. One of these films gets the award on the spot. So I made one and it got an award.

'That year's theme was resilience. When our script got selected, my agency said we are not going to pay for it. I said fuck man, this is bad shit. Jayant Kriplani was my executive creative director at that time, a super father-figure kind of guy. He finally paid for it, and he also told me, "You don't need a director, you have to direct it yourself, only then will I pay for it." It was Rs 20,000 or something. He made me shave my head, made me act and made me direct. Basically he made me do my first independent production.'

'So in a way he showed you the way.'

'He's definitely the switch, he made me believe I could

direct. But this was only ads, I had no clue about cinema and I was never interested in cinema also.

'After leaving Bombay I spent the next six years in Sri Lanka. Finally I was out of this Indian shit, because Sri Lanka had nothing to do with India. All these agencies were big and Singapore was their hub, not India. Suddenly even in advertising terms, my outlook shifted and I'd say for the better that is why I could be in advertising for sometime, but of course finally, I was out in the open. I did not have to hide my actual identity. We were all druggies and everyone was a tripper and everyone did their own thing, it was also very edgy because they were all mad people in one space. And I left that agency after two years and joined a production company.

'In Colombo, there was this video store, which I found in Wellawatte, the Tamil area of Colombo. This place was called Mohan Video Vision, those were the VHS days, and there were titles I had never seen. The cover of one tape had this chick in red hair running on the streets. I was like this looks interesting, the chick has red hair. So that movie was *Run Lola Run*, and then I came back home, and it was a Saturday or a Sunday, it was my day off and I watched it—completely head-fucked—I watched it again—totally head-fucked—and I watched it again. Third time I realised that I had now watched it nine times, because in the film, the same story happens three times.

'I suddenly realised this is another world; this is a different kind of trip. It is not like any other movie that I had seen in my life and then Mohan Video Vision became my temple. Then it was like three movies a day.

'There I wrote a story called *Myths*. It was a mash up of five myths that exist. Three Sri Lankan myths, two

Indian myths and I was making up the sixth myth. The head of Sri Lanka's National Film Corporation, a great guy called Tissa Abeysekara, a super maverick, liked the script very much and was ready to provide 75 per cent of the funding. So I came to Bombay and for seven months talked to everyone that could be talked to, and it was clear that the remaining 25 per cent was not going to come. That was the first failure.

'By this time, I had started coming to Calcutta every year, every holiday that I got. I had started making music videos for these musicians who were part of the scene that I had fled. They had all become superstars now but they still did not have money. Rock was displacing *aadhunik* music and becoming mainstream, but these guys did not have packaging ... nothing.

'By this time I had also found Dogme 95, a Danish movement which rewrote the rules of filmmaking. Three Danish filmmakers wrote this sort of bible for digital filmmakers, and the rules are that you cannot use lights, you cannot use special effects, you cannot do basically anything. It was a revolution in cinema at that time, out of which some severely cool directors came out. So that was a big, big influence on me.

'Soon I had another script ready, full Dogma 95 style, called *Tepantorer Mathe*—In the Land of Nowhere, which was a comedy, a sort of revisit of the old folk tales of Bengal. Suddenly I found a producer for this, because I pitched it as a movie that can be made in digital for fifteen lakh rupees. It was a big company in Bombay which was just setting up at that time, they had lots of money and my entire budget was like their hotel bill or something. Suddenly I had my first film. These guys had no idea what I was going to do and I knew that also.

'The film was shot with D100 and Cannon XL-1S, but in Calcutta, there was no infrastructure that could handle digital information for a feature-length film. Finally we went into a TV studio and painstakingly put together the film the analogue way. When I went back to the producers with the rough cut, they were horrified. That was the end of it.

'I had no money, I was bankrupt, I had some 40,000 rupees in the bank. I realised that I had to go back to advertising again. So I made calls and told people that I was available. And I had good contacts in Sri Lanka, so I got some offers. Since I knew I had to go back to a job, I decided that with these 40,000 rupees, I will make another film, and this time I will have to make something that works. It will still be my way, but how do I do that?

'This was the first time I was doing serious strategic thinking. I hit upon an idea: take some superstars and make a film about something that people really like: music. So I called all my musician friends who were now stars—they had bands like Moheener Ghoraguli, Fossils, Chandrabindu, Cactus—and shot for four days. I called the film *Le Pocha* (a Bengali expression, which roughly means "What rot!") which was a sort of throwback on the eighties street music thing.

'We designed the title like that, *Le Pocha*, to make it look like a French film. And I showed it in Café Coffee Day, which had just opened on Park Street. The guy who was managing it was quite cool and he was a stoner. So once we smoked up, I told him, "Dude, lets show a film, since there aren't too many people coming here anyway." This Café Coffee Day outlet has a glass façade and it's a space that fits about forty people. So I asked my friends to come. About 120 people turned up. Once the film started, within ten minutes there were nearly 500 people watching it from the pavement. There was a jam, and so the cops came, they too started to watch. So we placed one speaker outside the door so people could hear it. It was widely talked about, like the first public screening of a film. *Le Pocha* was my biggest hit till *Gandu* came.'

'How much money did you spend making *Le Pocha*?'

'Twenty-five or thirty thousand rupees. I didn't have any money left to send it to any festival at that time, but one festival called 0110—it was the first digital festival in India funded by the British Council—got to know about it and asked for the film. They showed the film and it got the best documentary award or some shit like that.

'So my trick worked. I had flouted all rules of cinema in the film. There were frames within frames; you could even see the camera falling at one point. The audience just laughed, and I knew I had achieved the desired effect. So I was very happy. I went back to Sri Lanka to take up a job with Ogilvy. It is every advertising person's dream to work with Ogilvy at some point. I was the creative director, handling Southeast Asia, like severe cool job, and I could make the commercials that I wanted to and my boss was great so everything fell into place.'

'Who was your boss?'

'My boss was a Sri Lankan woman, who was the CEO. So now I had some sense of purpose. I knew I had to come back eventually and by this time I had started Overdose (his production house, named after the brand he had set up as a teenager), even though it had nothing except my mom's address—that's it.

'While working there I kept coming back and kept

planning and kept meeting people, and through this exercise I got to know about Docedge. It is a platform for pitching documentaries. To them I pitched *Love in India*.'

'What? *Love in India* was made by *you*? It's a brilliant documentary, I mean I loved it. I chanced upon it on a porn website and therefore could not even share the link on my Facebook page. Now how unfortunate is that!'

'No, not unfortunate at all, I find it hilarious. In fact it was selected for the biggest porn festival of the world, which is the Berlin Porn Film Festival.'

'They have something called the Porn Film Festival?'

'Yeah, yeah, it's a very serious film festival at that. They have full-on porn sections, but erotic art basically. So as I was saying, after I pitched for *Love in India*, I went back and told my CEO that I wanted to make a film. She said, "You are working here. How can you make a film there?" I told her that it's going to take a long time because it's a process and I have to learn a lot and that I need some time off every now and then. She was super cool about it. So I started working on *Love in India*.

'Suddenly I had found sponsors: BBC; Arte from Germany—they are the biggest in documentary production, bigger than BBC; TV2 from Denmark; YLE from Finland; SBS from Australia; and Steps International. Making the documentary was a very difficult and a strenuous process, but it eventually got made and it was acquired by various countries.

'It did very well in India also. It was brought out on DVD and got a national award for best documentary on family values, even though you find it on porn sites and it actually deconstructs the idea of a family. I found this bizarre. I did not go to collect the award also. By that time,

I had done *Gandu* and it was all over the place, and while the ministry was having severe issues with (the explicit content of) *Gandu*, the same ministry was giving me a national award.

'When did *Gandu* happen?'

'*Gandu* happened in a *Le Pocha* moment. It was a fuck-you moment. Till *Le Pocha*, I would still think about what people would say. Now I did not. It was like completely liberating. I didn't think of anything when I made this film: who would watch it, what would people say. And it all worked out. We had the right camera, we had the right gear, we had the right actors, we had the right locations suddenly.'

'What made you think of such a title?'

'I wanted to tell the story that I told you, about those losers (who would gather at Gariahat). Those losers were all my friends, I know that life. So I was discussing this idea with my writer friend, who has been with me in everything, Surajit Sen, and I said let's make this hardcore punk film where the central character is a complete loser, who gets fucked from every quarter, everyday, a complete *gandu*, and everyone calls him that, so much so that he calls himself *gandu*. So we thought this can be the title of the film.

'I would also like to say that because my whole set up and my whole trajectory is about identity, I don't like many characters. In my films, you'd, very rarely find characters who have names, that have identity. They are characters who are trying to hide this whole identity thing. They could be anywhere, they could be anybody. They don't have an identity, that's their issue.

'This was the first film that I shot without a script. This

was a completely new process for me. I had an idea, the *Le Pocha* idea, of how to make people watch a film. But I also knew this film is not for here (India) actually. I am going to flout all rules, nobody (in India) is going to be interested in it, so let me make it for (the festivals). What do festival films have? What do Europeans love? Realism. I am not into realism, I am a documentary filmmaker, but I thought let me give them a realistic value. So I placed the character in a realistic situation and I started shooting. So in the first twenty minutes, you will see the character-study, of this guy in a situation. Europeans love that, they are suckers for that.

'So when we had all the rushes and I sat with my editor—he was a student, he had not edited a film before—we thought let's make a trailer first so we will have an idea if there is a fucking story or not and to get a sense of the narrative. Then we started editing the film, and as we got into it, we were not even half-way through, when we could feel that it's got to be a good film.

'At that point, I knew this one guy from this film festival, where we had shown *Love in India*, in New York. It was a ghetto festival. I didn't have any idea that any big festival will take it, so I asked this guy, "You want to watch this thing that I have done?" He said, "Yeah, yeah, punk film from India? Sounds great." So I sent him the trailer then he called back at whatever time it was in the US. He was completely demented, this guy. He said, "What have you done! Send me the film right now, let's see what happens." I said, "Will you show it?" He said, "Of course, this will be the biggest thing I have ever done."

'Then he showed it to some people, one of them was Todd Brown of Twitch.net, which is a big independent film portal. This guy saw it and went mad. He said. "Look I don't care, don't tell him anything, I am uploading this trailer right now." He uploaded it without telling me. Two days later we found out and by that time it was out. That's how the trailer hit and then he said something is happening in India. He said he could see on his servers that India is going bonkers on this.

'Now I was thinking: you have some hope, you have some future, you have to treat it carefully because already it's happening. So I set up a screening at Yale University. That was first time *Gandu* was screened—this was late 2010. It was an academic screening at Yale, it was academically stamped, so what would Bengalis say now? Anything Yale for a Bengali is fine.

'Then it went to New York, and New York went completely demented. Then Berlin came. Everyone went bonkers about it. So far we have been to 72 festivals with *Gandu*.'

'But you can't legally show it in India unless you give it to the censors?'

'No. And to get it censored I have to cut it, which I don't want to.'

'Did you make money from *Gandu*?'

'Yeah, even from *Love in India*.'

'How much?'

'Not humongous money, we don't believe in humongous money, but we always recover the cost and make enough to sustain ourselves.'

'The longish sex scene in *Gandu* (which features Gandu, played by Anubrata Basu, and a prostitute, played by Rii, Q's real-life girlfriend) is quite explicit by Indian standards, and yet it doesn't look crude. Did you not find it difficult to film?'

'These guys were in workshop for a month, to sort of lose all inhibitions about their body and not act with the face but embody the character really. It's a very elaborate and exhaustive method, very extreme method, called Grotowski's Method. What they did in the workshop, we didn't even do half of that in the film. Joyraj, who plays Ricksha in the film, took the workshop. He is a veteran on the method.'

'After the workshop it was easy?'

'It was much easier, but there were things. For instance, Rii is my girlfriend and Anubrata, the guy who played Gandu, is quite scared of me. So he was finding it difficult to get a hard on during the shooting.'

'But the sex scene was not even make-believe, it was very real. And to get your girlfriend to do it with another man—wasn't that a problem?'

'No, the best filmmakers have all stripped their lovers to the world. I don't have any emotional attachment. I am not a jealous person.'

'You think a film like *Gandu* could be made only in Calcutta and nowhere else?'

'Yes, totally.'

'So Calcutta has been an influence on you.'

'Also Colombo, to a certain extent. There are certain spaces that always influence you. Calcutta with its leftist sort of mind space is perfect for this kind of shit, this is the cheapest place in the world. Also, it's a space stuck in time, all this makes it a very interesting space. Like Berlin, like Rome—places that are stuck in time somehow but at the same time give you a sort of futuristic feel.'

'Has Satyajit Ray been an influence on you?'

'No, Satyajit Ray is no influence. I don't like him.'

'Have you watched him?'

'Yeah, yeah, you have to watch Ray, what are you saying? Being a Bengali most things are thrust upon you even if you don't want anything to do with it. You end up idolising them because you are pushed into it. Like with Tagore. Tagore and Ray are the two pillars holding Bengali culture together. And this entire morbid fascination with a guy who is obviously influenced by Hollywood does not work for me. I find Ray a huge influence in terms of typography design. His work is unparalleled in that area. I like his children's films, they were great fun. I find much more relevance in Mrinal Sen and Ritwik Ghatak. Then Tapan Sinha, brilliant filmmaker!'

'No matter how many films you make, you will always be known for *Gandu*. Like Ramesh Sippy will always be known for *Sholay*, no matter how many other films he made. But *gandu* happens to be a bad word, which means most polite people won't even mention the name of your most famous film. Does that bother you?'

'In fact, I am overjoyed how many people now say the word. Even my mom said *gandu*,' Q laughs. 'In a very scientific way, *gandu* is an adjective, a street adjective, but at the same time, it's a very old word. You find it in the Vaishnav Padabali. Back in the day, it was not considered an abusive word. Like many other things, *gandu* has fallen and become an untouchable word. My greatest achievement, I think, is that I have raised an untouchable word to being a Brahmin.'

7

ON 29 JULY 1911, something unthinkable happened. Eleven Bengali men, only one of them wearing boots and the rest barefooted, but all of them wearing impressive moustaches, beat the East Yorkshire Regiment team to lift the Indian Football Association Shield for Mohun Bagan.

The tournament took place at the Maidan, and the final was attended by nearly one lakh people. Only a fraction of them could get a direct view of the game, the rest of them were there for a feel of the historic moment, looking out for the green-and-maroon kites that carried the score.

Mohun Bagan won 2-1, and when the winning goal was scored, Calcutta burst into a jubilation never seen before or since then. From the time football came to Calcutta, in the 1850s, Bengalis had been restricted to the fringes of the Maidan as they gathered to watch the *sahebs* play. The natives began to play in their neighbourhoods and over time, sporting clubs were formed. Mohun Bagan was the first to be formed, in 1889, and twenty years later, in 1909, it was allowed to play for the IFA Shield. After poor performances in the first two years of its participation, the club created history on 29 July 1911—Mohun Bagan fans consider it the independence day of Indian football.

That evening—as the story goes—when the victorious team was being carried off the Maidan by jubilant spectators, an elderly man ran up to the players and, pointing to the Union Jack fluttering atop Fort William, asked, 'When are you going to bring that down?'

Perhaps it wasn't a coincidence that Bengal saw a sudden rise in militant nationalism after this unimaginable victory. The youth must have been guided by the idea that if the IFA Shield could be wrested with physical prowess, why not Fort William? However, less than six months after the win, Calcutta ceased to be the capital of British India, but it had become the capital of Indian football, a status it proudly retains even today.

Late one beautiful morning, after an invigorating walk at Central Park and a breakfast of *phulkas* and omelette, I take a taxi to Floatel, the floating hotel on the Strand. My destination, however, is not Floatel but the fortress-like State Bank of India building opposite it, where I am to meet Subrata Bhattaracharya, who played for Mohun Bagan for seventeen years and remains one of its greatest stars ever. He is an employee of the bank.

In the taxi, however, I think not about football but about that morning's walk in Central Park. I had woken up late and reached the park when free entry for morning-walkers had been closed and the idyllic landscape already taken over by lovers. As I walked in the direction of the exit after walking for an hour, I had been intercepted by a young couple.

'I just saw a snake,' the man stammered out of fear, 'this long.' He stretched out his left arm to indicate the length of the snake.

'Snake?'

'Yes snake. *Hum to ghabraa gaye*'—I got scared. His accent was Bihari.

His girlfriend, standing behind him, wore a smile of embarrassment. Her eyes clearly said: This boyfriend of mine, he got so scared at the sight of a snake, how is he going to face bigger problems in life?

With the air of a veteran forester, I had told the young man not to worry. The truth was that I myself now wanted to get out as quickly as possible: I am scared of snakes more than anything else in this world. I quickened my pace—the gate was still a long way off—and I found myself walking past another young couple. They were huddled against the wall of a platform, an open umbrella covering their torsos. Precisely at that moment, the couple decided to kiss and lifted the umbrella to cover their faces. That's when I got a glimpse of her bare breast. As the umbrella went up, she quickly pulled her dress down. I suddenly forgot all about the snake. I was determined to take a look at the girl.

Central Park is a maze of pathways, and I decided to encircle the patch of lawn on which the couple sat huddled, so that I could cross them again. That's when I ran into the snake: it was getting into a hole in the hedge, making a rustling sound as it hurriedly slithered over dried leaves. I froze for a moment, and then it became clear that the snake was more panic-stricken than I was.

How strange. For two years I have been coming to Calcutta to write this book, but only on the last day of what happens to be my final visit, as far as collecting matter for this book is concerned, do I sight a snake—and a bare breast—in Central Park. It is also a strange coincidence that on this last day, I should be sitting in a taxi going in the direction of Floatel, just as I had on the very first day two years ago.

In the State Bank of India building, I have no problem finding Subrata Bhattacharya's office. Almost everybody seems to know him, and they direct me to the Specialised Institutional Banking division on the fourth floor. But once I walk into the large air-conditioned hall that houses the division, I have a problem locating him. After all, I watch football only once in every four years, when the World Cup takes place, and I do not recognise any of the Indian players, except two: PK Banerjee and Baichung Bhutia.

I lower my voice and ask the first man I come across, 'Where can I find Mr Subrata Bhattacharya?'

He points to a desk across the hall, where a broad-shouldered man, resembling a retired soldier who has retained his ruggedness, is leaning back on his chair, lost in thoughts. I walk up to him and introduce myself. Subrata Bhattacharya sits up and asks me to take a seat and without wasting any time, begins telling his story:

'I was born in a village near Shyamnagar town, in Barrackpore. My village was *hatha daridra* (a region of extreme poverty). Sitting in a high-rise in Calcutta, it's difficult to even imagine a place as poor as that. Our family had eight members—six siblings and our parents. My father worked in NICCO.'

'What is NICCO?'

'National Insulated Cable Company. But you can write NICCO, everyone knows. We were very poor, though at the time we hardly realised it, but we did not even have enough to eat.

'What did your father do at NICCO?'

'He was a clerk, but we had a big family. We never had enough money. We lived in a modest house, just like that of the poor. When I went to the Sunderbans recently, I saw one such house near the guesthouse where I was staying. It reminded me of how we lived back then. The woman in that house was working as hard as my mother would when we were young. She was sweeping the house at dawn, flooring it with cow dung, milking the cow, lighting the mud oven, cooking—all this in the biting cold. I gave her the shawl I was wearing because she reminded me of my mother's hardships.

'Even though we were utterly poor, my mother was

quite enthusiastic about football because her brothers—my uncles—used to play football. I am talking about the fifties. We were quite close to the uncles, I still am. They also helped us financially at times.

'At the time there was this famous player called Keshto Pal, an Olympian. He played from 1952 to 1959 and was a part of the 1956 Melbourne Olympics team. Now, since I spent so much time with my uncles and they used to hang out with Keshto Pal, I got to know him too. That is when I started to get influenced by the game.

'Which team did your uncles play for?'

'They played for Bhowanipore Club.'

'Did you attend school back in the village?'

'I went to a primary school, which is now called Jawaharlal Nehru Vidyalaya, but at the time Nehru was alive and it was called something else which I cannot recall now. I studied there from class one to four and joined Kanti Chandra High School from class five onwards. But I would bunk classes and play football. I was in great demand for under-height tournaments in Shyamnagar. Do you know what under-height is?

'No.'

'It was a system where boys of similar height could play together in matches. For example, boys under 4'6" could play together, boys under 4'10" could play together, and so on. At this time I became friends with a young man called Subhash—his nickname was Buro—who ran a small club. He died last year. I would mostly play for his club.

'Buro contributed to my love for football and my career as much as my uncles did. He would come to Calcutta every year to watch Mohun Bagan play in the Calcutta Football League. In 1962, after I had won the final of an under-height tournament for his club, he brought me along to watch the matches. I must have been barely ten years old then.

'That particular under-height tournament remains in my memory. The tournament had taken place in Bhatpara (not far from Shyamnagar) and I had been adjudged the best player. Pradip Banerjee, the legendary footballer, who had just returned from the Jakarta Asian Games after winning the gold for India, had come to give away the prizes. Buro was so proud of me that he decided to bring me along to Calcutta to show me the matches.

'Although my grandmother lived in Calcutta, in Beleghata, I do not recall anything about our trips to her place. This is the first trip that I remember. There were no electric trains then, only steam engines. 'Buro and I had taken the Manpur local from Shyamnagar to reach Sealdah, from where we took tram no. 12 to Esplanade. The tram ticket cost us forty-five paise. We had walked from Esplanade to the Maidan. I remember Buro holding my hand throughout, just in case I get lost.

'At the time Mohun Bagan had stalwarts like Chuni Goswami, Jarnail Singh, Kempiah, Narsiah, Dipu Das ... We started coming back every year. As soon as the train pulled into Calcutta, we could see Pradip Banerjee's house near the Sealdah station. His house was like a tourist spot for us: Pradip Banerjee's house! Back home, I would go to school and also play under-height matches for Buro's club.

'These days they don't follow the under-height system anymore, they follow the point system.'

'What is point system?'

'There are now different categories under which boys

can play, such as 95-point category, 100-point category and so on. If a boy wants to play in the 95-point category, his height in inches and his weight, put together, cannot exceed 95. In our time however, the height was the only criterion.

'Then in 1966, I was disqualified for these matches because I had exceeded the height limit—I had grown much taller than the other boys. It got me very upset and I went and joined a club called Yuger Proti. It is a very old club, my uncles and even Keshto Pal had played there. The club still exists.

'There I met Murari Sur, he went on to become my first ever coach. He played for Calcutta. He's still alive. He had seen me sitting and watching the matches and asked me if I wanted to play. I said I would like to. He then said, "Look here, today I am allowing you to play barefoot, but from tomorrow, you would not be allowed to."

'Now, I was supposed to buy shoes and my mother had no money, but I could not have gone to play without the shoes. She somehow arranged for money and bought me a pair of keds for three rupees, and a pair of socks for one rupee fifty paise. So in 1966, my journey began, from Yuger Proti Club in Shyamnagar.

'I started to practise with Murari Sur and in 1967, I was selected for the district team, but I had no proper boots. Sometimes when I think about those times, I feel like crying. So I had no boots and my mother had no money to buy me any—a pair cost fifteen rupees. She then sold her gold chain to get me boots and socks.

'But how long can one play with a single pair, I needed more. Thankfully, by then, my uncles became senior players and they would give me their used boots. That's how I could play. I used their boots for long.

'In 1968, I watched Mohun Bagan play Eastern Railway at the Mohun Bagan ground. It was a dream for me at the time to play on a ground like that. But that very year, in September—I had watched the match in July—I played for the IFA Shield on the same ground. I was representing my district, 24 Parganas. Isn't it amazing how your dreams come true if you remain determined?

'Those days we would play only out of love for the game. We got no money. Money in football is a recent phenomenon. After a game, we would be at the most given a sweet and a *kachori*. And if we won a final, we got a cup and a T-shirt. The financial condition at home was only getting worse, because all of us had grown up now and our needs had increased.

'So in 1969, since I could not even afford boots, I joined the LIC'—Life Insurance Corporation of India—'team. One of my cousins had found me a place in the team. Here I would get boots and socks and daily, after each match, five rupees. That is the only reason I played for LIC.

'Here I met Rono Chakraborty. He was a referee and was conducting one of the matches that LIC were playing against State Bank of India. The SBI team had just been formed, and it was a great team, a terrific team. But we drew that match. Rono*da* was very impressed by my performance and asked me whether I would play for Bally Pratibha as well. It was one of the better clubs at the time. He was on the committee of the club. I agreed.

'Around that time, one of the commandants of the Border Security Force, PK Burman, who had seen me play, asked me to join the BSF. My elder brother had recently joined the BSF, and PK Burman had told him,

"If your brother wants to play for the BSF, we could take him."

'So, in late 1969, I joined the BSF, on a salary of Rs 185 a month. I still remember the happiness on my mother's face when I gave her my first salary. Rs 185 was a huge amount at the time. But life was very hard for me.

'I would take a train at 5.20 in the morning from Shyamnagar to Barrackpore and reach the BSF ground at 6 for parade. Although I would not be part of the parade, I had to be there. Then, from 7 to 9, I practised with the BSF team, after which I had a bath in the Ganga and ate the snacks provided to us.

'From there I would go to college, Rashtaguru Surendranath College, also in Barrackpore. After that I would take the 2.20 train to Dum Dum, from where I took a train at 3.05 to reach for the practice sessions for the Bally Pratibha Club at Bally.

'You know Bally, right? It's opposite Dakshineshwar. So I would practice at Bally and take the 6.05 pm train back to Dum Dum from where I had the connecting train to Shyamnagar at 6.40. Once back in Shyamnagar, I would go for tuition classes around 8 or 8.30. For an entire year, my life was very tough.

'Towards the end of 1970, Bally Pratibha went to play exhibition matches with BNR (Bengal Nagpur Railway) and Mohun Bagan on the Barrackpore grounds. BNR lost to us by two goals and Mohan Bagan drew the match with two goals each.

'This was when Debu Ghosh, the BNR coach, said, "Let's get this stopper (defender) into our office team." Playing for BNR meant I had to work there too, and I readily agreed. The salary was Rs 370. My mother was delighted. Our financial condition was slowly beginning to improve.

'BSF usually does not let people go, but they released me. I stayed with BNR from 1971–74. They had given me a clerical job, but I did not have to work really. I would go to office after morning practice, mark my attendance and leave. While in BNR I played the Santosh Trophy, I played in the all-India railways team, and, for the first time, played in the Indian team.

'In 1974, I was signed up by Mohun Bagan. I had to leave BNR. But since I had played for the Indian team, I got a job with the Central Excise. In 1979, I joined State Bank of India. By now I was completely free of financial worries. I had a club that paid me and a job which gave me a regular salary.'

Just then the air-conditioned hall fills with the smell of cigarette smoke. I turn around out to find a bearded gentleman, with a just-lit cigarette between his lips, settling into an adjoining desk with a cup of tea and a newspaper. I wonder whether Subrata Bhattacharya, being an athlete, minds the smoke, but he shows no reaction.

'How much did Mohun Bagan pay you?' I ask him.

'The money wasn't big in those days. When I started in 1974, my contract was for Rs 5,000 a year. It slowly increased, and by the time I retired, in 1991, I was getting Rs 90,000 a year. Today a player of my rank would be drawing Rs 60 lakh a year from the club.

'But then, my achievements remain unparalleled. I played for Mohun Bagan from 8 May 1974 to 19 April 1991, and during this period 1,244 matches for the club—the highest played by any footballer ever in India. I got seventy-eight trophies for the club—no one in India has got so many. As a defender, I scored fifty-eight goals in my career, forty-seven of them for Mohun Bagan. I got twenty trophies as a coach.

'Whatever I achieved, I achieved on my own. I never sought favours from anyone. I had to fight for everything that I have got. Throughout my career, I have often been overlooked by selectors and coaches (for selection in the national team) because I never went out of my way to please anyone.'

He pulls out a blue packet of 555 cigarettes from his shirt pocket and lights one up. He takes a long drag and continues:

'Once, when I was in Thrissur to play for the Santosh Trophy, even though I was adjudged the best player in the tournament, I was not considered for the national team which was selected in the room adjacent to mine at the hotel. How could the 'best player' not be in the national team? But the selectors had their preferences.

'I can give you many such instances but I won't because I don't want you to write about all this. I am an honest man and I have played with honesty—people know that. No one can take away my achievements.

'I came up the hard way, *gali thheke rajpath* (from the street to the palaces). I have seen poverty and success. I have known Uttam Kumar, I have also known the roadside tramp. Mithun Chakraborty is a friend, so is the common man. My circle is big.'

A peon comes over to him with sheets of paper. The former Mohun Bagan star goes through them carefully. It is almost impossible to imagine a footballer engaging in paperwork, that too in a government office in Calcutta, where employees are known to shirk work. Unable to contain my curiosity, I asked Subrata Bhattacharya what the papers are about.

'It is the list of invitees for my farewell. I am retiring at the end of this month,' he tells me.

'What is your designation in the bank?'

'You can say team manager.'

'Who all do you have in your family?'

'My parents are dead and my brothers are all working in different places. I have a son and a daughter. My son, Saheb, is an actor. My daughter has just returned home after completing her studies abroad, she's looking for a job. My children or my wife did not see my struggle. I was established by the time I got married, in 1982. My wife comes from a wealthy family.

'But I still go to Shyamnagar every Sunday. I have to maintain my parents' house. My friends from there, some of who are still not established, often come to me to seek help. I help those who I can. I got some of their children jobs.

'When you write about me, you must highlight my struggle. People must know that one can get up from abject poverty and still succeed in life with hard work. I started with nothing and achieved everything only through hard work and struggle.'

AS I WALK down the Strand, looking for a taxi, I stop at Baboo Ghat, the neo-Classical-style ghat built in 1830. I walk down the steps and gaze at the river. To my left is the Vidyasagar Bridge, and to my right, the Howrah Bridge. A sprinkling of bathers, men and women, are knee-deep in the water. On the steps, a masseur is at work. A large dark man is lying on his stomach on what resembles a hospital stretcher. The masseur, a skinny, cheerful man who has a *bidi* stuck between his lips, is rubbing his client's back with all his might.

After the massage, the man who is now lying on his stomach, wearing nothing but a *gamchha*, thin towel, will walk down the steps and scrub himself in the river. He will then go home, have lunch and take a satisfying nap, thus completing a ritual that has for long been quintessentially Calcutta.

For that matter, the steps where I am standing right now is truly, originally Calcutta: if someone were to turn the clock back by 350 years, I would be standing in Kalikata, the riverside village that gave the city its name.

8

AT SEVENTY-THIRTY in the evening, Park Street is at its liveliest. The red balloons from Valentine's Day are still intact in some of the shops. For two years I have been romancing Calcutta, sometimes longing for it and sometimes belonging to it, but never gathering enough courage to move in with my belongings.

This evening I have deliberately left my notebook behind because I would like to believe that I am done collecting material for this book. Calcutta is a never-ending city, at some point you need to call it a day so that you move on. I will return—as a visitor, as a son-in-law, as a lover of the city—but without the compulsion to constantly look around and fill up my notebook, the association isn't going to be the same. I know I won't give the fat pimp of Park Street a second glance hereafter.

This evening, he is sitting right on the sill of the Oxford

Bookstore. He now wears spectacles. He doesn't even look in my direction as I enter the bookstore, walking right past him. With his improved vision, he must have gauged from a distance that I am someone who knows Calcutta too well to require his services.

But how well do I know Calcutta after these two years? It is safest to leave that question hanging, rather than make proclamations that might come across as flawed, false or even foolish. If I say I know Calcutta well enough, I am sooner than later bound to meet, or be met by, another Bengali who knows the city better. There is always a Bengali who knows better.